THE

ŒDIPUS JUDAICUS.

THE

ŒDIPUS JUDAICUS.

BY

THE RIGHT HONORABLE

SIR W. DRUMMOND.

ŒDIPO conjectore opus est.

PLAUTUS.

RESEARCH INTO LOST KNOWLEDGE
ORGANISATION

c/o R.I.L.K.O. Books,
B. & J. Hargreaves,
10 Kedleston Drive,
Orpington,
Kent. BR5 2DR

Distributed by
THORSONS PUBLISHING GROUP LIMITED
Wellingborough, Northamptonshire

First Published 1811
This Edition 1986

Cover illustration
by
Joyce Hargreaves

British Library Cataloguing in Publication Data

Drummond, *Sir* W
   Oedipus Judaicus
   1. Bible. O.T.—Criticism, interpretation, etc.
   I. Title
   221.6   BS1171.2
   ISBN 0-902103-12-1

Printed and bound in Great Britain

TABLE OF CONTENTS.

——————

FOREWORD

Intended only for private circulation at the time of its first publication in 1811, *Oedipus Judaicus* is a remarkable book written by an unusually talented individual. Sir William Drummond was born around 1770 and died in 1828. Surviving records suggest that he was a student at Christ Church, Oxford, taking his degree in 1788. By profession he was first a politician (he was a Member of Parliament for a number of years) and then a diplomat, chiefly serving at the court of Naples. His main interest, however, lay in scholarship and he early showed himself to have a sharp mind for philosophical debate and a gift for languages. Both these talents would be important contributing factors to the composition of *Oedipus Judaicus*. Like his fellow Scot David Hume (1711-76), who figured prominently in his early work

Academic Questions (1805), Drummond was an empiricist and realized that much of the Old Testament, if taken literally, contains nothing but a brutal and self-contradictory collection of stories about a small and apparently insignificant race of people. This is the same sentiment which was so violently expressed in Thomas Paine's *Age of Reason* (1793):

'When we read the obscure stories, the cruel and barbarous executions, the unrelenting vindictiveness with which more than half the Bible is filled, it would be more consistent that we called it the work of a demon than the word of God. It is a history of wickedness that has served to corrupt and brutalise mankind . . .

In part, what Drummond set out to do in *Oedipus Judaicus* was to show that there is an alternative method by which to approach Biblical criticism, one which will lead to very different conclusions from those which are the inevitable products of a pure historicism. To achieve his aims he turned to the newly emerging science of comparative linguistics. As early as 1798 Drummond had translated *The Satires of Persius* and in 1810 he and Robert Walpole produced *Herculanesia, or Archaeological and Philological Disser-*

tions containing a manuscript found among the ruins of Herculaneum. At precisely the period when Drummond was doing this work, dramatically new and exciting discoveries were taking place elsewhere in the field of philology. As early as 1786 Sir William Jones had made a comparative study of Sanscrit, Greek and Latin in the context of modern European languages. Eventually this type of investigation would lead to the awareness that there must have been a now lost Indo-European ancestor linking a whole range of ancient and modern langauges, many of whose developments could be accounted for through a series of laws – the most important of which was enunciated in 1822 by Jacob Grimm (of the brothers Grimm). The comparative method, then, provided a radical breakthrough in the study of languages and, in a broader sense, in the study of Western civilisation.

Oedipus Judaicus represents, in many ways, a daring application of this same kind of method to the problems of Old Testament scholarship. Using linguistic clues and studying the Jewish culture in context rather than in splendid isolation, Drummond came to the conclusion that large portions of the Old Testament are allegorical in the broadest sense and that for the adept these books provide astronomical information of great complexity. In *Oedipous Judaicus* portions of the Book of Genesis, the Book of Joshua and the Book of Judges receive particular scrutiny. Personal names are handled with great erudition (Drummond was an expert in many languages) and are shown to have a variety of astronomical connotations. Reminding us that the Jewish Cabbala indicates a strong awareness of the arcane traditions of other Eastern religions, Drummond points out that it does not seem unreasonable to accept that the writers of the Old Testament:

> 'followed the example of all the East, in blending in their narratives real with fictitious events and involving important lesons to man-kind whether in morals, or in science, under the guise of recorded fact.'

In this case, Scripture has a much more universal significance than the mere historians would suggest; it also, however, stands in need of careful explication. Ultimately, so Drummond concludes, we must realise that the temple is an archetype of the universe. This accepted, one can see that much Old Testament narrative concerns calendrical and astronomical matters – the reconciliation of lunar and solar systems of reckoning, for example, and the Zodiacal com-plications caused by the precession of the equinoxes (as the story of the idolatrous worship of the golden calf makes apparent).

When first published, *Oedipus Judaicus* provoked bitter response and led to considerable controversy. An edition of two hundred and fifty copies was republished in 1866. The book has not, however, reached a wide readership and it had become virtually impossible to obtain until this republication by R.I.L.K.O. Historically, *Oedipus Judaicus* is interesting because Drummond's work anticipates certain generally accepted twentieth-century modes of Biblical scholarship, but – even more importantly – Drummond raises a number of issues in his examination of the Old Testament which have not been satisfactorily dealt with elsewhere. One does not have to agree with every conclusion in *Oedipus Judaicus* to find it a highly provocative and intellectually exciting work.

James P. Carley, Ph.D.

Cambridge   York University

1985   Toronto.

ADDITIONAL REMARKS.

⁎ These are become necessary from the fault of the Author, not of the Printer.

PAGE 14.

The reader will please to observe, that in this page the author is speaking according to the fixed zodiac.

PAGE 20.

For, " when the Sun is in the sign of *Capricorn,*" *read,* " when the sign of Capricorn rises."

PAGES 87. and 89.

For, " Civil year," *read,* " Sacred year."

PAGE 288.

After the word, " written," add, " according to the fixed zodiac."

immutarent, sed CCCLXV dies peracturos, sicut institu-
tum est ab antiquis. It follows from this, that when the
Priests reckoned by their sacred year, they would lose a
whole day every fourth year. This day, as I have said
above, was reckoned in the astronomical year; but as this
was against the religious law, the Priests seem to have
feigned, that during that day the course of the Sun and
Moon was suspended; and thus obtained their small canicular period mentioned by Bailly.

ADDITION.

_____

In speaking of the 12th verse of the 10th chapter of the Book of Joshua, I might have observed, that if the year be taken at 365 days, and if we suppose one day intercalated every fourth year, the meaning will come out more obviously. This one day was not admitted into the sacred, but into the astronomical, year of the Egyptians. An ancient and anonymous writer gives us the following account: In templo Ægypti Memphis, (lege Apidis Memphi) mos fuit solio regio decorari reges, qui regnabant. Ibi enim sacris initiabantur primùm, ut dicitur, Reges, satis religiosè tunicati: et Tauro, quem Apim appellant, jugum portare fas erat, —— et per vicum unum duci. Deducitur autem à Sacerdote Isidis in locum qui nominatur Adytos, et jurejurando adigitur, neque mensem, neque diem intercalandum, quem in festum diem

PREFACE.

IT will naturally be asked by those, who may chance to see this volume, why its author has caused a book to be printed, which he yet does not choose to publish. When, however, it is considered, that I have treated chiefly of things deemed sacred, and that there is considerable novelty in some of my opinions, I trust, that I shall be easily pardoned, if I confine the distribution of the copies of this work to a narrow circle.

a

I pretend, that the ancient Jews, like other nations of antiquity, had their esoteric and their exoteric doctrines. They concealed the former under innumerable types and symbols, the meaning of which is generally unknown among their descendants. It is the object of my book to explain the hidden sense of many passages in the Hebrew Scriptures; but as Christians are, for the most part, so well satisfied with the literal sense, as never to look for any other, except when it is thought that some allusion is made to the advent of Christ, I feel myself unwilling to publish any explanations of the original text, which may not coincide with those notions concerning its meaning which are most commonly received. Besides, there may be passages in this volume, which are capable of alarming the timid, and of provoking the prejudiced. Ignorance bears ill being told, that it has much to learn; and to instruct Pride is to affront it.

The Old Testament is a book, which we have all read in our childhood, when reason proposes no doubts, and when judgment is too feeble to decide for itself. But its early associations are generally the strongest in the human mind; and what we have been taught to credit as children, we are seldom disposed to question as men. Called away from speculative inquiries by the common business of life, men in general possess neither the inclination, nor the leisure, to examine *what* they believe, or *why* they believe. A powerful prejudice remains in the mind;—ensures conviction without the trouble of thinking;—and repels doubt without the aid or authority of reason. The multitude, then, is not very likely to applaud an author, who calls upon it to consider what it had hitherto neglected, and to stop where it had been accustomed to pass on. It may also happen, that there is a learned and a formidable body,

which, having given its general sanction to
the literal interpretation of the Hebrew
Scriptures, may be offended at the presump-
tion of an unhallowed layman, who ventures
to hold, that the language of those Scriptures is often symbolical and allegorical,
even in passages, which both the Church
and the Synagogue consider as containing
nothing else than a plain statement of facts.
A writer, who had sufficient boldness to
encounter such obstacles, and to make an
appeal to the public, would only expose
himself to the invectives of offended bigotry,
and to the misrepresentations of interested
malice. The press would be made to ring
with declamations against him; and neither
learning, nor argument, nor reason, nor
moderation, on his side, would protect him
from the literary assassination which awaited
him. In vain would he put on the heaven-
tempered panoply of Truth. The weapons,

which could neither pierce his buckler, nor break his casque, might be made to pass with envenomed points through the joints of his armour. Every trivial error, which he might commit, would be magnified into a flagrant fault; and every insignificant mistake, into which he might fall, would be represented by the bigoted, or by the hireling critics of the day, as an ignorant, or as a perverse, deviation from the truth.

Under these circumstances, I feel little inclination to make my opinions too publicly known. It may be hoped, however, that reason and liberality will soon again be progressive in their march; and that men will cease to think that Religion can be really at war with Philosophy. When we hear the timid sons of Superstition calling to each other to rally round the

altar, we may well blush for human weak-
ness. The altar, of which the basis is
established by Reason, and which is
supported by Truth and Nature, can never
be overthrown. It is before that altar
that I kneel, and that I adore the God,
whom philosophy has taught me to consider
as the infinite and eternal Mind, that
formed, and that sustains, the fair order of
Nature, and that created and preserves the
universal system.

To a small circle I think myself at liberty
to observe, that the manner in which the
Christian readers of the Old Testament
generally choose to understand it, appears
to me to be a little singular. While the
Deity is represented with human passions,
and those none of the best;—while he is
described as a quarrelsome, jealous, and
vindictive being;—while he is shown to be

continually changing his plans for the moral government of the world ;—and while he is depicted as a material and local God, who dwelt on a box made of Shittim wood in the temple of Jerusalem ;—they abide by the literal interpretation. They see no allegory in the first chapters of Genesis ; nor doubt, that far the greater portion of the human race is doomed to suffer eternal torments, because our first parents ate an apple, after having been tempted by a talking serpent. They find it quite simple, that the triune Jehovah should dine on veal cutlets at Abraham's table ; nor are they at all surprised, that the God of the universe should pay a visit to Ezekiel, in order to settle with the Prophet, whether he should bake his bread with human dung, or with cow's dung. In these examples the Christian readers of the Hebrew Scriptures understand no allegory.

They believe the facts to have happened literally as they are stated; and neither suspect, nor allow, that the language of the sacred writers upon such occasions may be entirely figurative. Very different is their mode of interpreting these same Scriptures, when they think there is any allusion made to the kingdom of Christ. Then they abandon the literal sense without scruple, and sometimes, it may be thought, without consideration. The Rabbins learn with astonishment, that the Song of Solomon, for example, is a mere allegory, which represents the love of Jesus for his church; and that the lady, whose navel was like a round goblet, not wanting liquor,—whose belly was like a heap of wheat, set about with lilies,—whose nose was as the tower of Lebanon, which looketh towards Damascus,—and who promised to her wellbeloved, that he should lie all night betwixt her breasts,—was not Solomon's mistress, but the Church, the spiritual spouse of Christ.

But since the Christians do admit allegory—since they even contend that the Old Testament abounds with figurative and symbolical language, descriptive of the advent of the Messiah; why will they so strenuously insist upon the strict interpretation of the text in other examples? Be their decision what it may, the theist is bound to vindicate the majesty of the Deity.

Cicero has said, that it is easier to tell what God is not, than what he is. Now every theist is surely prepared to say, that the Deity is neither unjust, nor cruel, nor liable, in any manner, to the frailties of human nature. Is it possible for the literal

interpreter of the Hebrew Scriptures to aver
this of Jehovah? The Lord hardened the
heart of Pharaoh;—was it just then to
afflict Egypt with so many calamities, on
account of Pharaoh's obstinacy? The
destruction of the seven nations, ordained
in the seventh chapter of Deuteronomy,
appears to be utterly irreconcileable either
to justice or to mercy. Their crime was
idolatry; but this was the crime of all
mankind with the exception of the Hebrews;
and the seven nations seem to have merited
so terrible a fate less than the Egyptians,
who beheld all the miracles performed by
Jehovah, and who yet continued to worship
the Gods of their country. But we cannot
wonder at these things, since the passions
of anger and jealousy, and the feeling of
repentance, or regret, which are human
infirmities, are frequently attributed to the
God of the Hebrews.

Is there a mind, capable of forming just notions of the Deity, that can believe any testimony, which records that the divine, infinite, and eternal Being is affected by accident, or is subject to passion? It is impossible for the theist to admit, that any thing is more powerful than God ; and, therefore, he cannot allow, that God can ever be in a state of passion ; for passion must always be the effect of action, and of action which cannot be resisted. Passion is sufferance, and no being suffers of its own accord. If any thing could put the divine mind into a state of passion, that thing would act independently, and in spite of God. Hobbes has said that passion is power. He should rather have held, that it proves power, for it is the effect of power.

From this view of the subject, then, I

am not afraid to state, that, if the writers of the Old Testament were really inspired, they must be supposed to have spoken figuratively on all those occasions, when they have ascribed human passions to the Supreme Being. It may be objected to me, that as the Hebrew Scriptures contain little else than the histories of squabblings and bickerings between Jehovah and his people, we might come in this way to allegorise the greater part, if not the whole, of the Old Testament. I confess, for my own part, I would rather believe the whole to be an allegory, than think for a moment, that infinite wisdom could ever waver in its judgments, could ever be disturbed by anger, or could at any time repent of what it had ordained.

These are opinions which I have no wish of promulgating to the mob; but I

call upon the theist, who has contemplated
the universe as the work of intelligence, to
consider, whether the Old Testament, if
literally interpreted, present him with such
exalted notions of the Deity, as natural
religion is itself capable of inspiring. I
must acknowledge, that the Jewish scriptures, thus understood, appear to me to
be contrary to all true theology. It is
monstrous to be told, if the sense be taken
literally, that the infinite Mind showed its
back parts to Moses. I read with pain, if
there be no allegory, that the God of nature
revealed himself to Jacob, in order that
that Hebrew shepherd should make a
journey to Bethel;—that this same keeper
of kine and sheep, after having wrestled
with a man all night, boasted in the morning that he had seen God ;—and that the
Lord of the Universe showed himself in a
vision to Jacob, standing upon the top of a

ladder. Then what are those things upon
the ladder, which our painters represent
with chubby cheeks, with wings at their
shoulders, and with long petticoats? If
Jacob saw all these things in a dream, it
must be evident that he was dreaming
indeed. Am I really to believe in the
existence of such singular conversations, as
are said, in the book of Job, to have taken
place between God and the Devil? " Skin
for skin," said Satan to Jehovah. The
expression is not very elegant, and it does
not sound very spiritual. The story of
Jonah in the fish's belly, if it be not allegorical, is a most surprising one, and the
whole must be a little puzzling to the natural historian. We are told in one of the
Psalms, that God rode upon a cherub. But
we learn from Ezekiel, that a cherub was a
strange creature with four heads, like a
man's, a lion's, a bull's, and an eagle's,—

with four wings,—with one hand,—and with
the hoofs of a calf.   This was a very singular equipage for Jehovah to choose, when
he went to take an airing.   I shall leave
the literal interpreters to explain these
things as they can.

There are, however, some yet graver
objections which I have to make against
them.   I cannot reconcile to my notions of
the perfectly wise and good Being the literal interpretation of the verse in Exodus;—
" And the Lord repented of the evil which
he thought to do unto his people."   Perfect
wisdom cannot repent of its intentions,
any more than perfect goodness can think
of doing evil.   When it is stated in Genesis, " that it repented the Lord, that he
had made man on the earth, and that it
grieved him at his heart," we can scarcely
suppose, that this was literally meant.

The prescient God cannot be imagined
to do any thing, which he foreknows he
will afterwards be grieved at his heart for
having done.

I have no doubt that the Jewish Rabbins
firmly believe, that the Deity conversed
with their ancestors upon the very various,
but not always very important, topics,
which the infinite God is said to have discussed with his priests and his prophets. It
is difficult, however, not to observe, that
some of the divine discourses are dictated
by an extraordinary spirit of vindictive
jealousy, while others are marked by a
prolixity, a garrulity, and a familiarity of
style, not altogether characteristic of the
wisdom and majesty of the Supreme Being.
The Platos, the Ciceros, and the Senecas
of the Pagan world would probably have
been astonished, if they had been assured,

that the following sentences had proceeded
from the highest intelligence.—" For I the
Lord thy God am a jealous God." (Exod.
20.) " I will bring evil upon this place."
(2 Kings, 22.) " Behold, mine anger and
my fury shall be poured out upon this
place, upon man, upon beast, upon the
trees of the field, &c." (Jer. 7.) " It
repenteth me that I have set up Saul to
be king." (1 Sam. 15.) The sages of antiquity would perhaps have thought the
tongue to be impious, which had pronounced that the God of the universe
could be in a state either of fury, or of
repentance.

The same sages, who have spoken so
divinely of the greatness and infinity of the
Supreme Intelligence, would have been
scarcely less surprised at hearing the following words.—" Go, tell my servant

b

David, Thus saith the Lord, Shalt thou not build me a house for me to dwell in? Whereas I have not dwelt in any house, since the time I brought up the children of Israel out of Egypt, even to this day, but have walked in a tent and in a tabernacle." (2 Sam. 7.)

We occasionally meet with a colloquial freedom of style, and a minuteness of detail in some of the discourses attributed to Omnipotence, which must appear rather singular to the disciple of Natural Religion. " And the Lord said unto Abraham, wherefore did Sarah laugh?" (Gen. 18.) " And the Lord smelled a sweet savor, and the Lord said in his heart, I will not again curse the ground any more, &c." (Gen. 8.) It is as difficult to conceive, how Sarah came to laugh in the presence of the Almighty, as it is to understand how the immaterial essence of the Deity dined at Abraham's table, after having had his feet washed by the pious Patriarch. The reason which is given, why the Lord said he would not curse the ground any more, appears to me to be very strange. God smelled a sweet savor ; and because his olfactory nerves were agreeably tickled, he would not curse the ground any more. It will be in vain pretended, that such a passage as this can be reconciled to a true system of theology, unless it be frankly acknowledged, that the Hebrew Scriptures are allegorical writings, in which the literal meaning is rarely the real one.

In the speeches ascribed to the Supreme Being, we meet with such sentences as the following. " And thou shalt make his pans to receive his ashes, and his shovels, and his basins, and his flesh-hooks, and his fire-pans, &c." (Exod. 27.) " Also thou shalt take of the ram the fat and the rump, and the fat that covereth the inwards, and the caul above the liver, and the two kidneys, &c." (Exod. 29.) When I lift my eyes to the starry vault of heaven, and when I recollect that God is the creator and preserver of more suns and worlds, than I can either count or imagine, I hope not to be obliged literally to believe, that the primordial, infinite, and ineffable Being talked to Moses, or to any body else, about pans and shovels, or about the fat, the rump, and the guts, of a ram.

My notions of the Divine Nature may be very heterodox, but they do not permit me to attribute human infirmities to God. I cannot suppose the Deity first creating our little earth, and then fretting because he had done so. I cannot ascribe to him

all the scolding and cursing about idolatry;
all the squabbling about capricious laws;
and all that prattling and gossiping about
insignificant rites and ceremonies, which
so frequently occur in the Jewish legends.
I cannot allow myself to imagine that the
Sacred Writers were speaking literally, when
they talked of these things; and I feel
myself compelled either to consider their
writings as impositions on the credulity of
mankind, or to believe that they are
chiefly, if not entirely, allegorical composi-
tions.

In the *Œdipus Judaicus* it will be found,
that I have adopted the latter opinion. I
recollect, that Moses was learned in all the
wisdom of the Egyptians; and I expect to
find traces of that wisdom in his works.
The learned among the ancient Egyptians
were pure theists, as Cudworth has proved.

They were deeply skilled in the sciences; but they carefully concealed their mysterious learning under innumerable symbols and allegories. May we not look then for the same things in the writings, which are ascribed to the Jewish lawgiver? It is what I have done; and I submit to the judgment of a few individuals, the result of my researches.

PRELIMINARY NOTICE.

PRELIMINARY NOTICE.

As I have had occasion to say a great deal on the subject of Astronomy in the following pages, I must take the liberty of requesting my reader to peruse them with his celestial globe beside him. He will of course make allowances for the retrograde motion of the fixed stars. There is one difficulty, which I ought to mention, and which I have felt during the whole of the time I was employed about this *opusculum.* It seems to me, at least, impossible to fix the time, when the books of the Old Testament, which I have examined, were

written. I have seen chronological tables,
where the death of Abraham is stated to
have happened in a certain year, and
where the periods, when Moses and Joshua
lived, are denoted. I confess I have very
little faith in such tables. It is likewise, I
acknowledge, not quite clear to me, who
were the authors of the books in question,
and when they lived. Circumstances have
been pointed out by Aben Ezra, by the
Pere Simon, and by others, which seem to
render it very questionable, whether Moses
were really the author of the Pentateuch.
Now without a more exact and certain
knowledge of these matters, I have thought
it better not to insist too much on the positions of the constellations, as referring to
dates given in the Chronological Tables.

I have made frequent use of the word
paranatellon; and it may be expedient to

explain it to some of my readers. The Oriental astronomers divided each sign of the zodiac into three parts. These were called decans, and amounted to thirty-six for the whole zodiacal circle. But the same astronomers also considered the constellations, or the asterisms, on both sides of the zodiacal circle, as connected with these decans. There was consequently a division of these extra-zodiacal constellations, amounting to thirty-six, the number of the decans. Now the extra-zodiacal stars, which are on either side of a decan, and which rise above the horizon, or sink below it, during the time that decan takes to rise or set, are what I call its *paranatellons*. The *paranatellons* of a whole sign may consequently be easily found. Many of the astronomical allusions of the Orientalists can only be understood by considering this theory.

There are a few observations concerning the zodiac, which I ought to make.

The constellations of the zodiac are necessarily displaced by the precession of the equinoxes. This has given rise to a distinction, which it is proper to state, because, without noticing it, we shall be led into mistakes. Astronomers, then, distinguish between a fixed and intellectual zodiac; and the moveable and visible zodiac. According to the former, *Aries* still stands as the first of the signs;—that is to say, the first thirty degrees of the zodiacal circle, reckoning from the equinoctial point in Spring, are allotted to *Aries* in the intellectual zodiac. The constellation, however, which is designed by the figure of a *Ram*, no longer occupies these first thirty degrees of the zodiacal circle. Its place is now held by *Pisces;* and the Ram has taken up the station formerly occupied by the Bull, which in its turn takes up the place formerly held by the Twins; and so of all the rest. Astronomers generally choose to reckon by the fixed and intellectual zodiac; and this seems to have been the case from a very early period. I am, indeed, inclined to think, that the ancient Egyptians and Chaldeans reckoned according to the intellectual zodiac; but that the first of the signs in their intellectual zodiac (I am speaking of very remote times) was *Taurus*. Perhaps it would not be amiss if astronomers brought the intellectual nearer to the visible zodiac. I have, however, now said enough to enable any of my readers, who may not have attended to these things, to understand, whether I be alluding, in different places, to the fixed and intellectual zodiac, or whether I be referring to that, which is retrograde and visible.

It now only remains for me to say a few words concerning the masoretic points. These, it will be seen, I have wholely discarded. If my reader wish to know why I have done so, he may consult Morinus, who in my opinion has set the question at rest. I believe, however, that there are now few Hebraists, who will think of undertaking to defend the masorah.

In addition to the above remarks, I find myself compelled to take particular notice of an objection, which has been made to my theory. I have briefly adverted to it in my dissertation on the Book of Joshua ; but I have not there given it so full a consideration as I should have done, if I had been aware of the importance, which has been attached to it by its supporters.

Some persons have contended, that when the first books of the Old Testament were written, the zodiac was not yet divided into twelve constellations ;—that when that division did take place, the zodiacal signs were not represented in the same manner by the Egyptians and Orientalists, as by the Greeks ;—and finally, that in the time of Moses the knowledge of the sphere did not yet exist.

To fix the time when the books of Moses and Joshua were written, may not be so easy a task as some of the objectors seem to suppose; but let them take the earliest period which they can reasonably assume, and I fear not to show, that before that period the division of the zodiac into twelve signs was known to the Orientalists ; and that the figures there represented did not materially differ from those, which were afterwards exhibited in the Grecian zodiac, allowing for a few exceptions, which cannot affect my general argument.

I believe, that no person will pretend, that the Pentateuch was written at an earlier era than 1500 years before Jesus Christ. My own judgment would lead me to fix the date at a much later period; but upon this point I shall not insist.

M. Bailly, in his History of Astronomy, tells us, that the zodiac of the Indians had two different divisions, one consisting of twenty-eight, and the other of twelve, constellations. He also observes, that they had two different zodiacs, the one fixed, and the other moveable. The discovery of the latter he states to have taken place about 2250 years before Jesus Christ, and consequently 750 years before the Pentateuch could have been written.

The same author places the invention of
the Persian sphere about 3000, or 3200
years before Jesus Christ, and consequently
1500 or 1700 years before the time, when
it is pretended, that Moses wrote the
Pentateuch.

To fix the exact date when the Egyptians first divided the zodiac into twelve
signs, would be very difficult. Macrobius
attributes the invention of the zodiac to
the Egyptians, and Jamblichus asserts,
that Hermes was the author of it. But it
is not easy to determine the time when
Hermes florished. The accounts concerning him are so vague and contradictory,
that it seems idle to say more than that he
lived at a very remote period of antiquity.
This second Hermes, however, seems rather
to have been the restorer, than the original
discoverer, of science; since he is said by

Manetho to have deciphered the hieroglyphics on the ancient monuments. I am
inclined to think, that the zodiac was
divided into twelve signs by the Egyptians
about the time, when they introduced the
twelve great Gods. Now the Egyptian
Hercules was one of these; and without
attributing to him the extreme antiquity,
which was claimed for him by the priests
in the time of Herodotus, we may easily
admit him to have florished long before
the age of Moses. (See Herodotus, l. 2.
c. 4. 43. 144.)

According to Diodorus Siculus, the
Grecian Hercules, whom we must not confound with the Egyptian, introduced the
knowledge of the sphere (τὸν σφαιρικὸν λόγον)
into Greece. Others have named Musæus,
and others Chiron. Be this as it may, the
Greeks appear to have become acquainted

with the sphere more than thirteen centuries before Christ; and consequently not
two centuries after the time of Moses.

We have now seen pretty clearly, I think,
that the Egyptians and Orientalists were
acquainted with the sphere and with the
zodiac, before the Pentateuch could have
been written; even allowing, what I think
to be extremely doubtful, that it was composed at so early a period as 1500 years
before Jesus Christ.

But I have passed cursorily over this
part of the subject, and have not even
noticed the high pretensions of the Chaldeans, who date their astronomical discoveries from so remote a period as the reign
of Belus. I imagine, that the objectors
are chiefly disposed to argue, that the forms
now exhibited in the Oriental zodiacs have

been copied from the zodiac of the Greeks. It is then to this subject that I must direct the attention of my reader; and although the due limits of a mere preliminary notice will compel me to be brief, I have yet no doubt that I shall be able completely to repel this objection.

M. Bailly seems inclined to think, that the Indian zodiac was the most ancient of any. We have already seen, that the Indians invented their moveable zodiac 750 years before the time of Moses. In the Philosophical Transactions for 1772, we find a representation of an Indian zodiac. Its resemblance to our's, though it differ in some respects, is exceedingly striking. *Aquarius* is represented by an urn. In *Pisces*, there is only one fish. In the two next signs we find the Ram and the Bull. Instead of the Twins, a man is represented

with two shields. The two next signs are
the same as our's. *Virgo* is depicted as a
young girl seated according to the Oriental
fashion. The *Balance* is exhibited as by
us; the image of the *Scorpion* is much
defaced; and *Sagittarius* is represented by
a bow and arrow. We denote *Capricorn*
by a goat with the tail of a fish; but in this
Indian zodiac the goat and the fish are
separated. The objectors pretend, that this
zodiac must have been copied from a Greek
zodiac after the time of Alexander. But
it is not the character of the Indians to
copy from other nations; and when they
do condescend to become copyists, they
are, I am assured, minutely faithful to their
originals. The very discrepancies, then,
which may be observed in the Indian and
the Grecian zodiacs, may lead us to believe,
that it was the Greeks who made the
changes. The love of change belonged as

much to the character of the Greeks, as it was remote from that of the Indians. Let us also observe, that this Indian zodiac is square. Now the Indians would hardly have taken this figure, if they had seen the circular zodiac of the Greeks. Then the goat and the fish are separated in the Indian zodiac, and united in the Greek; and this affords a strong presumptive proof of the former having been the original; because it is more natural for a copyist to combine two distinct ideas, than to separate them after they have once been united. Again, this Indian zodiac contains but one fish in *Pisces*. Of this there is no example in the Greek zodiacs; but it would seem from Kircher, that Ichthon, or rather Dagon, had his station in this sign in the Egyptian zodiac.

Sir William Jones was a tolerable judge

of these matters, and he strongly maintains the antiquity of the Indian zodiac. His translation from the Sanscrit verses, in which the Indians give an account of their own zodiac, is so curious, that I shall transcribe it. " The *Ram, Bull, Crab, Lion,* and *Scorpion,* have the figures of those five animals respectively: the *Pair* (the *Twins*) are a damsel playing on a *Vina* (a harp), and a youth wielding a mace: the *Virgin* stands on a boat in water, holding in one hand a lamp, in the other an ear of rice-corn; the *Balance* is held by a weigher, with a weight in one hand : the *Bow* by an archer, whose hinder parts are like those of a horse: the *Sea-monster* has the face of an antelope: the *Ewer* is a water-pot, borne on the shoulder of a man, who empties it : the *Fish* are two with their heads turned to each other's tails, &c." But I shall leave the objectors to answer the arguments of

Bailly and Jones concerning the zodiac of
the Indians, and shall proceed to consider
that of the Persians.

Diodorus Siculus tells us, that a God
was supposed by the Persians to preside
over each of the twelve signs of the zodiac.
But it appears from the Zendavesta, that
this division of the zodiac was made in the
time of Zoroaster.   Hyde has most erroneously placed Zoroaster as contemporary
with Darius.   Suidas fixes his era at 500
years before the Trojan war.   Plutarch
places him 5000 years before that time;
and though I shall not say with Pliny, that
Zoroaster lived many thousand years before
Moses, yet I have no great hesitation in
admitting, that the Persian preceded the
Jewish sage by several centuries.   (Consult
Plutarch, de Is. et Osir. and Pliny, l. 30.
c. 1.)   Now what are the figures of the

Persian zodiac described in that most
ancient book the Zendavesta? They are
thus named in their order :—The *Lamb*, the
Bull, the *Twins*, the *Crab*, the *Lion*, the
Ear of corn, the *Balance*, the *Scorpion*, the
Bow, the *Goat*, the *Pitcher*, and the
Fishes.

I shall not dispute whether the Egyptians were, or were not, the first inventors
of the zodiacal images. I must, however,
most strongly protest against the idea, that
they ever copied their symbols from the
Greeks. I have already shown, that there
is every reason to conclude, that the Egyptians had divided the zodiac into twelve
constellations, centuries before the age of
Moses. I shall now endeavour to prove,
that the Greeks copied the images of their
zodiac from the Egyptians and the Orientalists.

1. Hipparchus, if I do not err, was the first among the Greeks, who established what has since been called the fixed zodiac; and he placed *Aries* as the first of the signs. Theon, indeed, reproves Aratus for making *Cancer* the first of the signs, when the Egyptians, whom Theon intimates Aratus to have been copying, made *Aries* the first. This shows then, that the Greeks were in the habit of copying the Egyptians in these matters. It is besides obvious, that *Aries* has little or nothing to do with Greek mythology. The Ram was the well-known type of the Egyptian Ammon. In the planispheres of Kircher we find the Ram's horns. In those of Dendera the Ram is represented, as also in the fragment of the Egyptian zodiac found at Rome, of which an engraving is given by Bailly.

2. The *Bull* was a symbol of the sun,

known all over the East, long before it can be pretended that the Greeks had a zodiac at all. On many Indian, as well as on many Persian, monuments, we find the Bull. Then the worship of *Apis*, proved by the Pentateuch itself to be so ancient, may lead us to wonder how it can be fancied, that the Greeks were the first, who placed this symbol in the zodiac.

3. The Greeks claim the symbol of the third sign as their own invention; and the story of Castor and Pollux may have been the production of their imagination. Some of their mythologists, however, designate the twins by the names of Hercules and Apollo, while Plutarch calls them Harpocrates and Helitomemion, the sons of Isis and Osiris. But this sign proves pretty clearly the disposition of the Greeks to make the zodiacal symbols accord with

their own mythology; and may perhaps
tend to convince the objectors, that the
Greeks, and not the Orientalists, were the
copyists.   In the Sanscrit verses, to which
I have already referred, we are told, that
the Indians represented the sign in question by a damsel playing on a harp, and
by a youth wielding a mace.   The Greeks
converted these symbols into Apollo with
his lyre, and Hercules with his club.   Now
in the fragment of the Egyptian zodiac
found at Rome, the sign of the Twins is
represented by a female with a harp, and
by a man with a mace.   Is not this an
extraordinary coincidence between the
Indian and Egyptian zodiacs?   If the
Indians and the Egyptians had been the
copyists, how came they both to change
the form of Apollo into that of a young
woman? This could not have been arranged
by agreement; and it could hardly have

happened by accident. I am, however, very well convinced, that one of the twins in the ancient Egyptian zodiacs was represented by Anubis; and in this, I think, I am supported, not only by one of Kircher's planispheres, but by the great zodiac of Dendera, so accurately given in the plates, which accompany Mr. Hamilton's travels. In all events, the similarity between the Indian zodiac and the Egyptian fragment, seems to prove that the Greeks copied the symbol of the Twins from the Orientalists.

4. The more ancient Egyptians placed *Hermanubis*, or "Hermes with the head of an ibis," in the sign of *Cancer*. In the Grecian zodiacs we find the Crab, and the reason why that animal was stationed there is ingeniously given by Macrobius. But even this symbol appears to have been sug-

gested by the Egyptians. In the zodiacs of Dendera we find a Beetle instead of a Crab, and as the Beetle rolls its ball of dung in retrograding, it is not less a proper symbol for the sign than the Crab. I must confess, however, that I suspect that there is more ingenuity than truth in the conjecture of Macrobius.

I have likewise a great suspicion, that the same author has shown more imagination than judgment in the reasoning which he employs, when he endeavours to account for the position of *Capricorn* among the signs.

5. That the history of the twelve labors of Hercules refers to the progress of the sun through the twelve signs of the zodiac is, I believe, generally admitted ; but I cannot allow, that the lion was first placed among

the zodiacal symbols, because Hercules was fabled to have slain the Nemean lion. It would seem, on the contrary, that Hercules, who represented the Sun, was said to have slain the lion, because *Leo* was already a zodiacal sign. There are several reasons which induce me to think, that the Egyptians were the first, who placed the lion in the zodiac. The combat of Hercules with the lion was his first labor; and one of the several years of the Egyptians commenced at the Summer Solstice. The Grecian Hercules florished about 1350 years before our era, and consequently when, according to the fixed zodiac, the Summer Solstice accorded with *Leo*. Reckoning by the year in question, some of the Greek astronomers appear to have made *Leo*, (and afterwards *Cancer*), the first of the signs. Hence it was in compliance with what they believed to be the mode of reckoning in

Egypt, that the Greeks made the combat with the lion the first labor of Hercules. Theon afterwards showed them, that they were wrong in supposing, that the Egyptians had thus counted the signs from the Summer Solstice. There seems to be no reason why the Greeks should place a lion, an animal with which they could have had but little acquaintance, in the zodiac. The Egyptians had a most obvious reason. Diodorus Siculus (l. 3. c. 22.) mentions, that the lions appeared in great numbers, and became extremely formidable in Ethiopia, about the time of the Summer Solstice, and when the Nile is at its greatest elevation. Strabo, if I recollect rightly, speaks to the same purpose in his sixteenth book. It was then extremely natural for the Egyptians to place the lion, where we find him in the zodiac.

6. The Greeks have abundance of fables about the sign of *Virgo* : but this appears to have been originally no other than the symbol of the Egyptian Isis.

7. In the Indian zodiac, (in the Philosophical Transactions,) the sign of *Libra* is represented as by us. In Jones's Indian zodiac, a woman holds the balance. The Alexandrian zodiac is said not to have contained the balance, and its place was occupied by the Scorpion's claws. It is found, however, in the zodiacs of Esne and Dendera.

8. I believe, that the ancient Egyptians represented the eighth sign by various symbols;—sometimes by a snake,—sometimes by a crocodile—sometimes by a scorpion, &c. This last symbol is to be found on all the Mithraic monuments ; and it is pretty

d

evident, that those monuments must have
been constructed, when the vernal equinox
accorded with *Taurus*. I am, indeed, apt
to think, that the Mithraic monuments
might have been constructed, when the vernal equinox accorded with *Taurus*, as we
find that constellation in the sensible zodiac.
In all events, it appears vain to contend,
that the Greeks were the first, who employed
the Scorpion as an astronomical symbol.

9. Pococke, in his description of the East,
has exhibited a fragment of an ancient
Egyptian monument, on which the sign of
Sagittarius was represented as it is by us.
This symbol is likewise to be found in
Jones's Indian zodiac, and in the zodiacs
of Esne and Dendera.

10. The most general traditions, even
among the Greeks themselves, concerning

the sign of *Capricorn*, refer the origin of the symbol to Egypt. (Consult Hyginus, l. II. c. 29.—Theon, p. 136.—Germanicus, c. 27. &c.)

11. The Greeks have in vain endeavoured to reconcile the symbols of the eleventh sign to their mythology. *Canobus* with his pitcher is the evident prototype of *Aquarius* with his urn.

12. The sign of *Pisces* has nothing to do with Grecian mythology. The Greeks themselves appear to refer this symbol to the Chaldeans. It is, however, to be found in Jones's Indian zodiac, and in some Egyptian fragments, as well as in the zodiacs of Esne and Dendera. (See Pocoke's Description of the East—Kircher's Œdipus, Vol. 3.—Hamilton's Egyptiaca, &c.)

I shall conclude these remarks, which I have been obliged to put together more hastily than I could have wished, by observing, that the existence of the Indian zodiac, published in the Philosophical Transactions for 1772, and of the zodiac at Esne, are sufficient of themselves to establish my argument. It appears that the zodiac of Esne could not have been constructed at a later period than 4700 years before our era, because *Leo* is there placed as an ascending sign; and consequently this zodiac is, at least, 3500 years older than the Grecian zodiac, even if we suppose that Hercules introduced a zodiac into Greece. From this we may judge of the folly of talking about Eudoxus and Hipparchus—men who lighted their tapers at the embers of that nearly extinguished fire, of which the blaze had once illumined all the East. The Indian zodiac is yet

more ancient than that of Esne. The reasons which Dupuis, whose astronomical
knowledge was immense, has given, in order
to show that this zodiac was constructed,
when the Summer Solstice accorded with
Virgo, appear to me to be quite conclusive. Now the forms, both in the Indian
zodiac, and in that of Esne, nearly correspond with those in the Grecian zodiac.
The sign of *Virgo* is represented by a
sphinx, the symbol of Isis in the zodiac of
Esne; and, with this exception, the Greeks
have exhibited nearly the same symbols.
But even here, it must be observed, that
the figure of the *Virgin*, or of *Isis*, is to be
found in some very ancient Egyptian
monuments. In Jones's Indian zodiac the
figure of *Virgo* announces an Egyptian
origin. Be this as it may, the objectors to
my theory will be puzzled to show, that the

forms in the Grecian zodiac were not copied from the Orientalists; and I now boldly assert, that not only before the Greeks had a zodiac at all, but centuries before the Pentateuch was written, the forms and symbols of the Oriental zodiacs, as far as the twelve signs were concerned, without speaking of the decans and paranatellons, did not materially differ from those, which the Greeks copied into their own zodiac. I admit, that there were some discrepancies; but, as I have said before, these cannot affect my general argument.

It only remains for me to observe, that in a work in which so many various languages are employed, and in which so many subjects are placed in new points of view, as in the present work, it would be much too presumptuous in me to imagine, that I have not occasionally fallen into errors. For these I shall claim the indulgence of my readers; and the more especially as it will not be in my power to correct the press, or to revise the sheets. I am confident, indeed, that I am now in much safer hands, than when I was compelled by more important occupations, to leave the *Herculanensia* to the mercy of a Sicilian Printer, from whose edition that work was reprinted in England before my arrival, and consequently when it was not in my power to repair its numerous errors. But in spite of the well-known accuracy of Mr. Valpy, who has undertaken to print the *Œdipus Judaicus*, I must expect that errors of the press will probably occur. I trust that these will be few in number, because I am fully aware that there are critics in the world, who are ever ready to

take undue and disingenuous advantage of
every trivial fault which they can find,
whether it proceed from the inaccuracy of
the Author, or whether it be caused by the
inattention of his Printer.

Observations

ON THE

PLATES

ANNEXED TO THE

ŒDIPUS JUDAICUS.

OBSERVATIONS

ON THE

PLATES

ANNEXED TO THE

ŒDIPUS JUDAICUS.

Plates I. II. III. IV.

THE first four Plates are copied in miniature from the Egyptian zodiacs and planispheres exhibited by Kircher. To the accuracy of these, many objections have been made, but Bailly has certainly repelled the most important of them. (Histoire de l' Astronomie, p. 500.)

Plate V.

This Plate represents the fragment of a zodiac found at Rome. Bailly mentions it in the following terms: " M. De Fontenelle dit que ce planisphère est Egyptien et Grec; pour nous, nous le croyons purement Egyptien, et nous y reconnoîtrons des traces de son Origine Indienne."

Plate VI.

The twelve zodiacal signs are here copied in miniature from the engraving of the great oblong zodiac of Dendera, exhibited in the plates annexed to Mr. Hamilton's Ægyptiaca. Mr. Hamilton has shown, with his usual learning, that the temple of Dendera was either built or repaired about the time of Tiberius; but I am not quite satisfied with the reasons which he gives for supposing, that this zodiac was constructed at the same period. Mr. Hamilton says, that when this zodiac was constructed, the Summer

Solstice was about $\frac{400}{2225}$ parts of the sign of *Cancer* removed from that of *Leo*. The reasons which he gives for thinking so may be perfectly just; but it does not appear from the zodiac itself, that it was constructed about the time of Christ. The Summer Solstice seems to be placed in it, Mr. Hamilton says, in *Cancer*, about 400 years from *Leo*. But it must be remembered, that the stars of *Gemini* now occupy nearly the same space in the heavens, with respect to the Solstice, which was held by those of *Cancer* 2150 years ago. The Summer Solstice now takes place, when the Sun is in the first degree of *Gemini*. There are then about 54 degrees to reckon, in order to bring the Solstice back to $\frac{400}{2225}$ parts of *Cancer* removed from *Leo*. Lalande thought that this zodiac was constructed about the time when the Solstice was at 15° of *Cancer*; and that astronomer, therefore, fixed its date about 1200 years before Christ. But Mr. Hamilton puts the Solstice, when this same zodiac was constructed, about 24° or 25° of *Cancer*. Now if Lalande placed the date of the construction at 1200 years before Christ, because he reckoned from 15° of *Cancer*, Mr. Hamilton, who reckons the date from 24° or 25° of *Cancer*, ought to have placed it more than 1800 years before the same era. Lalande, however, is so far wrong. If the Solstice be marked at 15° of *Cancer*, Lalande should have fixed its date about 1350, and not 1200 years before Christ.

Plate VII.

In this Plate the zodiacal figures of the circular zodiac of Dendera are represented in miniature, from the engraving of them in Mr. Hamilton's work; but neither in this, nor in the preceding Plate, have I ventured to copy the forms given to the decans and paranatellons. This would have required too large a Plate for my little work.

Visconti thinks that when this zodiac was constructed, the Sun at the Summer Solstice was in *Cancer*, because he finds the *Balance* among the zodiacal forms, and this, he appears to believe, must have been always a symbol of the equinox. But it seems very doubtful to me, whether this proposition be true. Dupuis has fixed the date of the Indian zodiac, which contains the *Balance*, at a period when this sign could not have corresponded with the equinox. I shall presently have to show, that the same thing is true of the zodiac of Esne. It has been proved by Bailly, that those who have contended that the *Balance* had no place among the zodiacal forms until a comparatively late period, are altogether in an error. In fact I find no good reason for supposing, that the *Balance* was originally intended as a symbol of the Equinox. Macrobius pretended, that *Capricorn* and *Cancer* were symbols of the Solstices; but Bailly has clearly shown, that the reasoning of Macrobius cannot be admitted.

Plate VIII.

The representation of the Zodiac of Esne is here copied from the celebrated French work on "Egypt," lately published at Paris. Mr. Hamilton admits that *Leo* is here depicted as an ascending sign; and though he seems afterwards to take alarm at the great antiquity, which he consequently assigns to this Zodiac, he nevertheless in the first place fixes its date about 4500 years ago. When I observe, that

I myself have spoken rather loosely about dates, and especially in my dissertation on the 49th chapter of Genesis, I have, perhaps, little right to find fault with Mr. Hamilton for having done the same thing. In fact, all this confusion about dates, to be determined by astronomical observations, arises from speaking sometimes of the fixed and intellectual Zodiac, and sometimes of the moveable and sensible Zodiac. Thus, when Mr. Hamilton allows, that we cannot assign a less remote antiquity to the Zodiac of Esne, than nearly 4500 years, he evidently fixes the Summer Solstice, in the first degree of *Cancer*, where, however, the Solstitial colure has not really been for more than 2000 years. The vernal Equinox had been retrograding through the constellation of *Aries*, and the Summer Solstice through the constellation of *Cancer*, for more than 2000 years before the time of Eudoxus. " Eudoxe, astronome Grec," says Bailly, " rapporte que les Solstices et les équinoxes étoient fixés au quinzième dégré, c'est à dire, au milieu du Belier, de l'Ecrévisse, de la Balance, et du Capricorne. On verra que cette détermination, rapportée par Eudoxe, est antérieure à son tems, et qu'elle remonte au siecle de Chiron, vers 1353 ans avant Jésus

Christ. By the same rule then, if the Zodiac of Dendera were formed at the time when the Summer Solstice answered to 15° of *Cancer*, we must fix its antiquity at about 1353 years before Christ; and we must allow the Zodiac of Esne, which refers the same solstice to the 1° of *Virgo*, to be more than 3000 years more ancient than that of Dendera.

It may be proper to retract an opinion, that I have given elsewhere, namely, that the sign of *Scorpius* was represented by a crocodile in the most ancient Egyptian Zodiacs. Both the *Scorpion* and the *Balance* are to be found in the Zodiac of Esne.

If my reader wish to ascertain the precise date of the Zodiac of Esne, he must consult the French work itself. But I think it is evident that the Solstice could not yet have been in *Leo*, which is there represented as the last of the ascending signs. Let us then place it in the first degree of *Virgo*. But it is at the present day in the first degree of *Gemini*, and if, at a rough calculation, we allow 2150 years for the retrograde motion through each celestial sign, we shall easily find the age of this Zodiac. In fact, the Autumnal equinox now corresponds with the first degree of *Virgo*; and consequently if we find a Zodiac, in which the Summer Solstice was placed, where the Autumnal equinox now is, that Zodiac carries us back 90 degrees on the ecliptic, and its date must be fixed about 6450 years ago.

Plate IX.

The Indian Zodiac represented in this Plate is thus mentioned by M. Dupuis.

" Le Zodiaque Indien, publié dans les Transactions Philosophiques de 1772, est un quadrilatère, autour duquel sont distribués les douze signes, de manière qu'aux quatre angles se trouvent la Vierge, le Sagittaire, les Poissons, et les Gemeaux; et la Vierge, répétée une seconde fois, se trouve encore placée au centre du cadre, la tête environnée de rayons. Nous imaginons, que ce monument réprésente l'état du ciel, dans l'age, où la

Vierge occupoit le Solstice d'été, et où l'Equinoxe de Printems répondoit aux Gemeaux ; position qu'ont dû avoir les cieux, depuis l'invention de l'astronomie, comme l'a très-bien fait voir Bailly ; et voici comme nous procédons pour arriver à cette conclusion. Ceux qui placèrent les douze signes dans l'ordre où ils sont dans ce monument, où il n'y a point d'Equateur, ni d'Ecliptique, dont l'intersection puisse désigner un commencement du Zodiaque, dûrent naturellement placer aux quatre angles du Quadrilatère les quatre signes, qui occupoient alors les quatre points cardinaux de la sphère. Ils dûrent faire du signe, qui occupoit le Solstice d'été, le dernier des signes ascendans, et le premier des signes descendans ; le signe du Solstice d'hiver dut être également le dernier des signes descendans, et le commencement des signes ascendans. Or, c'est précisément la place que la Vierge et les Poissons, signes solstitiaux, occupent dans ce monument. Tous les animaux sont réprésentés, marchant dans la même direction, tels que le Belier, le Taureau, le Lion ; et le commencement du mouvement de haut en bas se fait à la Vierge, et celui de bas en haut se fait aux Poissons. La Vierge est donc le terme du mouvement du soleil en ascension, et le point où il commence à descendre, pour parcourir les autres signes. Elle occupe donc le Solstice d'été, ou le trône du Soleil, et voilà pourquoi elle est encore une fois répétée, et placée au centre du planisphère, comme la Reine des Cieux." (Dupuis, tom. 6. part 1.) To these observations Dupuis has added many others not less interesting, but too long for insertion here. It is evident that if he be right in his hypothesis, this zodiac must be at least as ancient as that of Esne.

Plate X.

This Plate can hardly be considered as interesting in any other point of view, than as exhibiting an Indian zodiac, with the figures drawn obviously from no Grecian copy. It seems to me quite clear, that it is not of a more ancient date than the zodiac of Hipparchus. Its antiquity, therefore, cannot recommend it to our attention. Sir W. Jones, who had this zodiac engraved, was a man of most extraordinary talents. As a linguist, he seems to have had few, if any, equals; but I am obliged to confess, that I do not exactly follow him in his notions concerning the antiquity of the Indian zodiac. In the treatise which he wrote on that subject he maintains, in opposition to M. Montucla, that the Indians took their zodiac neither from the Greeks, nor from the Arabs; and he argues that they obtained it, and their knowledge of the stars, from the Chaldeans, about 1000, or 1200 years before the Christian era. In the Supplement to his Essay on Indian Chronology, Sir W. Jones gives us the following extract from the Hindu astronomer *Varaha.*

" Certainly the Southern Solstice was once in the middle of *Aslesha,* the Northern in the first degree of *Dhanishta,* by what is recorded in former *Sastras.* At present one solstice is in the first degree of *Carcata,* and the other in the first of *Macara,* &c."

Upon this I observe, that, according to Sir W. Jones, *Aslesha* and *Dhanishta* are the Indian names of the first Lunar mansions in *Leo* and *Aquarius;* and that *Carcata* and *Macara* answer to the signs of *Cancer* and *Capricorn.*

It would seem, then, that *Varaha* lived, when the solstices were in the first degrees of *Cancer* and *Capricorn*, and when these solstices were removed by a whole sign at least from their places, according to the ancient *Sastras*. It is now above 2000 years since the solstices accorded with the first degrees of *Cancer* and *Capricorn;* and it is more than double that period since they corresponded with the first Lunar mansions of *Leo* and *Aquarius*. It would seem to follow then, that *Varaha* lived above 2000 years ago, and referred to the Sun's place in the zodiac, as described more than 2000 years before his own time. Sir W. Jones does not take notice of this very simple and obvious calculation; and draws a very different result from the words of *Varaha*.

" The Hindu astronomers agree," says he, " that the 1st of January 1790 was in the year 4891 of the *Caliyuga,* or their fourth period, at the beginning of which, they say, the equinoctial points were in the first degrees of *Mesha* and *Tula,* (*Aries* and *Libra;*) but they are also of opinion, that the vernal equinox oscillates from the third of *Mina* (*Pisces*) to the 27th of *Mesha,* and back again in 7200

years, which they divide into four *padas*, and consequently
that it moves, in the two intermediate *padas*, from the 1st
to the 27th of *Mesha* and back again, in 3600 years; the
colure cutting the ecliptic in the 1st of *Mesha*, which
coincides with the 1st of *Aswini*, (1st lunar mansion in
Aries) at the beginning of every such oscillatory period.
Varaha, surnamed *Mihira*, or the Sun, from his knowledge
of astronomy, and usually distinguished by the title of
Acharya, or teacher of the *Veda*, lived confessedly when
the *Caliyuga* was far advanced; and since by actual observation he found the solstitial points in the first degrees of
Carcata and *Macara*, the equinoctial points were at the
same time in the 1st of *Mesha* and *Tula*: he lived, therefore, in the year 3600 of the 4th Indian period, or 1291
years before the 1st of January 1790, that is, about the
year 499 of our era, &c."

All the reasoning, which the very learned author here
employs, is founded on the calculations of the modern
Hindu astronomers. But what is to be said of the calculations of astronomers, who place the equinoctial points at
the beginning of their *Caliyuga*, nearly 5000 years ago,

in the first degrees of *Mesha* and *Tula* (*Aries* and *Libra*
and who talk of the oscillation of the vernal equinox from
the 3d of *Mina* (*Pisces*) to the 27th of *Mesha* (*Aries*),
and back again; and who make the colure cut the ecliptic
in the 1st of *Mesha*, at the beginning of each such oscillatory period? Sir W. Jones says, that *Varaha* found the
solstitial points *by actual observation* in the first degrees
of *Carcata* and *Macara*, or *Cancer* and *Capricorn*. It is
utterly impossible, if he really did so, that he could have
lived 499 years after Christ: on the contrary, he must
have lived nearly 400 years before our era, when the solstices were in the first degrees of *Cancer* and *Capricorn*.

But it may be said, that *Varaha* calculated like the
modern Hindu astronomers; and that at the commencement of each oscillatory period he brought the colure to
cut the ecliptic in the first degree of *Aries;* and having
done this, he was compelled to make a similar arrangement for the solstices. *Varaha,* however, says nothing of
the kind, and only affirms that in his time the solstices
corresponded with the first degrees of *Carcata* and *Macara,*

but that, according to former *Sastras*, they were once in *Aslesha* and in *Dhanishta*.

But even admitting, that *Varaha* taught this strange doctrine of an oscillating equinox, it is evident that it was unknown in the time when the *Sastras* to which he refers were written. The modern astronomers of India, it seems, make the vernal equinox oscillate from the 3d degree of *Pisces*, to the 27th of Aries, and back again. The Summer solstice, then, ought to oscillate from the 3d degree of *Gemini* to the 27th of *Cancer* and back again; and this state of things has existed since the commencement of the *Caliyuga*, nearly 5000 years ago. If then the ancient Hindu astronomers, who were the authors of the *Sastras*, mentioned by *Varaha*, had had the same system with the modern astronomers of India, they never could have placed the Summer solstice, since the commencement of the *Caliyuga*, in the first degree of *Leo*, because the limits of the oscillation of this solstice are the 3d of *Gemini* on one side, and the 27th of *Cancer* on the other.

Varaha says positively, that the Summer solstice is recorded in the ancient *Sastras* to have corresponded with *Aslesha,* or with the first degree of *Leo.* It is a fact, that since the commencement of the *Caliyuga,* the Summer solstice has corresponded with the first degree of *Leo.* This must have happened about the 700th year of the *Caliyuga,* or about 4300 years ago; and I must consequently conclude, that the observation was made at that period by the authors of the *Sastras.*

I have shown, that the authors of the *Sastras* could not have had the same system with the more modern Hindu astronomers; and I now pretend, that since they had not the same system, it seems vain to make the modern system the basis of our reasoning with respect to the ancient. The ancient astronomers marked the Summer solstice in the sign of *Leo.* It was actually there 4300 years ago. The modern astronomers make the vernal equinox to oscillate from the 3d degree of *Pisces* to the 27th of *Aries,* and back again, for a period of 7200 years, of which they say nearly 5000 years are elapsed. But each solstitial point must invariably be at the distance of 90° from each equinoctial point. Then the Summer solstice can never have corresponded with the 1st degree of *Leo* for the last 5000 years, according to the modern Hindu system. How then shall we apply any calculations made by the more modern astronomers of India, to the observations of their ancient progenitors, who have left records of the position of the Summer solstice having been in the first degree of *Leo*?

Plates XI. XII. XIII.

These Plates represent the Mithraic astronomical monuments as they are exhibited by Hyde (Hist. Rel. vet. Pers. p. 113.) and which evidently refer to a time, when Virgil might have truly said,

> " Candidus auratis aperit cum cornibus annum
> *Taurus.*"

" L'équinoxe," says Bailly, " n'a pu répondre au dernier degré du Taureau que vers 4600 ans avant Jésus

Christ." The Mithraic monuments appear to have been constructed while the vernal equinox corresponded with *Taurus*,—the Summer solstice with *Leo*, &c. For further information concerning these monuments, my reader may consult Kircher's Œdipus, Vol. i. p. 216. and Hyde, *in loco citato*. But in order that I may satisfy those, who cannot immediately refer to Kircher and Hyde, I shall transcribe one sentence from the latter. D. Hieronymus per *portentosa simulacra* (words employed by St. Jerome in speaking of the cave of Mithras, and its sculptured images) videtur intelligere solem in duodecim signis secundùm singula Dodecatemoria, quæ (inquam) videntur fuisse ex supellectili antri Mithraici. This is sufficient to show, that I do not call these monuments astronomical upon my own authority. But if they be astronomical, it is clear, that they refer to a time when the Bull really did open the year, as the bare inspection of them is sufficient to prove.

I have ventured to suggest, in my Dissertation on the 49th chapter of Genesis, that these, or similar *simulacra*, must have been familiar to the mind of Jacob. In the symbolical language which he addresses to Joseph, I think, he makes a direct allusion to them.

I have directed my engraver to alter the attitude of one of the figures, (in Plate 13) whose action, however, may still be understood. The ancients were not offended with such representations as those, which are found on the Mithraic monuments, because they considered them as merely symbolical; but the moderns entertain very different notions concerning these things, and it is needless to shock delicacy, even where we may think it more fastidious than is necessary.

I have placed *Succoth Benoth,* the hen and chickens, in the 11th plate. For further information concerning this symbol of the *Pleiades,* my reader may consult Selden, *de Dis Syris,* and the *Pantheon Hebræorum.* The representation, which I have given, is copied from Kircher; but the Syro-Chaldean words in his plate are nearly illegible. I have written them out distinctly. As, however, the letters are extremely ill-formed in the original, I will not answer for having restored the true reading. The

Syro-Chaldean is a jargon ; but still as I have written out
the words, they will be understood by any person who can
read the language.   As the characters are placed in Kircher's edition, there are manifestly false readings.

I have also copied the figure of an Indian God, as it is
given in the 25th plate of Moor's Pantheon.   This is so
exactly the form of the Egyptian Ammon, that, I think,
the resemblance, if not the identity, must be evident.

Plate XIV.

The 12 signs, with the Sun, copied from the Indian
zodiac, exhibited in the valuable Pantheon of Mr. Moor.

I think this zodiac extremely interesting ; for though I
imagine the picture in Colonel Stuart's possession to be
modern, yet I am of opinion, that the painter must have
generally copied it from some very ancient monument.
The Persian names may have been written by the modern

artist; and even the *costume* of some of the figures may have been changed. From the position, however, of *Suriya,* or the Sun, the original may be supposed to be of not less ancient date than that exhibited in the Philosophical Transactions. *Suriya* is seated in a chariot drawn by seven horses, which are probably emblematical of the seven planets. But *Suriya* has his back turned to *Virgo,* whence we may suppose, that the solstitial point corresponded with that sign, when the zodiac was originally constructed.

Plate XV.

In this Plate a miniature copy is given of the Camp of the Hebrews, slightly altered from Kircher's edition of it. The reasons which have induced me to make these changes are stated in different parts of my work.

It may be necessary for me to observe here, that when I wrote my Dissertation on the 49th chapter of Genesis, I did not perceive so fully, as I do at present, the truth, or importance, of the system, which I have since adopted. I have consequently spoken with less attention to some astronomical facts than I should have done. Thus I have said, that astronomy was first cultivated in the East, when the Summer solstice answered to *Leo*. That this is a mistake, and that we ought to carry the origin of astronomy to a much more remote period, must be evident from the monuments, which I have been considering. There are also some other little errors of expression in the Dissertation, which, I trust, my candid readers will impute to my ignorance of the necessity of employing more precise and scientific language. I had almost unconsciously touched a part of a system; and I consequently did not suspect, that that part was connected with others, forming altogether the great whole, which has since opened on my view. When we speak of astronomical subjects, we too often employ a familiar language, which does not strictly in most instances, and which does not at all in others, correspond with the truth. I believe, that in a few examples I have been guilty of this sort of negligence; but I hope in very few, indeed, where it can be essential to my general argument. I must expect, however, that every advantage will be taken of every error which has escaped my pen.

There seems to me to be no doubt, that some changes were made in the arrangement of the standards of the tribes. I have as little doubt, that when Moses established the standards of Judah, Reuben, Ephraim, and Dan, as the principal ones in the camp of the Hebrews, that he did so rather in compliance with the prejudices of the people, than with his own judgment. The same thing must have influenced him in the choice of the cherubic heads. The solstitial and equinoctial points had ceased to answer to the Lion, to the Man with the pitcher, to the Bull, and to the Scorpion, for several centuries before the time of Moses. But the superstition of the people seems to have prevailed, and the ancient traditions confirmed the ignorant populace in all their notions.

Plate XVI.

It has been objected to me, that in my Dissertation on the 49th chapter of Genesis, I have so often appealed to Hyginus, Columella, and other writers, for the rising and setting of the constellations, instead of referring to the time when Jacob died. My answer to this is very simple; we know pretty exactly the time when the above-mentioned writers lived; but I avow, I do not know precisely when Jacob died. If, however, any person has fixed that period to his own satisfaction, he will easily find the times of the rising and setting of the constellations by the help of his globe. In the mean time the reader may arrange the decans and paranatellons for each of the standards upon the plan, which I have given for that of Judah in this plate.

The paranatellons are represented on the standard, as the Jews, Egyptians, Persians, and Orientalists, have described them; and the correspondence of the symbols with Jacob's words appears very remarkable.

The form of the

EGYPTIAN ZODIAC

constructed

by the

Second HERMES according to

KIRCHER.

T. Baxter sc.

EGYPTIAN PLANISPHERE
containing the

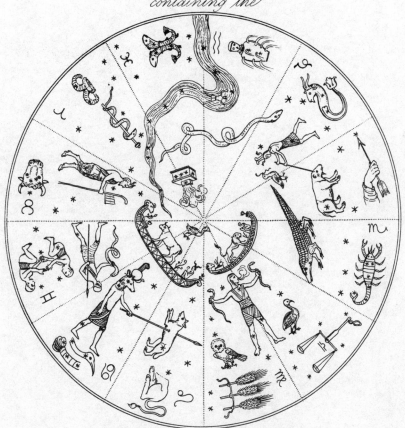

ZODIACAL SIGNS
with the
SOVTHERN CONSTELLATIONS
according to KIRCHER.

T. Baxter sc.

EGYPTIAN
PLANISPHERE
containing the

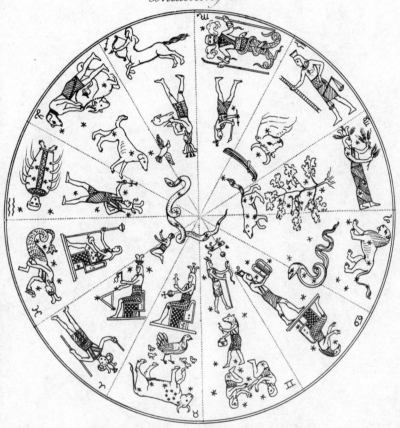

ZODIACAL SIGNS
with the
NORTHERN CONSTELLATIONS
according to KIRCHER.

T. Baxter sc.

4

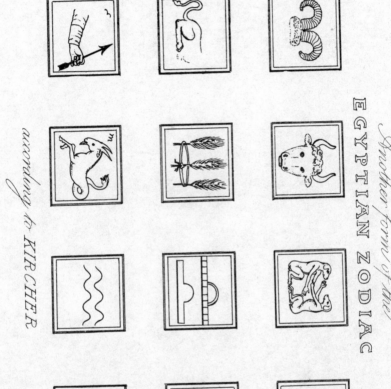

Another form of the

EGYPTIAN ZODIAC

according to KIRCHER

V. Baker sc.

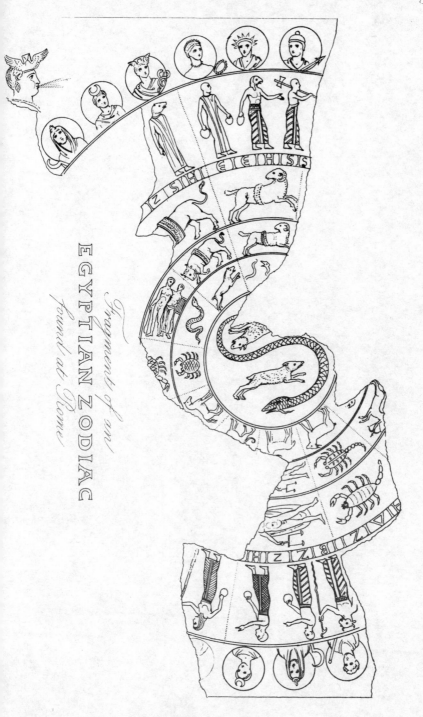

Fragments of an
EGYPTIAN ZODIAC
found at Rome

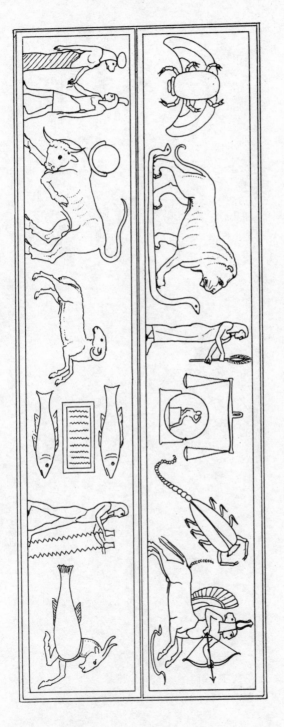

The Annular ZODIACAL SIGNS from the

OBLONG ZODIAC of DENDERA

T. Baxter sc.

The twelve
ZODIACAL SIGNS
from the

CIRCVLAR
ZODIAC

In the ceiling of one of the upper Apartments in the Temple of Isis

at
DENDERA

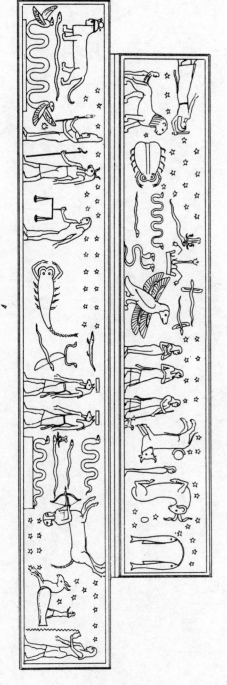

PART OF THE ZODIAC AT

ESNÉ (LATOPOLIS)

The form of the

INDIAN ZODIAC

as exhibited in the
Philosophical Transactions
for 1772.

T. Baxter sc.

The
ORIENTAL
ZODIAC
according to
Sᴿ W. IONES

T. Baxter sc.

11

LEO MITHRIACVS

AMMON

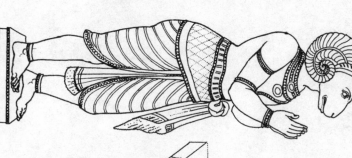

SVCCOTH BENOTH
or the
PLEIADES

according to KIRCHER.

This is the image of Succoth Benoth, or
the seven Gods of the Heavens with her chickens;—
or Hakpe in the Kingdom of Chaldæa.

J. Basire sc.

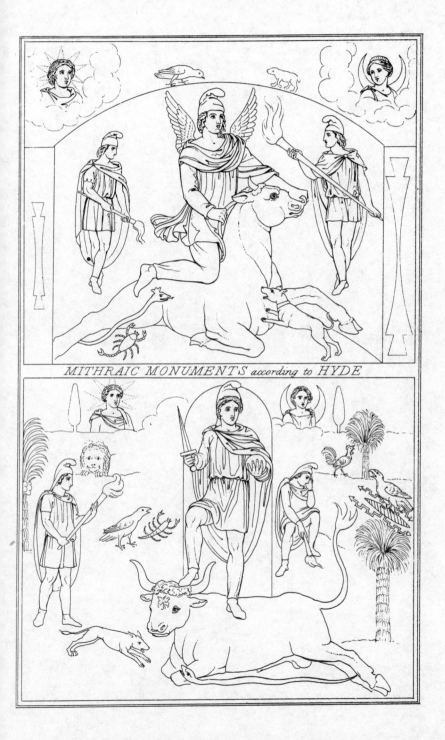

MITHRAIC MONUMENTS *according to* HYDE

T. Baxter sc

MITHRAIC MONUMENTS *according to* HYDE

T. Baxter sc

RASI
CHAKRA.
The
ZODIAC

from
MOOR's
HINDV
PANTHEON

T. Baxter sc

The CAMP of the HEBREWS
slightly altered from

OCCIDENS

SEPTENTRIO

ORIENS

Kircher's exhibition of it in his

ŒDIPVS ÆGYPTIACVS

T. Baxter sc.

The Sign of
LEO
the Standard of
IVDAH
with its three decans, and
with its paranatellons,
CEPHEVS, PEGASVS & EQVICVLVS

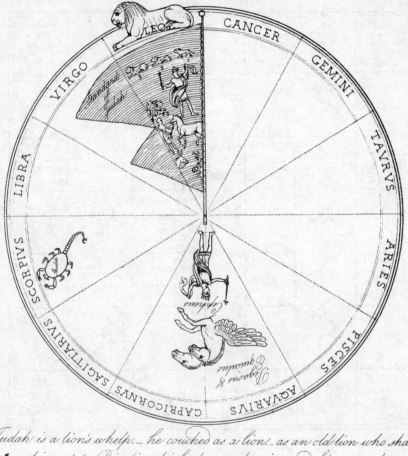

Judah is a lion's whelp._ he couched as a lion._ as an old lion who shall
rouse him up?_ Binding his foal unto the vine and his ass's colt unto
the choice vine._ The sceptre shall not depart from Judah, nor a
lawgiver from between his feet, until Shiloh come. Gen. C. 49.

In the Egyptian Calender we find the sign of LEO to
contain the figures of two lions & the head of a third, there are likewise
the figures of an ass bridled, and of a man leading a horse by the bridle

T. Baxter sc

I.

DISSERTATION

ON THE

FORTY-NINTH CHAPTER

OF

GENESIS.

This Essay is printed in the sixth Number of the CLASSICAL, BIBLICAL, and ORIENTAL JOURNAL, (a Quarterly Publication) with some few alterations.

Dissertation

ON THE

FORTY-NINTH CHAPTER OF GENESIS.

———————

JEHOVAH appears to have selected Abraham and his posterity from the rest of mankind, for the purpose of preserving among them the knowledge of the true religion; but this knowledge, it would seem from the 6th chapter of Exodus, was not bestowed on the Patriarchs in all its plenitude. ". And *Elohim* spake unto Moses, and said unto him, *I Am Jehovah;* and I appeared unto Abraham, unto Isaac, and unto Jacob, by the name of *El Shadai,* but by my name *Jehovah* was I not known unto them." The meaning is, that the true import

A

of the word was not explained to the Patriarchs; for had they understood it, they would have known that there was no God but *Jehovah*. Now that Jacob did not possess this knowledge is evident from his words:—" And Jacob vowed a vow, saying, if *Elohim* will be with me, and will keep me in this way that I go, and will give me bread to eat, and raiment to put on, so that I come again to my father's house in peace, then shall *Jehovah* be my God." No man, who entertained just ideas of the existence of the Deity, could have thought of making such a bargain with Omnipotence; nor if Jacob had comprehended the name of *Jehovah*,[1] would he have fancied, that he might

---

[1] *Jehovah* implies the Supreme Being, or the Being κατ' ἐξοχήν. It has been absurdly pretended by some of the Pagan writers, that the Jews worshipped their God under the form of an *Ass* in the temple of Jerusalem. In order to support this idle fable, they remark, on the authority of Apion, who was an Egyptian, that יהוה, which without the *Masorah* answers to the letters IHVH, signified an *Ass*. They say, that *Jehovah* was pronounced IAO, or IEO, and that this meant an *Ass* in Egyptian. They further remark, that we continually meet with *Pi-Jao* (פי יהוה, *Phi Jehovah*) the mouth of the

choose the God, whom he should adore. We must not be surprised, then, if we find traces of idolatry in the early history of the house of Israel:—if Rachel stole the *Teraphim* from her father Laban; —and if Jacob hid the strange Gods of his household under the oak of *Sechem.*

But since it appears from the Bible itself, that the Patriarchs were not acquainted with the divine nature in the same degree with Moses, and that they were not absolutely untinctured with polytheism, it cannot appear extraordinary, that they were influenced by minor superstitions, and that, with all their neighbours, they were addicted to divination and astrology. We know, that Joseph was a diviner; and there are many circumstances from which we may conclude, that Jacob was an astrologer. The streaked rods which were set up by

---

Lord: Thus repeatedly in the ninth chapter of Numbers we find על פי יהוה, which is translated, " at the commandment of the Lord ;" and it is pretended that *Pi*, or *Phi*, is nothing else than the Egyptian article, and that, therefore פי יהוה should be rendered *the ass*. The absurdity of this reasoning needs not to be pointed out.

the latter, in order to produce the breeding of the cattle, seem to have been formed in imitation of the rod which is held by the man, who occupied the sign of the Balance in the Egyptian zodiac, and who presided in the kingdom of *Omphtha* over flocks and herds. It appears from Eusebius,[1] that tradition, at least, represented Israel as an astrologer, who believed himself under the influence of the planet Saturn. Even at this day, the three great stars in Orion are called *Jacob's staff*, and the milky way is familiarly termed *Jacob's ladder*. This Patriarch had twelve sons, and tradition has allotted to each a sign of the zodiac. Kircher and Dupuis have pretended that the emblems, which were painted on the standards of the tribes in the camp of the Hebrews, were no other than the zodiacal signs; and Dupuis has endeavoured to corroborate this opinion, by the references which he has made to the 49th chapter of Genesis.

I have to lament that Kircher, with all his Oriental learning; and Dupuis, with all his

---

[1] Præp. Evang. L. IV. C. 16.

astronomical knowledge, should have so very briefly examined this curious question, as to leave it little elucidated by their vague and cursory observations; and I have to regret this the more, that after having read the 49th chapter of Genesis in the original Hebrew, I cannot doubt, that the prophecies which it contains, are all couched under astronomical symbols. It seems, indeed, extremely natural, that Jacob, who lived in times when mankind were almost universally addicted to astrology, should typify the future fortunes of his family by allusions to the celestial bodies.

Before I proceed, however, to analyse the chapter immediately under consideration, it may be proper to remark, that there is every reason to suppose, that the twelve signs of the zodiac were really painted on the standards of the twelve tribes of Israel. Aben Ezra reports, that according to the traditions, the figure of a man was painted on the ensign of Reuben, that of a bull on the ensign of Ephraim, that of a lion on the ensign of Judah, and that of an eagle on the ensign of Dan. If we turn to the Targum of Jonathan Ben Uzziel, we shall find that the lion is still ascribed to Judah, but that the bull is given to Reuben, the man to Ephraim, and a basilisk, instead of an eagle, to Dan. The captains of these tribes were each the leader of a host, and a host was composed of three tribes. Thus Issachar and Zebulon were associated with Judah on the eastern side of the camp— Simeon and Gad with Reuben, on the south— Manasseh and Benjamin with Ephraim on the west—and Asher and Naphtali with Dan on the north. Now the man, the bull, and the lion, evidently answer to the signs *Aquarius, Taurus,* and *Leo.* The basilisk may have been substituted for *Scorpius,* and the eagle appears to have been adopted as the symbol of that sign, which being deemed accursed, was rejected, if we can trust to Kircher, by the tribe of Dan. But one of the most remarkable passages to this purpose is to be found in the Chaldaic paraphrase of the 6th chapter of the Song of Solomon. After a curious description of the precious stones on the breast-plate of the priests, the paraphrase proceeds— *These* 12 *stones, which were typical of the* 12 *celestial signs, were lucid like to lamps, &c.* Thus we see, that the notion of the signs of the zodiac having been painted on the standards of Israel is not quite without foundation; and it will be strongly confirmed, when we come to examine the 2nd chapter of Numbers, which I propose to do in a succeeding dissertation. I shall now endeavour to illustrate my system by laying before my readers an analysis of the 49th chapter of Genesis.

I. Jacob, upon his death-bed, having called his sons around him, in order to tell them that which should befal them in the last days, thus addresses himself to Reuben his eldest son:—"Reuben, thou art my first-born, my might, and the beginning of my strength, the excellency of dignity, and the excellency of power: unstable as water, thou shalt not excel; because thou wentest up to thy father's bed; then defiledst thou it: he went up to my couch."

According to Aben Ezra, the figure of a man was painted on the ensign of Reuben; and this man is supposed by Kircher to have been *Aquarius*. In fact we find, that Jacob calls Reuben his first-born, the beginning of his strength, &c. and these epithets apply very well to the Sun in the commencement of his course,[1] after he has passed the winter solstice. The sign of *Aquarius* is typified by a man with a pitcher, whence he pours forth water. Reuben is said to be unstable as water. It is then remarked, that he shall not excel, because he went up to his father's bed; and we are thus reminded, that he had lain with *Bilhah.* The Oriental astronomers, and among others, Ulug Beig, still designate a remarkable asterism in the sign of *Aquarius,* by the name of *Bula,* or *Bulha.* This asterism rises, while the sun is yet in *Capricorn,* which is the domicile of Saturn, the star of Israel; and it sets towards the end of July, when *Aquarius* sets also with his head foremost, and when the ancients fabled, that he had made the Nile to overflow, by kicking down his urn. I know not, whether my reader will think that these circumstances, which have hitherto escaped observation, will tend, or not, to confirm the notions of Kircher and Dupuis.

---

[1] My reader will take into account the time when Jacob lived, or at least when the book of Genesis was written. Columella fixes the Winter Solstice at the 24th of December, and the next day the Sun was feigned to be born anew.

II. *Simeon and Levi are brethren.*

Kircher has allotted the sign of *Pisces* to these brothers, but without giving any reason for the conjecture. I shall endeavour to supply the deficiency.

Simeon and Levi are brethren.

In the astrological calendar, at the first degree of the first decan of *Pisces*, we find the following words;—*Duo viri unum caput habentes.*

Instruments of cruelty are in their habitations.

All the constellations, which are considered as noxious, are seen above the horizon, while the sun is in *Pisces*. It is then that *Sagitta* rises, that *Scorpius*, according to Columella, begins to set, accompanied with tempests; and that *Andromeda*, not yet delivered by *Perseus*, regards the monster that threatens to devour her. But this is not all; the descent of *Pisces* is fixed by Columella, for the fourteenth of the Ides of October, and consequently their disappearance was the prelude to the passage of the Sun into the sign of *Scorpius,* when the terrible reign of Typhon commenced. No sign appears to have been considered of more malignant influence than *Pisces ;* and it appears from the astrological calendar, that the emblems accompanying this constellation were chiefly indicative of death and violence. Thus we read in the second decan,

Vir in aquam mergens,

Duo equites confligentes,

Vir gladio se transverberans, &c.

and in the third,

Mulier, viro dormienti, caput securi amputat. &c.

O my soul, come not into their secret!

I am inclined to think that סר does not signify *a secret,* but *a fetter* or *shackle.* It will be recollected, that the fishes are united by a bond, or shackle, which the Greek astronomers called sometimes Δινὸν, and sometimes Σύνδεσμος.

*Unto their assembly my honor be not thou
united!*

The word כבד, which is here translated *honor*,
denotes in its primitive sense the action of light
in irradiation. The Patriarch seems to say, in
the language of astrology under which he veiled
his prophecies, — let not the light of my star be
united to their constellation.

For in their anger they slew a man.

Jacob seems to attribute all the effects produced
by the rising of *Scorpius* to the descent of *Pisces*.
In fact, we have already observed, that the latter
sign must descend before the former rises, and we
shall probably find reason to think, that the ancient
astrologers connected all the disasters of the
Typhonian kingdom with the setting of the
sign of *Pisces*. Columella fixes the passage of
the sun into *Scorpius* on the thirteenth of the
calends of November. We shall find, that this
period, then, nearly corresponds with that in which
Osiris was feigned to have been slain by Typhon,
and when the death of Orion was attributed to the
sting of the scorpion. The brilliant constellation

of Orion sets shortly after the descent of *Pisces*, and immediately after the rising of *Scorpius*.

And in their self-will they digged down a wall.

This interpretation rests upon the authority of Jerome; but I conceive it to be erroneous, and I appeal against it to the Septuagint, the Samaritan copy, and to the Hebrew itself. I translate—*in their self-will they castrated a bull.* Now the Oriental astronomers represent *Scorpius* as devouring the genitals of *Taurus;* and, indeed, the stars called *testiculi Tauri* set precisely when *Scorpius* rises.

Cursed be their anger, for it was fierce; and their wrath, for it was cruel.

I shall not trouble my reader with the fables which are told by the ancients, to account for the *Pisces* having been placed among the constellations. It suffices to say, upon the authority of Plutarch and other writers, that both the Syrians and Egyptians abstained from eating fish, which they seem to have held in singular dread and abhorrence; and Plutarch tells us, that when the Egyptians had to represent any thing as odious, or to express hatred by hieroglyphics, they painted a fish.

I will divide them in Jacob, and scatter them in Israel.

His standard was taken from Levi, and his tribe was divided in the camp of the Hebrews. We may observe, that the two zodiacal fishes neither rise nor set together, and that *Piscis Australis* might have been confounded with the zodiacal *Pisces.* Indeed, we find in some of the ancient zodiacs, that only one fish is represented.

III. *Judah, thou art he whom thy brethren shall praise. Thy hand shall be upon the neck of all thine enemies; thy father's children shall bow down before thee.*

According to all the traditions, a lion was painted on the standard of Judah; and I can have no hesitation in agreeing with Kircher, that the sign of *Leo* was thereby indicated. " Thou art he," says the text " whom thy brethren shall praise." While *Taurus* was the first of the signs, the summer solstice took place when the sun was in *Leo ;* and at that season of his highest elevation, the Sun was held in the greatest honor. The annual festival of the Egyptians upon this occasion is mentioned by several authors, and among others by Heliodorus in his ninth book. " Thy hand shall be on the neck of all thine enemies." The Sun in *Leo* was adored by the Egyptians as the King, Osiris; by the Syrians as the Lord, Adonis; by the Tyrians as *Melech-arets,* " King of the earth ;" and by the Greeks as Hercules, vanquisher of the Nemean lion. " Thy father's children shall bow down before thee." The sun being at his greatest altitude in *Leo*, the brothers of Judah are said to bow down before him. In the Indian sphere, in the second decan of the sign of *Leo*, a man is represented with a crown on his head, and a lance in his hand.

Judah is a lion's whelp : from the prey, my son, thou art gone up ; he stooped down, he couched as a lion, and as an old lion; who shall rouse him up?

The progress of the Sun through the sign of *Leo,* which, according to Aratus, was represented as a couching lion, is here clearly typified.

The sceptre shall not depart from Judah, nor a lawgiver from between his feet, until Shiloh come; and unto him shall the gathering of the people be.

The constellation of Cepheus, King of Ethiopia, is still represented as a man with a crown on his head, and with a sceptre in his hand. This constellation rises, according to Columella, on the 7th of the Ides of July. Thus Cepheus in the course of some days comes to rise under *Leo,* of which it continues to be the *paratanellon* until the Sun enters into the sign of *Scorpius.*

The word, מחקק, which we translate, *a lawgiver,* is shown by Bochart to be a corruption of חק *hyk,* which was the old Ethiopian word for a *King.* We may then suppose, with some appearance of reason, that *Hyk* was the ancient Ethiopian and Egyptian name for the constellation of Cepheus, or King of Ethiopia. It has been said, that the Egyptians were not acquainted with the constellation of Cepheus; but it is probable, that they only did not recognize it under that name.[1] The Arabians call it *Keiphus* and *Cheic*. The former of these names is evidently a corruption from the Greek, but the latter seems to be derived from *Hyk*, which should be pronounced *chyk*, with a strong guttural. But מחקק *mehukek*, "a lawgiver," being derived from *Hyk*, or rather perhaps being a corruption of this Ethiopian word, I cannot help thinking, that some allusion is made in the text to the constellation called the King of Ethiopia, which being seen very low in the northern hemisphere, when the Sun is in *Leo*, may be figuratively said to be under the feet of the lion.[2] Jacob

---

[1] The Jews were certainly acquainted with this constellation, which affords another reason for supposing that it could not be unknown to the Egyptians.

[2] It is to be recollected, that *Leo* at this time of the year is merged in the sun's rays. *The King with the sceptre,* therefore, rises under the *Lion,* while the latter is not visible.

thus distinctly says, " *the constellation represented by a King bearing a sceptre, shall not cease to be the paranatellon of the Lion, which is the sign of Judah, until Shiloh come.*

It remains to be inquired, what is meant by *Shiloh.* The answer in a sacred sense is obvious; but there is also an astronomical allusion. The King with the sceptre sets about the time that *Scorpius* rises, and then ceases to be the parana-tellon of the Lion. In *Scorpius* are two stars, which the Oriental astronomers call شولة *Sshulet;* and the brightest of these is named *Shuleh.*

Binding his foal unto the vine, and his ass's colt unto the choice vine.

In the first decan of the sign *Leo* in the Persian sphere, I find the head of a horse, and the head of an ass.

In the second decan of the Persian sphere (♌), I find the middle of the horse and ass advanced; and in the third decan their hind parts.

At the sixth and ninth degrees of the second decan (Ω) in the astrological calendar, formed from Egyptian monuments, I read the words,

Asinus frænatus
Vir fræno equum trahens.

In the last volume of Kircher's Œdipus, my reader will see the representation of an old Egyptian lamp, on which Silenus is drawn mounted on the head of an ass, which is girt round with grapes and vine leaves. Osiris, as we learn from Herodotus, was the same with Bacchus. His station was in *Leo,* and it is of him that Tibullus says,

Hic docuit teneram palis adjungere vitem,
Hic viridem durâ cædere falce comam ;
Illi jucundos primùm matura sapores
Expressa incultis uva dedit pedibus.

I believe, in all symbols of the physical world, where the operation of necessary causes is meant to be indicated, that *bonds* are chosen as the proper hieroglyphic. We have seen from indubitable evidence, that a horse, and an ass, were introduced into the ancient Oriental representations of the sign of *Leo;* and when Jacob says, " binding his foal unto the vine, and his ass's colt unto the choice vine," I conclude, that he alludes to the necessary influence of the sun in *Leo,* in ripening the fruits of the earth. This, indeed, is evident from his concluding words, in his address to Judah. *He washed his garments in wine, and his clothes in the blood of grapes: his eyes shall be red with wine, and his teeth white with milk.* The passage is well paraphrased by Onkelos: *Of fine purple shall be his raiment; splendid, and of various hues shall be his tabernacle: his mountains shall be reddened with grapes; his hills shall distil his wines; and his fields shall be whitened with corn, and with his flocks of sheep.* The writer is clearly speaking of the Sun, when he clothes the skies with fire, ripens the grapes, and turns the color of the corn.

IV. *Zebulon shall dwell at the haven of the sea; and he shall be for a haven for ships.*

The standard of Zebulon, according to Kircher, ought to have represented the sign of *Capricorn.* M.

Dupuis has adopted the same notion; but his reason for admitting it is certainly of no great weight. I must suppose, that Kircher had found some tradition on the subject; for, after a tedious examination, I am inclined to agree with him, though he has not given the slightest intimation, why he has referred this sign to Zebulon.

I ought, however, in the first place, to remark, that instead of *a haven for ships*, we should read *a haven for a ship*. A masculine noun ending in ', and assuming a feminine form in the singular, takes ת final rather than ה. Thus אנית is the regular feminine singular of אני, though sometimes written—אניה. In the plural the regular form is אניות. (Is. c. ii. v. 16.) We shall then translate, *a haven for a ship*. The ship *Argo* is one of the most remarkable of the constellations. It will be found that this ship descends under the horizon, when the Sun is in the sign of *Capricorn*.[1] But Hyginus will explain the matter better;—*Capricornus exoriens hæc sidera ad terram premere videtur; reliquam figuram Navis et signum, &c.*

---

[1] The rudder and the pilot *(Canobus)* are visible in Egypt.

This seems to indicate why Zebulon is called *a haven for a ship.*

And his border shall be unto Zidon, (Tsidon).

When we examine the countries belonging to the tribe of Zebulon, and to the Zidonians, we shall find, that they did not border upon each other. The allusion, therefore, seems to be astronomical rather than geographical. צידן *tsidon,* may be translated *the great hunter ;* and this probably was *Arcitenens,* or *Sagittarius,* who occupies the sign next to that of *Capricorn,* and whom the Greeks fabled to have been originally a famous hunter of the name of *Crotus.*

V. *Issachar is a strong ass couching down between two burdens.*

Kircher allots the sign of *Cancer* to Issachar; and Dupuis makes the following short remark upon the subject: *Le Cancer, où sont les étoiles appellées les ânes, forme l'empreinte du pavillon d' Issachar que Jacob assimile à l'âne.* I am upon the whole inclined to agree with these authors. The ass was the emblem of Typhon, and we learn from Plutarch, that in the month *Payni*, when the Sun is in the sign of *Cancer*, the Egyptians baked cakes, on which an ass was represented as bound. The Greeks, whose fables on the subject it would be useless to repeat, placed two asses in the sign of *Cancer*, where they still remain under that designation; and near to them we find the asterism called *Præsepe*, or the *Manger*. Now it will be observed, that the Hebrew words רבץ בין המשפתים, should not be translated *couching down between two burdens*, but *two partitions*, such as separate the stalls in a stable.

And he saw that rest was good, and the land that it was pleasant; and bowed his shoulder to bear, and became a servant unto tribute.

We shall probably be struck with surprise, when we find in the astrological calendar, taken from the Egyptians, the singular mixture which is there exhibited of rest and labor, of indolence and activity, in the three decans of *Cancer*. Out of the thirty emblems I shall select the following:

Mulieres duæ otiosæ.

Duo viri stantes coram duabus mulieribus sedentibus.

Virgo stans otiosa virum expectando.

Mulier dextrâ fusum tenens.

Navis stans in aquâ.

Vir spolium humeris portans.

Puer sedens.

Mulier stans otiosa.

Canis sedens in curru.

Vir stans otiosus.

Aqua profluens.

Equus equam insiliens.

Equus liber vagans in campestribus.

Aqua fluens ex montibus.

Equus frænatus.

Navis fluitans in aquis.

In the account of the Indian sphere I find these words at the third decan of *Cancer.*

Homo cogitans navem inscendere navigandi causâ, ad importandum aurum et argentum, annulis uxorum ejus fabricandis.

Issachar found that rest was good, but he bowed his shoulder to the burden, and became a servant unto tribute; and it is said in the 33d chapter of Deuteronomy, that Zebulon and Issachar shall suck of the abundance of the seas, and of the treasures hid in the sands.[1]

VI. *Dan shall judge his people as one of the tribes of Israel. Dan shall be a serpent by the way, an adder in the path; that biteth the horse's heels, so that his rider shall fall backwards.*

We have seen, that Jonathan, in his Targum, pretends that a basilisk was painted on the

---

[1] There seems to be something ambiguous in the original, as if an allusion were made to moisture or liquefaction. It was at the summer solstice, that the Nile came to its height: but I find this curious circumstance. The name of *Issachar* is formed of שכר with a *jod* appellative. In Buxtorf's Chaldaic Lexicon, the reader will find that this was the ancient name for a species of hawk. Now in the old Egyptian Zodiacs the sign of *Cancer* was represented by the *Ibis*, a species of hawk.

standard of Dan, and that Aben Ezra asserts, that it was an eagle. Kircher and Dupuis both concur in thinking, that *Scorpius* was the sign allotted to Dan; and, I trust, I shall be able to corroborate their opinion by proofs, of which they either had no knowledge, or which they have neglected to adduce.

Scorpius was considered by the ancient astrologers as a sign accursed. The Egyptians fixed the entrance of the Sun into *Scorpius* as the commencement of the reign of Typhon, when the Greeks also fixed the death of Orion, and the Persians the emasculation of the bull.

Kircher tells us that the *Scorpion* was refused by the tribe of Dan; but I am inclined to think, that that sign was originally represented by another emblem, both by the Jews and by the Egyptians. Most certainly the crocodile was an emblem of Typhon, and the Greeks may have changed the form of the crocodile into that of the scorpion. Be this as it may, the dreaded emblem was to be avoided, and Dan made choice either of the

Basilisk, or of the Eagle. Now the Eagle, or
Vulture, with the lyre, rises with the first part of
Sagittarius, and is to be considered as a paranatellon of *Scorpius ;* and *Coluber* (the Adder) is
placed on the Scorpion's back. But I am inclined
to think, that the Eagle, or Vulture, was commonly assumed as the ensign of Dan. There are
four great stars in opposite points of the heavens—
Fomalhaut, which is in the head of *Piscis Australis*,
may be said to belong to *Aquarius—Aldebaran*,
which is in the front of *Taurus*, is called his eye,
though in the ancient representations of the sign,
it was at a little distance from his head—*Regulus*,
which is in the middle of *Leo*, is frequently called
cor Leonis—and *Antares*, which is in the middle
of *Scorpius*, is denominated *cor Scorpii*. The Orientalists were much occupied with these four stars,
which had formerly answered to the Solstitial and
Equinoctial points. But *Antares* is found in the
midst of the accursed constellation. It was,
therefore, natural for Dan to look out for another
brilliant star, and to choose a constellation for his
ensign, which might not be affected by the evil
influence of *Scorpius*. In the Eagle, or Vulture,

shines the large star called *Asengue ;* and it probably helped to direct him to choose the constellation,
in which he found it.

Dan, it is said, *shall be a serpent by the way,
an adder in the path.*

Close to *Scorpius,* and by the Zodiac, which is
the solar way, we find the *Adder,* which is called
Coluber, or *Serpens Ophiuci.*

*That biteth the horse's heels, so that the rider
shall fall backwards.*

If we allow, that a man on horseback first gave
the idea of a centaur, we may easily admit, that a
man on horseback first occupied the place, among
the constellations, which is now held by *Centaurus.*
Now I believe it will be found, that the head of
the adder ascends at the same time with the feet
of *Centaurus,* who rises heliacally with *Scorpius.*

Perhaps the allusion may be to *Sagittarius,*
followed in his descent by *Scorpius* and the *Adder,*

his concomitant. But the allusion will also apply to *Hydra*, a paranatellon of *Scorpius*.

At etiam Centaurus occidit cum Hydrâ.   Hyg.

But the most surprising thing, which I have remarked on the subject of Dan, is what is mentioned in the 19th chapter of Joshua, and in the 18th chapter of the book of Judges. There we learn that the Danites took possession of a city called *Laish*, or *Lashem*, &c. to which they gave the name of *Dan*. It seems very remarkable, that there are stars in *Scorpius* still called *Leshaa*, *Leshat*, *Lesos*, &c. In fact the Greeks give this last name to *Antares*, from the Chaldeans, by whom it was called *Lesh*, or *Lesha*. My reader may consider these things, and then judge for himself.

VII. *Gad, a troop shall overcome him, but he shall overcome at the last.*

When I first read this, I was inclined to assign *Capricorn* to Gad. R. Solomon, and other

Rabbins, distinctly tell us, that a certain cluster of stars was called *Gad;* and these stars, we know, are to be found in *Capricorn,* which sign is called *Giedi* by the Arabians, *Gadia* by the Chaldeans, and *Gadi* by the Syrians, all of which are manifest corruptions from *Gad.* But it now appears to me that *Aries* was assumed by *Gad* as his ensign.

Columella fixes the 24th of December as the period of the winter solstice, and the 24th of March as that of the vernal equinox. Now the Sun was feigned to be born anew at the winter solstice, and was then represented by the Egyptians under the form of the infant Harpocrates. At the vernal equinox, he passed to the upper hemisphere into the region of light. But the new birth of the Sun had taken place, when he was in the sign of *Capricorn,* where a troop, or cluster, of stars, had received the name of *Gad,* which signifies *a troop;* and as this was considered a happy epoch, *Gad* came to be adored as a Deity, that presided over the fortunes of men, and that was known under the name of *Baal-Gad.* The appellation of *Gad,* which seems to have come in the end to signify the fortunate, was thus probably associated with the Sun, when he ascended to the upper hemisphere.

That *Gad* assumed *Aries* as his ensign is probable from the traditions, but I chiefly infer it from the text before us, and from a passage which I shall have presently to cite from Deuteronomy.

Gad, as I have already observed, originally signified *a troop ;* and we must remember, that the sign of *Aries* is called *Princeps Zodiaci, Ductor exercitús Zodiaci, Dux gregis, Princeps signorum,* &c. It is said, that a troop shall overcome *Gad,* but that he shall overcome at the last. *Aries* seems to be the symbol of the Sun, who after having descended to, and returned from, the lower hemisphere, contends for his place in the upper hemisphere; and the ancients accordingly represented him as struggling against the constellations, which they typified by a ram butting with his horns. In the 33d chapter of Deuteronomy we read, that " *Gad* had provided the first part for himself, because there, in a portion of the lawgiver, was he seated." The year of the Hebrews commenced in the month *Nisan,* when the Sun was in *Aries,* and thus we may understand how *Gad* provided the first part for himself. He was seated in a portion of the lawgiver, whom we have seen to be *Cepheus;* and according to Hipparchus, the Zodiac, *ab Arietis* 8 *mediâ parte ad* 14, descends with the crown and sceptre of *Cepheus.* In the Persian sphere, a young man is here represented sitting on a throne.[1]

Out of Asher his bread shall be fat, and he shall yield royal dainties.

The *Balance,* according to Kircher, was the emblem painted on the standard of *Asher.*

In the astrological calendar taken from Egyptian monuments, I find under *Libra* the following

---

[1] It is to be observed, however, that at the period when the text was written, *Aries* occupied the place now held by *Pisces.* I find that the star in *Ursa Minor,* which is next to *Cepheus,* the lawgiver, is called *Giadi,* or *Gadi,* by the Arabians. Perhaps the relative positions of these constellations with *Aries* may be alluded to in the text.

emblems of that abundance, which the text indicates as coming out of *Asher.*

Vir utrâque manu spiculum tenens.
Vir arvum equis arans.
Vir aratrum trahens.
Villa cum domibus benè ornatis.
Arbor frondosa in horto, &c.

In the account of the Indian sphere, and under the sign of *Libra,* I read as follows:

Homo in tabernâ institoriâ in foro manu tenens stateram ad emendum et vendendum.

In the 33d chapter of Deuteronomy, Moses thus addresses *Asher—Let Asher be blessed with children, let him be acceptable to his brethren, and let him dip his foot in oil. Thy shoes shall be iron and brass, and as thy days so shall thy strength be.* The happy season, when the Sun was in *Libra,* was represented by a man ταυροκέφαλος in the Egyptian Zodiac, who held a streaked rod in one hand, and a balance in the other. We often find the balance alone. Perhaps when it is said, *thy shoes shall be iron and brass*, some allusion is made to the scales of the balance.[1]

IX. *Naphthali is a hind set loose; he giveth goodly words.*

This seems to me to be unintelligible. I have no hesitation in translating with Bochart, *arbor surculosus edens ramos pulchritudinis.*[2] The traditions allot the sign of *Virgo* to *Naphthali.*

A tree then was probably the symbol painted on the standard of *Naphthali;* but what has *a tree* to do with the sign of Virgo? R. Avenar, the Jewish astrologer, tells us that a tree was represented by the Egyptians beside the sign of *Virgo.* In the Zodiacs found at Dendera, *Virgo* is represented

---

[1] Two of the sons of Asher are called *Jimnah* and *Ishuah* —he that shall distribute or weigh out any thing—and he who shall equalise—evidently alluding to the sign of the balance.

[2] Consult also the Septuagint.

c

with the branch of a palm-tree in her hand. In the calendar, to which I have so often referred, I find under the sign of *Virgo* the following emblems :

Vir sub abiete sedens.
Arbor frondosa in gramine.

When, then, we consider, that instead of translating *Naphthali is a hind set loose, he giveth goodly words ;* we should render, *Naphthali is a tree shooting forth, producing goodly branches ;* we shall have no great difficulty in fixing the sign, to which we may suppose Jacob made allusion.

We read in the 33d chapter of Deuteronomy, *O Naphthali, satisfied with favor, and full of the blessings of Jehovah, possess thou the west and the south.*

Let us take the summer solstice in the sign of *Leo,* where it had been in fact, when astronomy was first cultivated in the East. After the solstice, then, the Sun entered the sign of *Virgo,* which I suppose to have been the emblem of *Naphthali.* The possession of *Naphthali* was consequently to be in the South and the West, for the Sun had begun to return from the northern hemisphere towards the equator. It will be observed, that this address of the sacred historian can be by no means applied to the geographical position of the tribe of *Naphthali.*

X. *Joseph is a fruitful bough, even a fruitful bough by a well, whose branches run over a wall.* In the original the words are as follow:

בן פרת יוסף בן פרת עלי עין בנות צעדה עלי שור.

According to the traditions, *Taurus* was the emblem of *Ephraim,* who assumed the standard of his father Joseph, whom Moses compares with a young bull.

I find the *Hebrew* words, above cited, full of allusions to the sign of *Taurus.*

The words בן פרת, which are translated a *fruitful bough,* may be rendered *filius vaccæ.* Thus we find in Job פרתו, *his cow.* Should my reader, however, prefer the usual interpretation, he will find that

Theon compares the *Pleiades*, the concomitants of *Taurus*, with clusters of grapes; and Onkelos, in his Targum, gives us to understand, that the *fruitful bough* in question was a *vine branch*.

That עיין *ain*, in a metaphorical sense, may signify *a well*, is undeniable; but its proper meaning is *an eye*. Now it will be recollected, that the great star, which the Arabians commonly call *Aldebaran*, is also named by them *Ain-al-tor*, " the bull's eye;" and, (if I understand Riccioli rightly) it is sometimes termed simply *ain*, " the eye." I cannot help thinking that *ain*, in the passage before us, means *ain-al-tor*, " the bull's eye."

בנות *benoth* properly signifies *daughters*, and it seems very strange to translate it " *whose* branches." But I imagine, that an allusion is here made to the *Pleiades*, which the Chaldeans called *Succoth Benoth*, and the Arabians بنات النعش *Benat Alnash*. This group of stars was represented by a hen and seven chickens; and *Succoth Benoth* is thus symbolised in the Mithraic monuments, and in the Egyptian Zodiacs. But my reader will find this more fully explained in the *Pantheon Hebræorum*.

The word שור *shor* is translated *a wall:* its more obvious signification is *a bull.*

The archers have solely vexed him, and shot at him, and hated him.

Immediately after the Sun has passed into *Sagittarius,* the head of *Taurus,* according to Columella, begins to set.

But his bow abode in strength, and the arms of his hands were made strong by the hands of the mighty God of Jacob: from thence is the shepherd, the stone of Israel.

I cannot help suspecting, that the word קשת is not always properly translated *a bow.* The bow, indeed, is only called קשת from its being stiff, and hard to bend.

Arms in English may signify either *arma* or *brachia,* but it is only in the latter sense that זרע can be translated *arms.* Now *brachia manuum ejus* seems to me to be very like nonsense. I conceive the proper meaning of זרע is *semina.*

The Patriarch seems to be alluding to that season when the Sun is in *Taurus*, and when all nature may be said to germinate.

From thence is the shepherd, the stone of Israel.

I am unable to say what is the astronomical allusion intended in this place. Perhaps reference is made to the brilliant constellation of Orion. I observe, that the Arabians call one of the stars of Orion by the name of *Al rai*, " the shepherd." Perhaps an allusion was made to *Horus*, the type of the vernal Sun, and the representative of the principle of generation among the Egyptians.

We may then translate the whole passage literally —*A son of a cow*, (meaning the celestial bull, or sign of *Taurus*) *is Joseph, a son of a cow beside Ain ;* (meaning *Ain-al-Tor*, the great star commonly called *Aldebaran*,) the *Benoth* (meaning *Succoth Benoth*, or the *Pleiades*, whose station is on the back of *Taurus*) *walk upon the bull. The archers* (probably alluding to *Sagittarius*) *have sorely grieved him, and shot at him, and hated him. But his bow* [1] *abode in strength, and the seeds of his hands were strengthened from the hands of the mighty one of Jacob, whence the shepherd, the stone of Israel.*

Now let my reader turn to Hyde, *Hist. Rel. Vet. Pers. p.* 113. where he will find four representations of the Sun in *Taurus*, taken from the Mithraic monuments, and let him compare them with the passage before us.

Mithras is represented upon the back of a young bull, which he pierces with a dagger, and its blood, the symbol of fertilisation, trickles down upon the ground. At some distance is seen the head of another bull, and a fruit-tree is placed over its head. If, therefore, we prefer the common translation of בן פרת, *a fruitful bough*, we shall have the sense explained by this monument, where we see a fruitful bough upon the bull's head, where is the star called *Ain*, or *Aldebaran*. In the next copartment, a hen and seven stars, called *Succoth*

---

[1] *Anne membrum genitale intensum ?*

Benoth, or the *Pleiades,* are seen on the back of a bull, and the text says, the *Benoth* walk upon the bull. A flying arrow is represented as ready to pierce the breast of *Taurus,* and we are told, that the archers shot at Joseph. But his bow abode in strength, and the seeds of his hands were made strong by the hands of the Mighty One of Jacob. Before Mithras and the bull stands the personified principle of generation, who sheds his seed upon the ground. Now be it observed, that the God *Hor* was the *Priapus* of the Egyptians, and Kircher has proved, that *Taurus* was the station of *Hor.* Lucian has described this God—but I must give the translation of the passage in Latin— *dextrá manu sceptrum tenebat—lævá suam ipsius mentulam arrectam, quòd semina humo tecta in apertum emittat.*

If Jacob really meant to make no allusion to the sign of *Taurus,* it seems very strange that we should find so many circumstances which seem directly to relate to it.

XI. *Benjamin shall ravin as a wolf: in the morning he shall devour the prey, and at night (evening) he shall divide the spoil.*

I differ from Kircher and Dupuis concerning the ensign of Benjamin, which I suppose to have been the *Twins*.

The entire appearance of the constellation of *Centaurus*, and his *Wolf*, is fixed by Columella for the 5th of the Nones of May.

Among other Oriental symbols of the sign which we call *Gemini*, Avenar, the Jewish astrologer, reckons the *Wolf*, which he calls זאב *zeeb*, the very word in the text.

In the account of the symbols contained in the Persian sphere, I read, at the second decan of *Gemini—Homo tenens instrumentum musicum aureum, quo canit. Bestia arbore insistens. LVPVS, in cujus anteriore pede est signum.*

My reader may also take the following circumstances into consideration :

1. Among the Egyptians, *Gemini* was the sign in which *Anubis* had his station.

2. *Anubis* was the type of the planet Mercury, which is sometimes a morning, and sometimes an evening, star.

3. The horison, immediately before the rising, and immediately after the setting, of the Sun, was symbolised by *Anubis*.

4. Diodorus Siculus represents *Anubis* as hunting for prey.

5. Julius Firmicus calls him *Anubis Venator*.

6. Bochart has shown, that the wolf was called זאב *quasi* זהב, that is, *zeeb*, *quasi golden*, from its color; and Jablonski pretends, that *Anubis* signifies *gold* in Egyptian, and that the God received that name *quasi golden*.

It may be observed, that Joseph and Benjamin were the sons of Rachel. But Rachel is Hebrew for *a sheep*. The signs taken by these brothers properly follow the sign of the sheep, which was variously called a ram, a sheep, and a lamb, in different languages.

12. The sign of *Sagittarius* alone remains for *Manasseh*: and if I be right in my former conjectures, I cannot be mistaken in this; but having already written so much on the standards of the tribes, I shall leave it to the ingenuity of my readers to supply what I have left unsaid on the subject of *Manasseh*.

It then is only incumbent on me to add, that Jacob's employing astronomical symbols, in order to convey his prophecies, can by no means take away either from their truth, or from their importance; nor do I conceive, that their application is less obvious now, than it was before.

II.

Dissertation,

&c. &c.

Dissertation

ON THE

FOURTEENTH CHAPTER OF GENESIS.

THE fourteenth chapter of Genesis, if taken merely as a piece of history, certainly appears to contain a very extraordinary relation of events. Eight Kings, among whom one was King of Admah, (that is, King of the earth,) and another was King of Nations, had been subject during twelve years to Chedorlaomer, King of Elam. In the thirteenth year, five of these Princes rebelled against their chief, and in the fourteenth year were defeated by him in the vale of Siddim, where four kings strove against five. But after this splendid victory of the King of Elam, he had, it seems, the rashness to carry away the shepherd Lot among his captives ; and this mighty monarch, this King of Kings, who had subdued the King of the Earth, and in whose train was the King of Nations, is in his turn pursued, defeated, and slaughtered, by the shepherd Abraham and his household servants.

I presume not to deny, that this may be a true narrative. It seems difficult, however, to understand, who the monarchs were, who came to contend in the Vale of Siddim ; and it appears singular, that we know nothing of the kingdom of Elam,—that the vague title of the King of the Earth should be given to a tributary prince, —and that another of these potentates should be indicated by the equally indefinite description of King of Nations. I shall not take notice of the idle conjectures of those, who have supplied by bold assertions, whatever has been left doubtful, by the silence of the sacred historian. I shall only observe, that since Chedorlaomer and the kings that were with him, before they vanquished the rebels in the Vale of Siddim, had already overthrown the

Rephaims, the Zuzims, the Emims, the Horites, the Amalekites, and the Amorites, their force must have been, indeed, considerable; and that, while we are still unable to discover where were their dominions, we can entertain no doubts of the magnitude of their power, or of the terror, which must have been inspired by their arms.

I acknowledge, that I believe the chapter before us to be rather a typical illustration than an historical narrative. I am aware of the objections which may be urged against those, who too fondly seek for allegory in the Scriptures; but I am not convinced that we are bound either by reason, or by faith, to assert that allegorical illustrations were never veiled by the sacred penmen, under the guise of recorded facts.

It is well known, that Tsabaism, or the worship of the hosts of heaven, had seduced mankind from the religion of Nature and of God. The Deity, therefore, appears to have instructed Abram and his posterity in the knowledge of the true religion, not only that this knowledge might be transmitted from generation to generation among the chosen people, but that the world might not be without witnesses of the continued exercise of the divine Providence; when, at last, the Gentile nations should be called upon to partake of the blessings produced by the most glorious of its dispensations. But so powerful is example;—so prone are men to fall into error :—and so favorable were the Heathen superstitions to the gratification of the passions, that the Hebrews, amidst an uninterrupted succession of miracles, were continually relapsing into that idolatry, from which the divine interposition was still necessary to rescue them. Separated from the rest of mankind,—with all his natural liberties abridged,—the slave of institutions which were as rigid as they were singular ;—Israel sighed for the comparative freedom, the milder laws, and the religious tolerance, of the Gentiles. He remembered Egypt—her wealth, her magnificence, her wisdom, her power, and her luxury. He beheld himself an emigrant and a wanderer. His way was the path of the outcast—his possession, the gloom of the Desert. When he hoped, it was as a robber; and when he thought of enjoyment, it was as a plunderer and a spoliator. He had no leisure for contemplating the divine nature and

attributes, while he fled from before the face of
Pharaoh; while he murmured for bread in the
wilderness of Sin, or while he thirsted for water by
the rock of Horeb. He saw, indeed, that miracles
were worked in his favor; that Jehovah had led
him through the sea; and that, if there were other
Gods, his God was mightier than they were; but
he conceived not the existence of a supreme and
immaterial Being, whose throne is the Heavens,
and whose empire is the Universe. He beheld
Jehovah descend in fire on Mount Sinai, and heard
the voice of the trumpet that made him tremble in
his camp; and yet his soul longed for the superstitions of the Heathen, and his heart still clave
to the dark idolatries of Egypt. Even the sight
of the promised land could not conquer the stub-
bornness of Israel. He could not learn to refer
the existence of all things to a single and primary
principle; he could not imagine the operation of
power which was to be attributed to an invisible
and incorporeal agent; and where he could not
account for many, and for extraordinary effects,
he was tempted by example, and perhaps inclined
by superstition, to seek for the causes in beings,

whom his credulity exalted to the rank, and whom his fears invested with the power, of Gods.

The opinions and example of others seem to have had much influence on the Hebrews. From the Nile to the Nubian Desert on one hand, and to the Euphrates on the other, the infatuated nations adored the Sun, the Moon, and the Hosts of Heaven. After men had lost the knowledge of the true God, it may be easily conceived that they fell into this species of idolatry. The human mind is ever restless until it has associated effects with causes; but when this association is once made, we seldom give ourselves the trouble of examining whether it be just or not. In a fine climate, and under a serene sky, the attention of the people was naturally, and seems to have been continually, directed to the observation of the celestial bodies, the movements of which soon came to be connected in their minds with the fate of individuals, and with the destinies of Empires. But where there is influence, there is power; and where there is power, there must be both choice and knowledge. Men probably did not mark the gradations by which they came to attribute life and action to inanimate objects; and yet where superstitious ignorance once acknowledges an undefined and superior power, the steps are few which lead it to all the rest.

There can be no system of religion but the true one, which is capable of satisfying a reasoning and reflecting mind. We may believe, that as the Chaldeans and Egyptians advanced in knowledge, their learned men secretly renounced, while they continued openly to teach, the errors of Tsabaism, which, in the hands of such men, could have been nothing else than a system of astronomy imposed on the people as a system of religion. Accordingly we find, that the popular Gods of Egypt were in fact mere astronomical symbols. The Sun, the Moon, and the Stars, were personified and deified; the conjunction and opposition of planets were made subjects of joy or of lamentation; and blessings, or misfortunes, were supposed to follow the rising, or the setting, of the unconscious constellations. When the learned had to mark the commencement of new cycles, or to denote the periodical revolutions of the Stars, new gods were introduced into the Pantheon, as regularly as changes were noticed in the calendar. As astronomical periods succeeded each other, the Sun, under new appellations, was adored on the throne of the heavens; and even as he proceeded in his annual course through the signs of the zodiac, he was hailed by new names, and was worshipped under different attributes. Hence the Egyptian figments concerning the dynasties and the wars of the Gods; and hence all the marvels and the monsters, which sprang from the allegorical mythology of Egypt.

From the most impartial examination which I have been able to give to the subject, I believe the mythology of the Chaldeans and Egyptians to have been chiefly founded on astronomy, and I think that hero-worship was ever unknown to those ancient nations. This was, indeed, the clumsy invention of a more degraded superstition; and I attribute it with pain to the most amiable and ingenious, but not the most scientific, people of antiquity. Still, however, hero-worship seems to have been connected with Tsabaism. The mob of deified mortals, composed of heroes, of tyrants, of women, and of boys, was stationed in the starry heavens. Cepheus, Perseus, and Hercules, were, from remote antiquity, fabled to have ascended to the sky, where Cassiopeia and Andromeda have each a portion of the celestial sphere, where Orion leads on the most brilliant of the constellations, and where his eagle had borne the favorite of Jupiter, ages before a place was there allotted to the minion of Adrian.

When then we consider the general prevalence of Tsabaism among the neighbouring nations, we shall wonder less at the proneness of the Hebrews to fall into this species of idolatry. Neither shall we be surprised at the anxious efforts of their lawgiver to persuade and convince them of the vanity of these superstitions, when we recollect, that though he could command the elements, and give new laws to nature, he could not impose fetters on the free-will of others. With such a power as this he was by no means invested; for the Almighty, in offering to the Hebrews the clearest proofs of his existence, by no means constrained their belief. It cannot be doubted, that by an act of power, God might have coerced submission, and have commanded conviction; but had there been no choice, there could have been no merit in the acceptance of his law.

Since, then, Jehovah did not compel the people to acknowledge his existence, by fettering their free-will, it was natural for his servant Moses to represent, by types and by symbols, the errors of the Gentile nations; and it is in no manner surprising, that the past, the existing, and the future, situation of the Hebrews, as well as the religious, moral, and political state of their neighbours, should be alluded to in symbolical language by an historian, who was also a teacher and a prophet.

Above all things, however, it is evident, that the establishment of the true religion was the great object of the divine legation of Moses. To attain this purpose, it was not enough that he performed the most surprising miracles. His countrymen acknowledged the existence of Jehovah; but with him they reckoned, and were but too willing to adore, other Gods. Is it then surprising, that the false notions of religion entertained by the Gentiles should be pointed out in the writings of Moses and that their religious systems should be there made to appear what they really were,—the astronomical systems of scientific idolaters?

In the chapter before us, I see nothing that does not accord with this notion. It seems to me, that Moses intended to typify the history of the Gods of Egypt, and to show, that they were astronomical symbols. After having done this, he clearly intimates the overthrow of idolatry, and the establishment of the true religion; and insinuates in no ambiguous terms, that the superstitions of the Gentiles, though interwoven with the laws, and countenanced by the prejudices, of mighty empires, should be at last destroyed through the means of a people, insignificant alike from their power and their numbers. Finally he introduces the Priest of the Most High God, whose appearance in this place is surely symbolical.

But it is time that I proceed to the proof of what I have been hitherto generally stating. I must observe, however, in the first place, that I assume the acquaintance of my reader with Egyptian mythology and astronomy, to be sufficiently extensive, to enable him to follow the observations, which I shall have to make concerning both. It is only necessary then, that I remind him, that for the most part in all the ancient oriental languages, and almost invariably in Hebrew, proper names are significant. Let us now proceed to our analysis.

And it came to pass in the days of Amraphel.

The Chaldeans were accustomed to call the sign of *Aries* אמרא *amra,* or אמר *amar,* and the Syrians اٮرو *amro*—i. e. *agnus.* אמרפל *amarphel* or *amraphel,* seems to be a contraction for אמרפלא *amraphela,* " the wonderful lamb," or for אמרפלה, " the lamb of separation."—*Ammon,* or the Sun in the sign of *Aries,* was probably intended to be typified.

King of Shinar.

Melech, Moloch, or King, was a common solar title.

Shinar, I conceive to be a compound word, שו-ער; I imagine שו *shan* to be the name, under which the annual Sun was worshipped. A temple was built to this God by the Philistines, who fastened the body of Saul to the wall of the house of Shan.

עַר *ar* signifies " an enemy." *Aries* is certainly the station of Mars; but I rather think that עַר should be written יַעַר *iar*, because the Arabians call the plain of Babylon, to which this name of *Shinar*, or *Shanar*, was transferred, *Shaniar*, or *Shiniar*. It would then be *Shan* of the wood, or grove. Now Strabo [1] mentions that the temple of Ammon was placed in the midst of a grove, which formed a singular contrast with the surrounding desert. [2] See also Lucian *de Deâ Syriâ.*

I am inclined to think, then, that *Amraphel, Melech, Shan-ar*, are only so many titles, or symbols, descriptive of the Sun in the sign of

---

[1] L. 17.

[2] Upon further consideration I am inclined to believe, that שנער ought to be read שֶׁן נַעַר *shan-naar*—the year or annual sun, personified as a boy. In effect, the boy Harpocrates was represented in the sign of *Aries* in both the Egyptian zodiacs found at Dendera.

Aries, who was worshipped by the Egyptians under the name of Ammon.

Arioch, ארי *ari,* is the Hebrew for *a lion,* but it is peculiarly applied in the cognate dialects to the sign of *Leo.*

Och, or *Uch,* was a term of honor, and *ari-och* probably signified *Leo præclarus.*

King of Ellasar. Where was this Kingdom of Ellasar, which must have been read Sellasar by some of the Greek translators, and Tellasar by Jonathan? Hieronymus understood that it was Pontus, but I know not on what authority. In Hebrew the word is written אלסר, and without any *masorah* may be read *Elsar.* אל *El,* may signify *mighty,* or it may signify *God.* סר *Sar, Ser,* or *Sir,* (for the sound of the supplied vowel is of no manner of consequence) was a title frequently given to the Sun by the Egyptians, but particularly in the sign of *Leo.*

Osiris was a symbolical name of the Sun, and, like other enigmas, was probably intended to convey several meanings. There may be reason to think, as I have stated elsewhere, that the initial vowel, which we know to have been changeable, was frequently left out. The termination in *is* is evidently Greek. The name may then be expressed in Coptic letters CIP *Sir*, or, if the article be prefixed, OϤ-CIP, which comes sufficiently near to the Greek Ὄσιρις. *Leo* was the domicile of Osiris, or of the Sun.

The river Nile, which had assumed its greatest height, when the Sun was in *Leo*, was called *Siris*, or rather *Sir*, by the Ethiopians. Thus Stephanus says, Συήνη, πόλις Αἰγύπτου καὶ Αἰθιοπίας ἐπὶ τῷ Νείλῳ· μεθ᾽ ἣν ὠνόμασται Σίρις ὁ ποταμος—*Syene is a city of Egypt, and of Ethiopia, upon the Nile; beyond which the river is named Siris.*

This name was undoubtedly given to the Nile, because it had already attained its greatest eleva- tion, when the Sun was worshipped under his character of *Osir*, or *Sir*. Hence, indeed, the river was said to owe its origin to Osiris. Plutarch strongly expresses this. Νεῖλον τὸν πατέρα καὶ σωτῆρα τῆς χώρας, καὶ Ὀσίριδις ἀπορροὴν ὀνομά-

ζουσι,—they call the Nile the father and saviour
of the region, and a fluxion of Osiris.

There seems to be a strange corruption which
is made by the Greeks of the name of the Egyptian
month, which is said to have answered to August.

$$\text{Καὶ Μέσορι Νείλοιο φέρει φυσίζοον ὕδωρ.}$$

I cannot help suspecting the initial *me* in *mesori*
to be nothing else than the Egyptian sign, which is
usually prefixed to a noun to denote it to be such.
The vowels were probably supplied by the author
to suit his verse.

The stars in the sign of *Leo* now occupy the
place, which was held by those of *Virgo* a little
more than two thousand years ago.

The Dog-star was probably called *Sir* (in Latin
Sirius) from its rising heliacally, shortly after the
time that the Sun was in *Leo,* and while that
luminary was worshipped under the name of *Sir,*
or *Osir.*

The Persians and Indians still call the sign of *Leo*, by the name of *Shir*, or *Sir*.

I have already observed, that it imports little with what vowel we supply the radicals S. R. *Serapis* evidently combined the names of *Ser* and *Apis*. That *Sir*, or *Osir*, whom the Greeks called Osiris, was the same with *Apis*, may be proved from Strabo and other writers, whose words I have cited in another place.

But the word *Sar*, *Ser*, or *Sir*, also denoted a certain cycle. Its duration was 3600 years according to Berosus. Suidas gives a different account of it, for he makes it consist of only 222 months and a half. The *Sar*, or Chaldean cycle called *Saros* by the Greeks, has embarrassed astronomers. Halley having found the cycle mentioned by Pliny to consist of 223 lunar months, and not of 222, as wrongly printed in the common editions, has pretended, that this period is no other than the *Saros*, and that the text of Suidas should be corrected in the same manner. The reasoning of Halley upon this point is generally rejected; and has been refuted both by M. Goguet and by M. Le

Gentil. We must then adopt the text of Berosus and his followers, and read 3,600 years. But this period, says M. Goguet, (like that assigned by Suidas,) is one to which we can apply no astronomical operation.

Now this does not appear to be quite correct. The cycle called the *Neros* was of 600 years duration ; and M. Goguet agrees with Cassini in thinking it one of the finest periods which has yet been found. But after the completion of this period for the sixth time, that is to say at the end of 3,600 years, it would be found that a very sensible disorder had resulted from it. Cassini, I believe, allows the error of one second for each lunar month; and makes the Solar year of the Chaldeans to amount to 365 days, 5 hours, 51 minutes, and 36 seconds. In order not to be embarrassed with fractions, let us assign the error of one second to each solar month in the Chaldean calculation. Then at the completion of the sixth revolution of the *Neros*, or at the end of 3,600 Chaldean solar years, there would be an error amounting to about 63 hours and a half for the whole period. It can scarcely be supposed, that a people so scientific as the

Chaldeans would fail to remark this; and they consequently would reform their calendar. Thus the Egyptians, when they perceived that the *Sothis*, or the *Thoth* as it was sometimes called, did not make a perfect period, multiplied this cycle by 25, and obtained their great year. This has always appeared to me an extraordinary proof of the science of a people, whom we affect to treat with contempt.

M. Goguet further observes, that the name of *Sar*, given to this period, would suffice to prove, that it was composed of lunar months, because the Chaldean word *sar* signifies *menstruus*, or *lunaris*. This statement is not quite accurate. The word סהר *sahar*, or סהרא *sahara*, signifies *the moon* in Chaldaic; but that luminary is only so called from its globular form, because the proper and original signification of *sahara* is *rotundity*. I rather imagine, therefore, that the cycle was called *sar* from its being a round period, at the conclusion of which the Sun and the Moon ought to return to the points, at which they were found at its commencement.

E

That *Ari-Och, Melech, El-Sar*, were words
expressive of some astronomical symbol I can
hardly doubt. Concerning the enigmatical manner
of writing and speaking among the Egyptians, I
conceive it to be unnecessary to make any remarks;
but that this manner has been copied in the text
appears sufficiently evident.

Chedorlaomer King of Elam.

The name of Chedorlaomer is thus explained by
Jonathan in his Targum.

דהוה קישר מתהפיד בעומרין.

*This is the ligament revolving itself about the
sheaves.*

This seems a very singular name for a great
monarch. Nevertheless Jonathan's explanation
of the word appears to be nearly just. I confess,
however, I can only understand it as an astronomical symbol. According to the Egyptian mythology, Isis was said to have dropped a sheaf of

corn as she fled from Typhon, who scattered it over the heavens, as he continued to pursue her.

In the Egyptian Zodiac Isis, whose place was supplied by *Virgo*, was represented sometimes with the leaf of a palm-tree, and sometimes with three ears of corn in her hand.

But I think it highly probable, that the signs of the zodiac were compared with corn bound in sheaves. ' This notion is not unsupported by evidence.

The Chinese call the zodiac the *yellow road ;* as resembling a path over which the ripened ears of corn are scattered.

The Syrians and Chaldeans appear to have had a similar idea. Mor Isaac says

ܘܐܠܡ ܣܒ̈ܠܬܐ ܚܣܝܢܬܐ ܕܟܠܡܘ
ܘܒܢܗ ܣܒܝ ܝܚܠ ܚܠܝܐ.

' The symbol of *Blaundus* in Phrygia was four ears of corn tied together.   Geb. tome 9.

*and the zone of the zodiacal circle is called the
path of straw.*

That the signs of the zodiac were assumed as
the twelve ensigns of the tribes of Israel, I have
proved in another dissertation. Joseph seems to
allude to this, when he says, " the Sun and Moon,
and the eleven stars (constellations) made obeisance
to me." But he had already said to his brethren,
" your sheaves stood round about, and made
obeisance to my sheaf."

I confess then, that I cannot help considering
Chedorlaomer, or *that which girds the sheaves*,
rather as a symbol expressive of the zodiac, than
as the name of a real monarch.

The Sun in his progress through the signs of the
zodiac was called *Chon* by the Egyptians, whom,
as I have shown elsewhere, they considered as the
God of Time.

מלך עילם, *King of Elam—King of Time.*

Tidal King of nations. The word תרעל *Tidal*,

(if this be the true reading) is Chaldaic. It is compounded of תד (Chaldaic for שד), a *breast*, and על, *exalted*. There can be no doubt, that the Heathens worshipped idols under the form of *paps* or *breasts*, which the Hebrews called *Shedi*, or *Shedim*, and the Chaldeans *Tedi*. Isis, or Diana, or the *Dea Multimammia*, will present a ready emblem of this species of idolatry to the mind of the mythologist. Isis, then, whose type was *a cow*, may have been meant by this *exalted breast*. But it seems to me, that for תדעל *Tidal*, we should read תרעל *Tiral*, or *Taral;* and in this I am supported by the Septuagint.[1] There is, however, no such word in Hebrew, as תרעל, unless we bring it from רעל, which is out of the question. It follows then that we must look to the Chaldaic; and there we shall find תר-על, or תור-על would signify *Taurus excelsus*.

מלך גוים *Melech Goim*, "King of Nations." The Syrian interpreter writes *Melech Geleth*, " King of

---

[1] The LXX always write a *gamma* for the Hebrew *ain.* They consequently have θαργαλ in the Septuagint. They ought to have had either θαρααλ, or ταρααλ.

the revolving sphere," whence one would think he held *Tor-al* to be an astronomical personage. In fact, before the time of Abraham, *Taurus* was the leading sign—the conductor of the celestial hosts. Rather more than 4000 years ago, that title was transferred to *Aries*. But I would rather read *Goim*, as in the text, and with the LXX. *Goa*, or *Gao*, is the ancient Persian name of the sign of *Taurus*.

That these made war with Bera.

ברע *Bera*, according to the *Targum* of Jonathan, is compounded of the preposition ב, and רע, and consequently signifies *in evil*. This seems, at least, to have been the manner in which Jonathan understood the word. But I rather suspect that ברע *Bera* is an erroneous reading for פרע *Pera*; where we find רע preceded by the Egyptian article פ. *Pera* then would signify *the evil one*, if רע be Hebrew in the name before us; but I rather think it to be that Egyptian word which signified *King*, and which I have explained in my "Essay on a Punic Inscription." If, however, we follow the orthography before us; I must take the meaning from the Arabic, in which

בֵּרַע *Bera* signifies *excellence,* and which was probably an ancient solar title.

מלך סדם *Melech Sodom,* " King of Sodom." This last word is not Hebrew, and in truth few of these proper names are. They are all either Egyptian, or Chaldean, or ancient Persian. In Hebrew *Sodom* might signify *a secret,* or *a shackle,* as derived from סד. The meaning, however, is *order,* or *regularity,* or the beauty which proceeds from both. [1]

Birsha. Jonathan translates this word ברשע ; and some again translate him as rendering the name " in *opprobrium,*" and others, "against *opprobrium.*" This can have nothing to do with the sense. No man ever had such a name. The personage here is an astronomical one. ברשע *Birsha,* is Chaldaic. It is a name compounded of בר *filius,* and שעה, or שע, *hora, tempus,* &c.

King of Gomorrah. This last word was principally used to signify either *a certain measure,* or *a sheaf of corn.* We have already seen that this last was an astronomical type.

---

[1] See Rumelin.

Shinab King of Admah. Without attending to the points, which every Hebrew scholar must know to have been invented at least six hundred years after the Christian era, we may conclude, that *Shinab* is compounded of *Shan,* "the annual Sun," and *ab* (a well-known solar title), which signifies *father.* This may then indicate the year, or period, of Saturn. It is certain, that the Sun was worshipped under the names of Rephan, Moloch, Chon, and Saturn; and that Saturn was fabled to have been dethroned by his son Jupiter. When, therefore, we find *Shan,* the title under which the year, or perhaps the Sun in his annual course, was deified and worshipped, coupled with אב *ab, pater,* we may naturally associate it with the name of Saturn. *Shan-ab* is called "King of *Admah,*" that is, "King of the Earth;" and Saturn was fabled to have fled to the earth, after having been driven by Jupiter from the throne of the heavens.

Shemeber.

This signifies *the name of the mighty one;* but both the Samaritan copies have *Shemabad,* i. e. *the name of destruction,* or perhaps, *of the destroyer.*

May not this destroyer be the great serpent, feigned
by some to have been slain by Apollo, but which
is said by Pausanias to have been killed by Κρίος,
that is, by Ammon, or the Sun in *Aries?*

I think it is mentioned by Aratus, that the
Dragon was not to be found among the figures, by
which the Egyptians represented the constellations.
I cannot, at this moment, refer to Kircher, in order
to discover upon what authorities he placed the
Dragon in the planispheres, which he has exhibited;
but that dragons, or serpents, were represented in
the Egyptian planispheres, I cannot doubt. Hor-
Apollo mentions, indeed, that the hieroglyphic
which expressed the heavens was *a serpent*, and
that the stars were denoted by the scales; and
Clemens Alexandrinus tells us, that the oblique
course of the stars was indicated by the tortuous
folds of a serpent. It appears, that from the
most remote antiquity the two points, at which the
ecliptic and the Moon's orbit intersect each other,
were called the head and tail of the Dragon. As
these are the points at which eclipses happen,
astronomers fabled the existence of a monster that
devoured the sun and moon.

It seems not impossible to me, that the word may have been originally written שפף-אבד, or שף-אבד, *the serpent of destruction.* But this is merely conjectural. My reader may, however, consider what has been stated, with some plausibility, by M. Dupuis on the *Abaddon* of the Apocalypse.

That the *Dragon* is alluded to in the text appears more clearly from the following words, since *Shemabad,* (or *Shemeber* as we have it in the Hebrew text) is called *King of Zeboiim.* Now what sense shall we affix to *Zeboiim?* If we follow the present reading, *Shemabad* must be either *King of decorations,* or *King of she-goats,* or *King of hyænas;* for which several meanings consult Buxtorf, *in voce* צבי, and Bochart Hieroz. Part first. Now I confess that I suspect צביים to have been written by some scribe for צבאים; and if this be so, I shall have no scruple in translating *King of the starry hosts.* We have already seen from Hor-Apollo, that the stars of heaven were hieroglyphically expressed by the scales of a serpent.

And the King of Bela.

בלע *Bela* signifies *to swallow up.* Is there not here another allusion to the celestial Dragon, feigned by astronomers, and believed by idolators, to have swallowed up the Sun? *Bel,* the God of the Babylonians, was no other than the great Dragon, though *Bel* has been sometimes confounded with *Baal.* The name of *Bel* seems to me to have been taken from *Bela;* for the great Dragon was evidently called *Bel,* as the devourer, or as the swallower. This is apparently alluded to by Jeremiah, where he says—

ופקדתי על בל בְּבבל

והצאתי את בלעו מפיו.

" And I have punished Bel in Babel, and have made him eject his *bela* (what he hath swallowed) from his mouth."

Which is Zoar; that is *the little.*

The greatest space between the Moon's orbit and the ecliptic is called the belly of the Dragon. As the Moon approaches to her nodes, this space becomes smaller, and of course is least just before the point, where she crosses the Ecliptic.

It appears, that the whole passage, as far as I have hitherto gone, is symbolical; and I find it not a little remarkable, that the greater part of it can be expressed in hieroglyphics, with considerable accuracy. Is it not probable then, that the text is an interpretation of a hieroglyphical writing, which the sacred historian thought it necessary to introduce into his work?

That the symbols here expressed were originally denoted by hieroglyphics, I think evident from the facility, with which they may again be rendered into their primary forms.

Ammon, or the Sun in *Aries*, here denominated *Amraphel*, *agnus mirabilis*, was represented by a man with the head of a ram. See my " Essay on a Punic Inscription," p. 50.

We are told by Ammianus Marcellinus, that a King was represented in hieroglyphics by *a bee*.

If I be right in reading *Shan-iar*, the hieroglyphic of this ought to be the image of the Sun, and a grove of trees; or if the etymology be *Shannaar*, we ought to have the more common symbol of Harpocrates.

The words *Arioch, Melech*, are to be expressed by *a lion* and *a bee.*

If *El-sar* be the same with *El-Sir*, there can be little doubt that reference is made to the God *Sir*, whom the Greeks called *Osiris*. The hieroglyphic of Osiris was *a sceptre* and *an eye.*

Chedorlaomer was probably denoted by a sheaf, or sheaves of corn. The bee again recurs. Time, or eternity, which is the signification of *Elam*, was typified by a serpent biting his tail.

Tor-aal, or *the exalted Bull*, is itself a hieroglyphic. The word Melech is again to be denoted by *a bee*. If for *Goim* we read *Geloth*, a hieroglyphic must be found for the spheres. Two present themselves: *First* an onion, of which the coats were the symbols of the spheres: (This was the reason why onions were so much venerated in Egypt :) *Secondly* two serpents, represented in the following form:

These made war.

Upon the authority of Hor-Apollo, we may state that a battle was designed by two hands, one of which held a bow, and the other a shield.

But I have said enough on this part of the subject, and shall leave others to exercise their ingenuity upon it.   Let us return to our analysis.

All these were joined in the Vale of Siddim, which is the salt-sea.

שדים *Siddim ;* These were Deities worshipped by the idolators.   They were probably so named from שד, *a breast.* See Parkhurst, *in voce.*   I shall attempt at the end of this Dissertation to give a rude sketch of one of these many-breasted idols,

of which there are various representations in the
7th volume of the Thesaurus of Gronovius.

Which is the salt-sea. It appears from Josephus, whose words I have quoted in another
Dissertation, that the sea was a symbol of the
hemisphere, as Isis, or the *Dea Multimammia,*
seems to have been a lunar emblem.

*Twelve years they served Chedorlaomer, and in
the thirteenth year they rebelled.*

The astronomical allusion, here intended to be
made, may be well illustrated by the words of M.
Goguet. " Nous voyons que dans les premiers
ages, l' année, chez presque tous les peuples, n'étoit
composée que d'un mois ; et encore ce mois étoit-
il lunaire." Now it is evident, that at the end of
the 12th lunar month, neither the solar nor the
sidereal year would be complete. The Sun would
neither rise, nor set, at the same time, or in the
same place, as when the lunar year commenced ;
and the constellations would not be found, where
they had been at the beginning of the period. In
following this mode of calculating, the whole order

of the seasons would be found to be reversed in the space of 17 years. We cannot suppose then, that the Chaldeans and Egyptians continued to count long by the lunar year, which is composed of 354 days. A reform appears to have been made at a very early period; and M. Goguet has proved that the year which Moses employed was composed of 360 days. This has led some to suppose, that Moses was very ignorant of astronomy. The chapter before us, I think, will justify him from that reproach.

To complete the year employed by the Hebrews, no less than five days and a quarter were wanting. Now the Priests of Egypt knew this. Herodotus says, that they added the five days; and if he makes no mention of the remaining hours, it is, probably, because the Priests did not confide to him the secret. The science of the learned Egyptians was their religion. Hence all the mysteries with which it was enveloped. We know, however, that Plato, Eudoxus, Diodorus Siculus, and Plutarch, were aware that the Egyptians computed the year rightly. The truth then was likely to be known to Moses, who was versant in all the learning of Egypt.

I have already stated that *Chedorlaomer* seems to have been the symbol of the Zodiac, or rather, perhaps, of the course of the Sun through the signs. It is by observing that course, that the true length of the year is to be determined; and the omission of the five days, and the consequent disorders in the computation of the year, seem to be symbolised by the rebellion of the five Kings.

Plutarch, when he informs us, that the five days were intercalated by the Egyptians, mentions that on each of these days a Deity was born. There are various fables told by the Greeks concerning this celebrated intercalation. For my own part, I cannot help thinking, that the fourteenth chapter of Genesis, and the tenth of the Book of Joshua, are only different editions of the same astronomical histories, of which the Greeks have again given new accounts, and which they told after their own manner.

And in the fourteenth year came Chedorlaomer, and the Kings that were with him, and smote the Rephaims in Ashteroth Karnaim, and the Zuzims

*in Ham, and the Emims in Shaveh Kariathaim,
and the Horites in their Mount Seir, unto El
Paran, which is by the Wilderness.*

Here all the confusion produced by the use of
the civil year seems to be pointed out. The five
days having been omitted in the old year, and
being reckoned in the first month of the new year,
at the end of the 12th lunar month; it is obvious
that in the second month of this new year, the Sun
would not be in the same part of the Ecliptic, as
he had been in the second month of the preceding
year. It will be observed that, since months were
denominated years, the fourteenth year in the text
really answers to the fourteenth month, or to the
second month of the new year. But each month
containing 30 days only, the error of the calculation would be perceived from the Sun's place in the
second month of the new year, fourteen months,
(or, as they were then denominated, fourteen years,)
after the commencement of the period stated to be
annual. Chedorlaomer, or the Sun in his progress
through the signs of the Zodiac, is consequently
typified as making war with the constellations.
He smote the Rephaims in Ashteroth Karnaim.

The Rephaim (not Rephaims) were adorers of the Moon, and probably those who principally adhered to the use of the Lunar year. (See Parkhurst, *in voce* רפאים.) If, however, we take the more common translation, we must understand the Rephaim to have been *giants*. Now the constellations were called giants, terrible ones, mighty ones, &c. as is evident from the catalogues of their names in use among the Oriental nations. Ashteroth has been generally supposed to be the title of the Moon, corruptly written Astarte by the Greeks. In fact it appears, that the idols, representing the Moon under her several phases, were called Ashteroth. Samuel tells us of Saul, that the Philistines

ישימו כליו בית עשתרות.

placed his armour (in) the house of Ashteroth. Kimchi says, *est nomen, (nempe Ashteroth,) imaginum ovium formam habentium, quas pro Deabus colebant Tsidonii et Philistæi.* See also Mor Isaac quoted by Kircher, Œd. V. 1.

Karnaim signifies *horns;* and Ashteroth of horns must consequently mean the lunar crescent.

Herodotus observes, that *Io* was represented with horns. *Io*, or *Ioh*, is still the Coptic word for the Moon.

And the Zuzims (read Zuzim) in Ham.

The *Zuzim* are generally understood to signify *strong ones, giants;* but I derive the word from זיז, *to shine,* or *to move.* The Zuzim were then probably *the shining ones,* or *the stars.* I know not the meaning of *Ham.* According to the Samaritan copy we should read *in Laish,* or in *Lisha,* and this name I shall show to have indicated *Scorpius,* when I come to examine a subsequent verse.

And the Emims in Shaveh Kariathaim.

The *Emim* were *giants,* or *terrible ones. Shaveh,* שוה, is the Chaldaic word for the *Equator. Shaveh Kariathaim,* the *Equator of the cities,* can hardly be mistaken for any thing else than for an astronomical expression.[1] The points seem to be indicated,

---

[1] The Persians designate the celestial houses, as we call them, towers, citadels, and cities.

where the Equator and the Ecliptic intersect each other, and where the Equator divides the celestial mansions, or cities, into equal parts.

And the Horites in their Mount Seir.

I translate, *and the wrathful ones in their mountain of the goat.* Whether, or not, any allusion be here made to *Capricorn,* I am unable to judge. The Horites may have been the stars in *Taurus,* where *Hor,* according to Kircher, had his station. *Taurus* rises early in the evening, when the sun is in *Capricorn.*

Unto El Paran, which is by the wilderness.

איל *el,* (rather *eil,* or *ail*) signifies *a ram,* and there seems to be some allusion to the sign of *Aries.* The word *Paran* is less easy to be explained. Perhaps it is פאר, with the addition of an intensive *nun.* It will then signify *an ornament for the head.* Eusebius, see my " Essay on a Punic Inscription," mentions that Ammon, or the Sun in *Aries,* was represented with a disk over his head. *El Paran,* or the Ram with the ornament on his head, is said to be by the wilderness. Now by the wilderness I understand the lower hemisphere, the region of darkness, and the kingdom of Ahriman. Four thousand five hundred years ago, the vernal equinox took place when the Sun was in *Taurus*, and consequently *Aries* and *Libra*, were the uppermost signs of the lower hemisphere. That the wilderness was the hieroglyphic, by which the lower hemisphere was expressed, I am led from many things to suspect. Jupiter Ammon, or El Paran, or the Sun in *Aries*, was fabled by the Egyptians *to have lived in the desart*, until he was brought out of it by Isis. Does not this allude to the period, when the equinox first happened when the Sun was in *Aries?* Plutarch says, φησὶ περὶ τοῦ Διὸς ὁ Εὔδοξος, μυθολογεῖν Αἰγυπτίους, ὡς τῶν σκελῶν συμπεφυκότων αὐτῷ μὴ δυνάμενος βαδίζειν, ὑπ' αἰσχύνης ἐρημίᾳ διέτριβεν. Ἡ δὲ Ἶσις διατεμοῦσα καὶ διαστήσασα τὰ μέρη ταῦτα τοῦ σώματος, ἀρτίποδα τὴν πορείαν παρέσχεν.

The anomalies created by the use of the year of 360 days seem to be manifested; and the incongruity of the vulgar year with the real, is figuratively expressed in the Hebrew; for after the first revolution of the former, the Sun cannot be in his true place according to the Calendar ;—His progress through the signs having been miscalculated, the order oft he seasons must have been in a short period reversed. The rising and setting of the constellation could not be according to computation. It would appear, that the text has marked these anomalies ; and that they are hitherto indicated from the commencement of the second civil year, (which took place when the Sun was in *Cancer*,) to the time of the vernal equinox. The Sun smites the giants in Ashteroth Karnaim ; that is, his place among the constellations, even from the first crescent, or first quarter of the lunar month, is at variance with the computation, and does not agree with the Calendar. The same thing is found, as he advances to *Lisha*, or to *Scorpius*, and as he comes to *Shaveh Kariathaim*, or to the Equinox ; as he proceeds to *Seir*, " the goat," or as it would seem to *Capricorn*, and thence to *Aries*, denoted *El Paran, the ram with a decoration on his head.*

But Chedorlaomer, and the Kings that were with him, *returned and came to En Mishpat, which is Kadesh, and smote all the country of the Amalc-*

*kites, and also the Amorites that dwelt in Haze-
zontamar.*

The Sun, having passed the vernal equinox,
returns to the upper hemisphere; but what relation does *en mishpat*, which is generally translated
the fountain of judgment, bear to the subject, as I
have hitherto understood the meaning of the text?
The proper meaning of עין *en* (rather *ain*, or *oin*,)
is *an eye*, and it is only metaphorically that it is
used to signify *a fountain*. But *ain* may be also
figuratively employed for *observation*, or *speculation*. The Rabbins often understand it as signifying *speculative knowledge*. It seems clear to
me, that the word corresponded with a hieroglyphic; and we are informed by Plutarch and Hor-
Apollo, that an eye was the hieroglyphic, by which
knowledge was expressed. Without much difficulty,
then, we may translate *ain, observation*, or *science*.
משפט *mishpat*, is frequently used in Chaldaic as
signifying *astrology*. בעלי משפט *Baali mishpat* is
synonymous with אשפים, *astrologers*. The meaning then seems to be, *they returned and came
according to the science of astrology, which is*
(*Kadesh*) *a holy thing;*

And smote all the country of the Amalekites.

The Sun, in his course through the Zodiac, ought now to be described as returning to the point whence he set out. At the end of the second revolution of the civil year, the Sun would indeed return to *Cancer,* whence he had proceeded at the commencement of the first year, but he would be ten degrees and a half from the place where he had then been. The incongruity of the civil with the solar year would consequently be manifest to astronomers. But how is the return of the Sun to *Cancer,* the sign in which he had been at the commencement of the first civil year, indicated in the text? Chedorlaomer and his allies *smote all the country of the Amalekites;*— that is,—*all the country of the people of the Beetles.* See Buxtorf, *in vocibus* עם et ילק. [1] Now it appears from the Zodiacs found at Dendera, that the Egyptians denoted the sign of *Cancer* by two beetles.—That the year began when the Sun was in that sign, may be proved from the passages to

---

[1] ילק also signifies *a locust.*

which I have referred on the subject in my " Essay on a Punic Inscription."

And also the Amorites that dwelt in Hazezon-tamar.

For the words אמר and הצץ I refer my reader to Parkhurst, only observing that to the last word an intensive *nun* is added in the text.

The literal translation then is—*and also the upper branches, (or perhaps the lambs) that abode in the division of the palm-tree.*

Now without being able to explain this passage entirely to my own satisfaction, I request of my reader to consider how far it may relate to astronomy. Perhaps his better knowledge of the astronomy and mythology of the ancient Egyptians, as well as of their hieroglyphics, will enable him to elucidate what remains obscure to me. In the mean time I shall offer a very few remarks.

That groves, trees, and branches of trees, were employed as symbols of the starry hosts, of constellations, and of asterisms, appears, I think, from various monuments. In the planisphere exhibited by Kircher, a tree is represented in the sign of *Virgo*. In the Zodiacs of Dendera, *Virgo* is drawn with a palm-branch in her hand. The constellation of *Cassiopeia* is called سدر اُل *al seder*, by Ulug Beig, and the *seder* is a species of *tree* well known in the East. In the Mithraic astronomical symbols we always find trees designated. The idolators appear to have worshipped groves as types of the starry Hosts. *And they set them up images and groves in every high hill, and under every green tree.* [1] *Manasseh reared up altars for Baal, and made a grove, and worshipped all the Host of heaven;—and he set up a graven image of the grove which he had made.* [2] *Josiah commanded all the vessels that were made for Baal, and for the grove, and for all the Host of heaven, to be brought out of the temple.* [3]

The Gentile nations seem to have generally entertained the same superstitions concerning trees.

---

[1] 2 Kings, C. 17.   [2] 2 Kings, C. 21.
[3] 2 Kings, C. 23.

Olim quas vellent esse in tutelâ suâ
Divi legerunt arbores ; Quercus Jovi,
Et myrtus Veneri placuit, Phœbo laurea,
Pinus Cybelæ, populus celsa Herculi.

Phæd.

Callimachus says, in addressing Ceres,

Tibique illìc pulchrum lucum posuerunt Pelasgi,
Arboribus undique densum, &c.

Lucretius has the following lines :

Sed nemora, atque cavos monteis sylvasque colebant,
Et frutices inter condebant squalida membra,
Verbera ventorum vitare imbreisque coacti.

See the stories in the Edda concerning the Ash *Ygdrasil.*

Pliny says, *Arbores fuere numinum templa.* L. 13. See also Diodorus Siculus, and Lucian, concerning the consecrated groves of the Egyptians. The Cabbalists represented the 12 signs of the Zodiac on the tree of life ; and the Arabians typified the starry heavens by a fruit-tree. See Kircher's Œdipus, Vol. 2 and 3. Groves and trees, then, being considered as symbols of the starry heavens, the upper branches probably denoted the constellations at their highest elevation.

It will be remembered, that in the Apocalypse the tree of life is represented as growing in the street, and as bearing *twelve fruits,* one of which it yielded every month. Some have thought that an allusion is here made to the Solar walk, where are found the 12 signs of the Zodiac.

The palm-tree appears to have been a solar symbol. I shall have occasion to say more concerning it in another place.

It may, however, be proper to state the words of a French writer. Le palmier fut consacré aux mouvemens célestes, et surtout à la révolution annuelle du Soleil; on lui attribuoit autant de propriétés, que l'année a de jours. I think, therefore, that we can have no great difficulty in understanding what was meant by the upper branches, which abode in the division of the palm-tree. *Amorites* is certainly a difficult word to interpret. It signifies either *teachers,* or *lambs,* or *upper branches.* I am inclined to give it the last signification here. But see Castelli *in voce.*

And there went out the King of Sodom, and the King of Gomorrah, and the King of Admah, and the King of Zeboiim, and the King of Bela, (the same is Zoar), and they joined battle with them in the Vale of Siddim—with Chedorlaomer King of Elam, and with Tidal King of Nations, and Amraphel King of Shinar, and Arioch King of Ellasar,—four Kings with five.

The Sun coming round to the point whence he set out, is thus figuratively represented as encountering the 5 days.

And the Vale of Siddim was full of slime-pits—

Literally—and the valley of the *Siddim,* (the many-breasted idols of the Moon, worshipped as the *Magna Mater)* wells, wells, of bitumen. But, as my reader will find by turning to Stockius, the original meaning of *Beer,* which we always translate a *well,* is *clearness,* or *lustre.* Again the word

חמר, which we render *bitumen,* and which signifies *muddiness,* is not very unlike to חמור. Indeed
Bochart tells us, that an ass is so called from its
color. Now this may have been the reason why
the Orientalists placed asses in the sign of *Cancer,*
when the Nile is approaching to its height. Most
certainly the ancient Persians called the Asterism
in *Cancer,* which we call the asses, by the name
before us. [1] Now I think it very possible, that
allusion is made to these stars. The commencement
of the vulgar Egyptian year took place, when the
Sun was in *Cancer;* and this may have been the time
fixed for the intercalation of the 5 days. *Beeroth,
Beeroth, Chemor,* may then typify the asterism of
the Asses. But the passage is too obscure for me
to speak with any pretensions to certainty in
endeavouring to explain it.

And the Kings of Sodom and Gomorrah fled,
and fell there. It appears that there is some
confusion in this passage. If these Kings fled,
they did not fall there.

And they that remained fled to the mountain.

---

[1] Consult Ulug Beig.

They that remained could scarcely have been *they that fled;* but I think the fault lies with translators.

The destruction and defeat of the five Kings seem to indicate the period, when the five days ought to have been intercalated.

And they took all the goods of Sodom and Gomorrah, and all their victuals, and went their way.

But the discovery of the real period of the solar year, did not prevent the use of the civil, and of the vague year among the Egyptians. The disorder, though perceived, was not remedied, except among the learned.

And they took Lot, Abram's brother's son, who dwelt in Sodom, and his goods, and departed.

לוט *Lot* is so clearly to be traced to לט *absconsio,* that I cannot doubt the meaning. אברם *Abram* evidently signifies *Pater excelsus.* Now it is manifest, that the former is here a type of the **Moon**, and the latter of the **Sun**.

The Greeks appear to have taken *Lethe*, and *Leto*, (*Latona*) from this word לט *lat*, which was probably the root of the Latin *lateo*, &c. The Greeks and Latins made *Leto*, or *Latona*, a female; but, as I have observed elsewhere, the Egyptians worshipped the Moon sometimes as a male and sometimes as a female Deity. Thus *Ioh*, one of the types of the Moon, was a male. It is still the Coptic name for the Moon, and is in the masculine gender. Ammonius says, Καὶ γὰρ εἰ ἀρσενίκως Αἰγύπτιοι τὴν σελήνην ὀνομάζειν εἰώθασιν, ἀλλ᾽ ὡς πρὸς τὴν γὴν, (οἶμαι) αὐτὴν παραβάλλοντες, οὐχ᾽ ὑπὸ ἡλίου μόνον, ἀλλὰ καὶ ὑπ᾽ αὐτῆς φωτιζομένην—" For if the Egyptians have the custom of naming the Moon in the masculine, I think it is because they consider her with respect to the earth, which is lighted not only by the Sun but by her." The Greeks made *Io* a female. But there are several things in the story of *Lot*, "the hidden one," which may recal the fables related of other lunar emblems. The Moon was feigned under different symbols to have been forcibly carried away to the realms of darkness, and to have hid herself from the sight of Mortals. Proserpine borne away to Tartarus; Latona, who hid herself in the island of Delos; Io, who concealed herself in the cave of mount Sipylus; and Lot "the hidden one," whether carried away by Chedorlaomer, or dwelling in the cave near to Zoar, are all so many astronomical allegories illustrative of the same thing.

With respect to the exalted father, I have only to observe that this is clearly a Solar title. According to M. D'Herbelot, the appellation of Father was peculiarly and emphatically given to the Sun by the Orientalists.

And there came one that had escaped, and told Abram the Hebrew.

The Hebrew. The word עבר signifies " one that passes over from, or to, a place." Now when we come to consider the feast of the *Passover*, or of the *Transition*, we shall understand, who were truly *Hebrews*. But I reserve this for my remarks on the Book of Joshua.

For he dwelt in the plain of Mamre.

I translate באלני, *among the oaks;*—Consult the

Septuagint. The oak, as is well known, was a tree sacred to the Sun. ממרא *Mamre,* is apparently derived from מרא, to *lift up,* to *exalt,* &c; but I conceive it to be the same in signification with the Chaldaic מר or מרא, *Dominus, Doctor,* &c.[1]

The Amorite.

I have already noticed the various meanings of this word, and must leave my reader to decide for himself; but I am rather inclined to think that the *Amorite* here signifies " an expounder, a teacher, a person employed to speak on, or to explain, a subject." It is possible, however, that the *Amorites* were those, who first showed the transit of the vernal equinox, and consequently of the commencement of the year, from the sign of the *Bull* to that of the *Ram,* or *Lamb.* The *Amorites* were, therefore, in the beginning, associates with Abram, who substituted the *Ram* as a sacrifice instead of his son Isaac. But these *Amorites* probably became afterwards idolators, and worshippers of Ammon, or of the Sun in the sign of *Aries.*

---

[1] See Buxtorf's Chaldaic Lexicon, in מרן.

אשכל *Eshcol.* Rumelin seems to consider this word as the same with אשכיל, *a vine-branch.* I would rather derive it from שכל, and consider the servile *aleph* as merely formative. I understand it to denote " an intelligent or scientific person. "

ענר *Aner.* This is a collocation of letters, which, I think, could scarcely have been made by the author. I therefore suspect it to be one of those names, which the scribes have mutilated. It is clear, indeed, that the LXX must have read עונן. Now this word signifies *an augur,* or *astrologer.* [1]

And these were confederate with Abram.

But according to the original we must read, *and these were Baali-Berith of Abram.* Now *Baal-Berith* appears to have been one of the Gods of the Tsabaists ; [2] and the *Baali-Berith* were probably idols adored in later times by the apostate Israelites. Here, however, they seem to indicate

---

[1] See Buxtorf.   [2] Jud. 8. 33.

the astronomers, who were employed in correcting the Calendar. *Baali-Berith* have generally been understood to signify *Lords of the covenant;* and this has been taken as an idiomatic expression, which signifies *Covenanters,* or *Confederates.* In the same manner *The Lords of Arrows* have been translated *Archers.* But I suspect, that this is not quite accurate. *Baali-Berith* appear to me to signify *Lords of purification;* [1] or perhaps, rather, Lords of Clearness. [2] They were those by whom the exalted father (the Sun) was purified, or rendered clear. But if *confederates* be the sense, the verse may be explained as follows.

And there came one that had escaped, and told the exalted father, him that passeth over ; for he dwelt among the oaks of him that teacheth, the instructor, or expounder, brother of him that is scientific, *and brother of the astrologer ; and these were confederates* (Lords of the Covenant) *with the exalted father.*

In spite of the difficulty and perplexity, which

---

[1] See Parkhurst.   [2] See Buxtorf, in ברי.

these names present, I cannot help thinking that the passage contains an astronomical allegory.

In the next verse we learn, that the exalted father followed with 318 of his trained servants, born in his house, and pursued Chedorlaomer unto *Dan.* This last word is a manifest interpolation. It is evident that Moses must have written *Laish*, or *Leshem.* [1] *Laish* then was called *Laisha* by the Chaldeans, with the emphatic *alepha.* But from the way in which the word is written in the Book of Joshua, I think we ought to trace it to לש, (not to ליש) a root now lost in Hebrew, but existing in Syriac ܠܫܐ *lesha*, which signifies *destruction.* The Danites then changed the name from *Lesha*, "destruction," to *Dan*, "justice." Now let us observe, that *Scorpius*, as I have proved elsewhere, was the sign of the Zodiac allotted to the tribe of Dan; —that the Chaldeans call the sting of *Scorpius*, *Lesha*;—and that a name not very dissimilar to this may be still found on the celestial globe, denoting the sting of *Scorpius.*

---

[1] Josh. 19. Jud. 18.

The number 318 is very remarkable. Plutarch relates, that a connexion having been discovered between *Saturn* and *Rhea*, the Sun threatened that the latter should not be delivered of a child in any month or year. But Mercury, who was in love with Rhea, having won from the Moon at dice the 20th part of each of her annual lunations, composed of them the 5 days, which were added to the year, and by which it was augmented from 360 to 365 days. On these 5 days Rhea brought forth *Osiris, Arueris, Typhon, Isis,* and *Nephte.*

I have already endeavoured to show, that these 5 days were typified by the 5 Kings in the Chapter before us.

We shall find a curious illustration of Plutarch's story in the 318 servants of the exalted father (the Sun) born in his own house. By these servants I understand days.

Now the old year being composed of 360 days, the 20th part amounts to 18 days. Let us then take 12 lunations at 28 days each, and we shall get a period of 336 days. Deduct a 20th part of the old year of 360 days from the 12 lunations at 28 days each, and the remainder will be 318 days. The equation may be given as follows.

$$28 \times 12 - \frac{360}{20} = 318.$$

And he divided himself against them, he and his servants by night, and smote them, and pursued them unto Hobah, which is on the left hand of Damascus.

Hobah signifies " concealment," and *Damascus* is " an angle."

Now let us suppose that astronomers educated in the temple of the Sun, had to correct the errors introduced into the Calendar by the omission of the 5 days. They would have found at the end of the second year, that the Sun did not arrive at the Summer solstice, until ten days and a half after the computed time. In following the solar course from the solstitial to the equinoctial point, they would have discovered, that by the omission of the five days, the calculation of the Sun's place conti-

nued to deviate more and more from the truth.
But in measuring the space from the solstice to the
equinox, the astronomers would perceive, and might
correct, the errors made by those, who had limited
the duration of the year to 360 days. They seem
really to have done so according to the text.

The circle is divided into four parts, each consisting of 90 degrees. It is easy to see whence arose
this division. Thus in fact the year was divided
into four parts, and was measured from each
equinox and from each solstice. The four Kings,
perhaps, among other significations, for all symbolical enigmas have many meanings, may represent
the four quarters of the year. But as 90 days
only were allotted to each of these quarters, the
anomalies produced by the omission of the five
days, typified by the five rebel Kings, would soon
be obvious. Between the solstice and the equinox,
the error would amount to about 31 hours and a
half. The astronomers, then, seem to have
followed the solar course from the summer solstice,
(when the new year began, when the five days and
a half should have been, and when they were not,
intercalated) until the arrival of the Sun in the

sign of *Lesha*, or of *Scorpius*, in which he arrived at the Autumnal equinox. By *hobah, concealment,* (for I derive it from חבה) I understand " the season when the Sun passes the equinoctial point." In fact the lower hemisphere was typified by mythologists as the hiding place of the celestial bodies. Hence Saturn, and hence Latona, clearly derived their appellations. Hence *Latium* was named, as the spot to which Saturn had retired; and hence the waters of forgetfulness were denominated from *Lethe.* This place of concealment, this *Hobah,* was on the left hand of *Damashek,* or of the *angle.* May not this be the angle formed by the ecliptic with the equator, where they intersect each other at the equinoctial point?

In the next verse we are told, that he (the exalted father) brought back his brother *Lot*—that is—" the hidden one."

The astronomers, who had to reform the Calendar, would find it necessary to correct the calculations made concerning the lunar month. A period of thirty days being allotted for each month, the calculations would be yet falser for the lunar than for the solar year.

It is impossible not to be struck with the passage before us, where we find the exalted father bringing back *Lot, the hidden one,* from *Hobah, concealment.* The three-headed Cerberus, like the triform Hecate, was a lunar symbol; and Cerberus brought back to the day by Hercules, appears to be only another type of the astronomical fable, which is here indicated in the story of Lot.

In the following verse we are told, that the King of Sodom (that is " of order, or regularity") went out to meet the exalted father at the valley of *Shaveh,* which is the King's dale.

But *Shaveh* in Chaldaic signifies *the equator;* and the true annual period being fixed, the exalted father is properly said to have met the King of order.

The purport of the Chapter, as far as we have hitherto gone, seems to have been to explain the astronomical mysteries of the Egyptians, and to show, that the Deities adored by the vulgar were merely scientific symbols. It appears, that the text is itself a translation from some hieroglyphical monument; and I am very far from pretending, that I understand all the various meanings and bearings of the symbols. It is highly probable, that the philosophical secrets concealed in these hieroglyphics were reverenced as sacred by those, who were inclined to become, or who already were, idolators among the Hebrews. They must have seen there almost all the symbols most venerated by the Egyptians. They might then have naturally mistaken them for the types of those very Gods, whom their own superstitions were constantly prompting them to adore. The sacred lawgiver appears to have unfolded the latent meaning of the hieroglyphics. He seems to have chosen such oral symbols in his own language, as suited the painted or sculptured symbols of the monument, which he thought proper to explain; and from this explanation it might be evident to the Hebrews, that the history of Egyptian theology was to be found in the Egyptian calendar. Thus it would be proved to their own conviction, that the Gods of their idolatry were mere fictions of the brain—

conventional marks and signs, intended to facilitate the acquisition of science to those, who were to be initiated in it, and contrived to impede the progress of knowledge among those, who were thought unworthy of being intrusted with the mysterious secrets of the wise.

To all those who were capable of comprehending it, this lesson from their lawgiver must have been deeply impressive. They must have seen, that they had been adoring allegories, and worshipping symbols; and that the religion of the people was only valued, inasmuch as it was science among the learned. They must have blushed for their own infidelity to the God of their fathers, when they came to understand who were the Gods of Egypt, and when they found, that the births, the lives, and the deaths of those Gods,—their victories and their defeats—all the changes which they underwent, and all the forms which they wore— were mere types and emblems, by which the history of astronomy was recorded.

The sacred lawgiver, having explained what appears to have been the hieroglyphical narrative of the reform in the Calendar, now introduces a type which relates not to human science. Melchizedek, or the Kings of justice, who are the King of Salem, that is, the King of Peace, bring forth bread and wine, and he is the Priest of God most High. But who are these Kings, that are a King? Who is this Priest of God most High—this King of Peace, that are the Kings of justice? In what calendar shall we find the answer to these questions? What mythology contains a likeness to this mysterious person, who being more than one is one? Is there no allusion here to the triune God, and to the ministry of Christ? At the period fixed, the Prophet seemed to say, when dynasty shall have succeeded dynasty among the contending and revolutionary Gods of idolatry; and after the Gentile nations have adored age after age, and cycle after cycle, the Sun, the Moon, and the hosts of heaven; the true religion shall be revealed, and the world shall behold the glorious fabric reared on the ruins of a thousand superstitions. Then shall mankind turn from their material idols and images to contemplate and to acknowledge the spiritual existence of a sole and infinite Deity. Then it will not be symbols, and devices, and allegories, nor yet the shining and unconscious orbs above, nor yet the seasons as they revolve, that will be addressed under divine appellations. The existence and the order of all things, and the laws which govern nature from the world to the atom, will be referred to a living source, and to a primeval and intelligent cause. The period of the year shall be told even to a second; the march of planets shall be calculated; and the orb of the Sun shall be measured. The Moon shall be followed from node to node, and in spite of her wanderings, her course shall be known. She shall not hide her face that it shall not be predicted, nor rob the Sun of his glory, that the hour of partial darkness shall not be expected. Time shall move as Science directs his pace. Nor Sun nor Planets shall conceal their distance from our earth; Comets shall not wander so far into space, that their return shall not be calculated; nor light fly swift enough that its speed shall not be measured. But the Priest of God most High shall have offered the expiatory sacrifice: The Kings of Justice, who are the King of Peace, shall have revealed the true religion: the Deity shall be adored as the God of Nature, and the works of the Creator shall no more be mistaken for Him, who is the cause of their existence.

Such to my humble apprehension appears to have been the design of Moses, in placing before his readers this mysterious account of Melchizedek.

I shall now conclude my remarks on this Chapter by expressing my hopes, that my endeavours to elucidate its meaning have not been fruitless. I cannot expect that my learned readers will agree with me on every topic. Indeed I have seldom seen two Hebraists, who read, and who translated, two chapters alike throughout the whole Scriptures; but it will be a subject of great satisfaction to me, if my observations may prepare the way for others, who shall be better qualified to carry on similar researches.

DEÆ MULTIMAMMIÆ IMAGO.

ADDENDA.

1. Having left it doubtful in the preceding dissertation, whether *Amraphel* should be translated the *wonderful Lamb*, or the *separated Lamb*, I think it necessary to add, that the latter appears to me to be the proper translation. The word is composed of the Chaldaic אמר and פלה, the ה in פלה being omissible, as is remarked by Parkhurst.

2. It has been observed to me, that צביים, *Zeboiim*, may signify *Tsabaists*. I am aware, that Maimonides and other Rabbins have thus written the word. But I am still inclined to think, that צביים is a corruption for צבאים, which I take to have been the ancient and regular form of the plural of צבא, of which the usual plural form is צבאות. I observe, that we commonly write *Sabaoth* and *Sabeans*, (sometimes *Zabeans*) but the true orthography is *Tsabaoth*, &c.

3. I have not been able to find the Persian word *Gao*, or *Go*, to which I refer *Goim*. I know not, therefore, whether it may not have been written with an *ain*. In all events the word employed by the Syrian interpreter shows, that allusion was made to *Taurus*.

4. It may be proper to acknowledge, that the Rabbins do not admit that Melchizedek implies a name including a plural form. It must also be confessed that Melech, or Moloch, was a very common solar title.

5. From a passage in Sanchoniatho, it may be thought, that the Sun was worshipped by the Tsabaists under the name of עליון. My learned readers will perceive, from these things, that it is possible to come to a different conclusion, from that, which I have drawn at the end of the preceding dissertation.

III.

ESSAY,

&c. &c.

Dissertation

TABERNACLE AND THE TEMPLE.

———

It would be difficult to imagine a more singular history, than that which relates to the construction of the Tabernacle and of the Temple, contained in the Old Testament. The Deity is represented as giving the pattern of both; as ordering the whole furniture; and as descending to the most minute details concerning the arrangement. Nothing is left unnoticed by the divine architect, who condescends to speak with amazing precision and familiarity both of the ornaments and of the utensils,—of lintels, curtains, fringes, rings, tongs, tables, dishes, bowls, spoons, and candlesticks.

This, however, is not all. The Tabernacle and the Temple were inhabited by the Deity. The God of Nature and of the Universe—the Creator and Preserver of all things—the ineffable and primordial Being, who called into existence all those Suns and Planets, which roll through the boundless regions of space—the sole God fixed his residence on a box made of Shittim wood, and overlaid and lined with gold. Upon this box too, the Deity was carried about by a barbarous horde of robbers, until King Solomon built a temple at Jerusalem, where the box was deposited, and where Jehovah dwelt between the Cherubim. And what were these Cherubim? They were whimsical and monstrous images, each with four wings, and four faces; the face of a man, the face of a lion, the face of an ox, and the face of an eagle.

The whole of this history, if literally taken, is surely very strange and astonishing. There can be no doubt, however, that it obtains implicit credit among the generality of Christians, who, without inquiring into the spirit and character of the ancient Oriental writings, are firmly persuaded, that facts only are recorded in the books of the Old Testament. He, indeed, who ventures to think otherwise, and who holds those books to be chiefly typical and allegorical, must expect to meet with that sort of reprehension, which zealous men think it incumbent to bestow on all, who differ from themselves.

I have often been struck with the different feelings, which manifest themselves in different persons, when questions of this nature are discussed. I confess myself to be one of those, who find it impossible to reconcile the histories related in the Old Testament, if literally taken, to my notions either of the goodness, or the greatness, of God. This is surely a subject of much importance; and yet it is managed in a very singular manner. No sooner is it started, than men of education in general endeavour to get rid of it. They seem to fear too rude a shock to their faith; and for the greater part, it must be pretty evident, that the question is one, on which few are prepared to speak. But such timidity, or such indifference, whichever it be, is little worthy of men of understanding. It is true, on the other hand, that Superstition has but too many champions and supporters, against whose decisions it is not always prudent to appeal. These men, sometimes vaunting, and sometimes disclaiming, their enthusiasm, are indeed at any time sufficient both from their numbers, and by their means, to raise such a clamor, as must drown the still voice of philosophy in the uproar. Some by their talents and learning engage the attention of the wise; others by their zeal and industry confirm the prejudices of the weak and ignorant; some affect to reason and persuade; while others seek to terrify and dismay. In their hands is the Press,—that guardian of civil liberty in the state—that tyrant over free opinion in the Church. With them is the cry of the multitude—with them the silent sanction of the laws. The weapons with which they fight are either borrowed from the armory of heaven, or forged in the fires of hell. When they condescend to reason, their logic is governed by rules of its own. Bold assumptions, though constantly disputed by their adversaries, are yet constantly repeated by them; and the entire mis-statement of an opponent's argument is not with them an illegitimate mode of carrying on a controversy.

But their strength, and none can know it better than themselves, lies not in reasoning; and hence the scurrilous invective, or the bitter taunt,—the opprobrious epithet, or the scornful sneer,—so often supplies the place of the forgotten argument.

From these champions of superstition, who falsely call themselves the friends of religion, I ask no indulgence ; but from the real friends of religion, from fair and dispassionate men of every sect and persuasion, I shall claim a candid investigation into the merits and demerits of my work, before they condemn it. I wish to call the attention of men of sense and learning to the interpretation of a Book, upon which so many think that so much depends, but about which only a few choose to allow themselves to reflect or to reason.

It may be, I admit, historically true, that Moses constructed a Tabernacle, and that Solomon built a Temple; but I cannot persuade myself, that the Deity inhabited either the one or the other, or that God at any time ceased to be omnipresent to the world which he made. I conceive the Tabernacle and the Temple to have been types of the universe, which is the true abode of the Godhead. Typically speaking, then, the Tabernacle and Temple were the residence of the Divine Majesty; and, in truth, it seems to me inconceivable, that men in an age like this should seriously believe, that the sacred writers meant literally, that the God of the Universe was cooped up in a Temple at Jerusalem, or any where else.

It is to be observed that God ordained the pattern of the temple; by which I understand that the sacred writers intended to say, in their usual allegorical manner, that the Universe was formed after the exemplar in the divine mind.

We shall find upon examination, that every thing belonging to the temple served as a symbol; and I am convinced that when these symbols are considered, there will remain no doubt of the temple itself being a type of the universal system. In fact it seems to me, that by this manner of viewing the subject, we obtain an infinitely more exalted notion of the ideas of the Jewish writers concerning theology, than we could possibly entertain, while we followed the literal interpretation. Who, indeed, that has any just notions of the Supreme Being, can believe that the Deity did in fact either sit down to breakfast with Abraham, or talk to Moses about pans, and shovels, and fleshhooks, and firepans? Who can believe, that the eternal and unchangeable God did that in anger one day, for which he was sorry the next? If these things be taken literally, there can be nothing more inconsistent with true theology; and most surely we should be the first to laugh, if an Indian were to tell us that *his* God was so very apt to change his mind.

I am equally persuaded, that the accounts, which we have of the Tabernacle and of the Temple, are mere allegories. " *Will God indeed dwell on the earth? Behold the heaven, and heaven of heavens cannot contain thee: how much less this house that I have builded?* " This language of the Royal Sage is at once reasonable and sublime, and sufficiently shows that Solomon did not believe, that the omnipresent Deity dwelt in a cloud over the ark. This cloud, which was probably produced by the smoke from the censers, filled the house, and was the emblem of that spiritual intelligence, which pervades the universe.

I shall now proceed to examine the various symbols, which were contained in the Tabernacle and in the Temple. I shall first consider the images called the *Cherubim*.

1. These singular images have been fully described by Ezekiel. I have observed elsewhere, that the four faces answered to four signs of the Zodiac— that of the *Man*, to *Aquarius*; that of the *Lion*, to *Leo*; that of the *Ox*, to *Taurus*; and that of the *Eagle*, (which emblem was assumed by Dan in place of *Scorpius*,) to the accursed sign represented sometimes by a *Basilisk*, and sometimes by a *Scorpion*. These four signs are in opposite parts of the heavens; and when astronomy was first cultivated in the East, the two *Solstices*, and the two *Equinoxes* took place, when the Sun was in those signs.

Aben Ezra says distinctly, that the four emblems

of Reuben, Judah, Ephraim, and Dan, were the same with the four faces of the *Cherubim.* Now we have seen in a former Dissertation, that the emblems of those four leaders in the camp of the Hebrews, answered to the above-mentioned signs of the Zodiac.

Philo Judæus, in speaking of these images, seems to consider them as astronomical symbols. " *Now let us consider,*" says that learned Jew, " *what may be subindicated by the Cherubim, and flaming sword turning every way. What, if this ought to be thought the circumvolution of the whole heavens?*" — Again —" *But of the flaming sword turning every way, it may be thus understood to signify the perpetual motion of these (the Cherubim) and of the whole heavens. But what if it be taken otherwise?—so that the two Cherubim signify both hemispheres;*" &c. pp. 111, and 112.

The *Cherubim* are thus noticed by Clemens Alexandrinus, the most erudite of the Christian Fathers. " *Moreover there are those golden images. Each of them has six wings, whether they typify the two Bears, as some will have it, or, which is better, the two hemispheres. The name, indeed, of Cherubim would express great knowledge. But both have twelve wings, and thus through the circle of the Zodiac, and of self-carrying time, they typify the world perceived by the senses.*'"

It must now, I think, be obvious, that the sacred writers never meant to say literally that Jehovah dwelt between the golden images, called the *Cherubim*, in the Temple of Jerusalem. To me, at least, it appears that they spoke figuratively, and really meant to represent the Deity as every where residing through the infinity of space.

In one of the psalms we find the following verse.

And he rode upon a Cherub, and did fly ; yea, he did fly on the wings of the wind.

There may be readers who think this very fine. For my part I pretend, that such readers have

---

' Strom. L. 5.

mistaken the sense. It by no means appears a fine image to me, to say, that the God of the Universe is flying on the wings of a current of air, over any tract of country on the surface of our little globe. I am of opinion that the word רוח *ruah* does not signify the *wind*, but the *spirit*. Then to fancy God riding on a *cherub*, as the word is commonly understood, offers no very sublime conception. What, if we consider the verse with reference to the explanations, which we have just received from Philo and Clemens? It appears to me, that the image will then be sublime indeed.

We are told by St. John, that round about the throne of God there were four beasts full of eyes before and behind—that these beasts were like a lion, a calf, a man, and an eagle—and that these four beasts had each six wings. Now it is plain enough, that these are no other than the *Cherubim* described by Ezekiel. But who can imagine, that such animals are really placed round the throne of the Almighty? We might as well suppose that the *Lamb* of God was any thing else than a symbol. The faces of the *Cherubim* are evidently types of the four signs of the Zodiac mentioned above. These are properly said to be round the throne of God; for to the Suns and worlds of a thousand systems, from equinox to equinox, and from solstice to solstice, the Deity, whose domicile is the Universe, and whose throne is the Heavens, is always present. To him all created nature is typified as chanting forth praise, and the celestial Hosts are figuratively represented as hailing the Creator, the Word, and the Spirit, in union, the threefold holy one, Lord God of Tsabaoth. It appears to me then, that the *Cherubim* typified the spiritual influences, which, proceeding from the Deity, produce the order and march of the celestial bodies. These influences were represented by the man *Aquarius*, in which the Sun descended to the lowest point—by the *Lion*, in which he ascended to his highest elevation—by the *Eagle* (assumed instead of *Scorpius*) when the orb of day began to sink from the upper hemisphere—and by *Taurus*, when the Sun rose from the lower hemisphere.

The Egyptians had images with the heads of different animals, which seem to have served as astronomical symbols. The *simulacrum* of Serapis, mentioned by Macrobius, was of this description.

2. Of all the Jewish symbols, the *Ark* is, perhaps, the most mysterious. I cannot help remarking, however, that a similar symbol was not unknown to the Egyptians. Plutarch tells us that the body of Osiris was inclosed in a chest, or ark, in the month of *Athyr*, when the Sun was in *Scorpius;* and the people annually held a great festival at this season of the year, when the ceremony of inclosing Osiris in the chest, or ark, was represented. Now it probably will not escape the notice of my readers, that the Israelites were defeated by the Philistines, after they had taken the *Ark* out of *Shiloh*, where it had been deposited. But *Shiloh*, as has been shown in a former dissertation, was the name of an asterism in the sign of *Scorpius*. The Egyptians also held, that the body of *Apis* was placed in an ark; and Varro gives the following curious etymology of *Serapis*. *Quia arca, in quá positus erat Apis, Grœcè seu Ægypti-acè dicitur σόρος, unde Σοραπὶς, quasi arca Apis, deinde, uná literá mutatá, Σεραπὶς dictus est ; ille autem bos, quem penè attonitá veneratione Ægyptus*

in ejus honorem alebat, non Serapis, sed Apis vocabatur, quoniam eum sine arcâ vivum venerabatur. Clemens Alexandrinus speaks nearly to the same purpose.[1] There is a curious passage which Kircher cites from Rossi; and from it the notions of the idolators concerning the Ark may be inferred. *Cùm verò projicerent aurum in ignem, in cuppam fusoriam, seu meliùs in modulos, venerunt Magi, Arab et Rab, qui ascenderunt cum filiis Israel ex Ægypto, et fecerunt vitulum arte magicâ, dicentes,—Ubi est Deus iste qui egressus est de medio operis lateritii,* (דמוסי I rather think means *the payments of tribute) in quo exercitabuntur filii Israel in Ægypto, et fuit in manu ejus nomen et lamina, in quâ Moses scripserat hæc verba,* עלה שור–עלה שור, *ascende bos, ascende bos, ut ascendere faceret in iis* ARCAM *Joseph è medio Nili ; et his dictis projecerunt in medium cupellæ fusoriæ, et egressus est vitulus.* It will be recollected, that the ancient Jewish idolators held Joseph to have been no other than *Apis;*[2] and the Bull, beyond doubt, was the symbol of that Patriarch. It

---

[1] Strom. L. 1.   [2] See Kirch. Œd. Vol. 1. p. 197.

is pretty clear then, that the ancient Egyptian and Jewish idolators considered the *Ark* as a symbol of their own erroneous superstitions. When the Sun, in the sign of *Scorpius*, descended to the lower hemisphere, they mourned his imaginary death, and feigned that their God had gone down to *Hades*. It was then, that *Osiris*, or his symbol, Apis, was said to be inclosed in an Ark. On the seventeenth of the month the ceremony of his being inclosed in this Ark took place; and, on the third day after, the Priests again opened the Ark, and pretended to find the lost *Osiris*. But the accounts of the Greeks are very confused on this subject. From some passages we might be led to imagine, that the death of Osiris was fixed at the Winter Solstice, and his resurrection at the Vernal Equinox. In all events we easily see, why the Ark was a symbol held in so much veneration by the idolatrous worshippers of the Sun. It is not so easy to determine at first sight, though we shall soon see the reason, why it was figuratively made the residence of Jehovah. The venerable St. Chrysostom tells us, that the Ark *had its origin from the rudeness of the Gentiles.* There can be no doubt, indeed, that an *Ark*, as I have already stated, was an object of reverence among the heathens. Plutarch says, (in describing the Ark which was supposed to contain Osiris,) *that the Stolistæ, together with the Priests, carried about the-sacred chest, which contained a golden ark.* In like manner Apuleius [1] mentions a chest which was carried by a priest in the religious ceremonies of the Egyptians. Pausanias [2] informs us *that the simulacrum of Bacchus was found in an ark, which was said to be the work of Vulcan, and which was the gift of Jupiter to Dardanus.* It appears from Eusebius [3] that the Phœnicians had an ark, or chest, before which they celebrated the mysteries of the *Cabiri.* Suidas seems [4] to indicate that chests, or arks, were sacred to Bacchus, and to the Goddesses, Ceres and Proserpine.

But the reason why an *ark* was adopted as a sacred emblem by Jehovah may be explained in this way. The temple was a type of the Universe, and every thing in it was intended to show, that

---

[1] L. 2.　　[2] L. 7.　　[3] Præp. Evang. L. 2.

[4] *In voce* Κισσοφόρος.

Jehovah was no local or national God, who was less than the Lord of all things. This supreme and spiritual ruler had been worshipped, as Cudworth has proved, from the most remote antiquity by the learned Egyptians. Now we shall find that there was a reason, why the *Ark* might be properly taken as a symbol, and why Jehovah should be figuratively said to dwell upon the *Ark*, and between the *Cherubim*. Synesius, speaking of the Egyptian hierophants, observes that *they have Κωμαστήρια, which are arks, concealing, they say, the spheres*, &c. Now a type, which represented the Deity as dwelling above the *spheres*, is one that can easily be reconciled both to reason and to religion. It will be said by some literal reader, that there was nothing contained in the *Ark* but the ten commandments ; but the text on which this assertion is founded, I believe to be an interpolation. If nothing had been in the Ark, but two stones, with a few sentences ingraved upon them which were known to every one, where would have been the crime of looking into the *Ark?* There was clearly a mystery, which was to be kept from the people, and I think, I may now assert, that the *Ark* and the *Cherubim*, were both symbols, which tend to prove my general proposition, that the Tabernacle and the Temple were types of the universal system, of which Moses, who was learned in all the wisdom of the Egyptians, seems to have had a very distinct notion.

3. I have probably already so much offended the literal translators, that, if any have begun to read my observations, it is very unlikely that any have read thus far. Why should not the God that has created, and who governs, ten millions of worlds —why should not that infinite Being condense himself into a cloud, and sit upon a box made of Shittim wood, overlaid and lined with the precious metal, *gold?* Go, ask, ye wise men, though ye be not of the East—go, ask of all Nature.

The next symbol of which I shall take notice is the *table.* For the description of it, my reader will of course consult his Bible. Clemens Alexandrinus thus explains the symbol. *But the table, as I think, signifies the image of the earth ; it is sustained by four feet, answering to the Summer, Autumn, Spring, and Winter, by which the year proceeds,* &c. [1]

---

[1] Strom. L. 6.

4. *The Shew bread.* Of this bread there were twelve loaves, which were placed upon the table. Josephus tells us distinctly, that these twelve loaves were typical of the twelve months of the year.[1]

5. *The golden candlestick with seven lamps.*

This symbol is thus explained by Clemens. *But moreover the candlestick was placed on the south of the altar of incense, by which were manifested the motions of the seven luminaries making their revolutions in the south—for there are three branches inserted into the candlestick on each side, and upon them are lamps; because the Sun, even as the candlestick, being also placed in the midst of the other planets, imparts light both to those above him, and to those below him, according to a certain divine harmony.*[2]

6. *The bowls, knops, and flowers.*

These were all astronomical emblems. Josephus

---

[1] Antiq. Jud. L. 3. [2] Strom. L. 5.

says, that the candlestick was divided into 70 parts, answering to the number of the Decans. The number of Decans in this instance must consequently be calculated upon the plan, which I have pointed out in my observations on the Book of Judges.

7. The veil.

Speaking of this, Clemens says, that *it was distinguished by the variety of the blue, purple, scarlet, and linen; and that it therefore typified, that the nature of the elements is, in effect, a revelation from God;—for the purple comes from the water—the linen from the earth—and the blue is assimilated to the air when dark, as the scarlet is to fire.*[1] Josephus speaks to the same purpose. *The veil, says he, which is woven of four colors, manifests the nature of the elements. The byssus (Βύσσος) seems to typify the earth, because linen (λίνον) springs from it ; the purple, the sea which is purpled with the blood of the murex ; by the*

---

[1] Strom. L. 5.

blue the air is signified ; and the scarlet (or crim-
son) is to be considered as the symbol of fire. [1]

8. *The molten sea*—a type of the hemisphere. [2]

9. *The chapiters of the pillars of Solomon's*
temple.

These have been shown by Hutchinson to have
been a kind of *Orreries,* representing the motions
of the planets, &c. [3]

10. *The pomegranates.*—These were emblems
of the fixed stars. [4]

11. If we now examine the dress of the High
Priest, we shall find that it suited the plan and the
type, according to which I pretend the temple was
built. Let us hear Clemens Alexandrinus. *But*
the long robe of the High Priest is a symbol of

---

[1] Antiq. Jud. L. 3.   [2] See Josephus.

[3] See Parkhurst, *in voce—*כתרת. [4] See Parkhurst, *in voce* רמון.

the world perceptible to sense. The five gems, and the two carbuncles, are symbols of the seven planets,—the two last are for Saturn and the Moon;—since the former is to the south, and humid, and earthy, and of a heavy aspect; and the other is airy, for which reason its name Ἄρτεμις *is by some explained* Ἀερότομος, *or air-cutter: But the air, or atmosphere, is obscure, &c.*[1]

The same writer informs us, that the number of bells attached to the Priest's robe amounted to 366, equal to the days of the year, of which the bells were symbolical. But the learned Father should have observed, that the year here implied was not the solar but the sidereal year, which last contains 366 days. In fact we find that the bells were placed alternately with the pomegranates. which were types of the fixed stars.

The same Clemens shortly afterwards tells us, *that the bright emeralds upon the ephod typify the Sun and Moon; and that the twelve precious*

---

[1] Strom. L. 5.

stones, arranged in four rows, describe to us the zodiacal circle, relatively to the four changes (seasons) of the year.

Josephus gives us a somewhat different account of these emblems; but still it is evident, that he considered them as typical of the general system of Nature. *The tunic of the High Priest,* says he, *since it was of linen, represents the earth; but the blue the pole of heaven—the lightnings were indicated by the pomegranates,—the thunders by the sound of the bells;* &c. He then observes, that the ἐσσήνη in the middle of the ἐφαπτὶς, and the zone with which it was girded round, signified *the earth* and *the ocean. But,* continues the Jewish Antiquary, *the two sardonyxes, with which the pontifical garment is clasped, denote the Sun and the Moon; but whether any one wish to refer the twelve stones to the twelve months, or to the same number of stars (constellations) in the circle, which the Greeks call the Zodiac, he will not wander far from the true meaning.* [1]

---

[1] Antiq. Jud. L. 3.

12. The Tabernacle has been styled, and not inaptly, a portative temple. Now it appears that the Tsabaists had also these portative temples, by which they represented the material system of the Universe. *Ye have borne the tabernacle of your Moloch and Chiun, your images, the star of your God.* [1] The idol of Moloch is described by Kimchi; and a curious account of it, extracted from the book *Jalkut*, may be found in Buxtorf. This idol, according to Kimchi, had the head of a bull; and in the body were seven cells, or receptacles, filled with fire. It seems to have been the exact prototype of the idol of Saturn at Carthage, described by Diodorus; for its arms were extended over a chasm filled with fire which gaped before it, and the children to be immolated were placed on the arms. But *Moloch,* or *Rex,* was a type of the solar heat and light, diffused through the planetary system. The Tsabaists, then, had tabernacles which were types of the Universe materially considered; and here lay their error. There were evidently two sects in ancient Egypt. The first

---

[1] Amos, C. 5.

taught a sublime, and, I believe, the true system of theology, on which the ideal system of Plato was afterwards built, though the Grecian sage seems not to have always clearly comprehended his Egyptian masters. This sect referred the whole existence of the sensible world to what is perceived and understood. Another, and probably a more numerous sect supported the doctrine of materialism; and it is against these hyloists, that the Priests and Prophets of Judea seem to me always to inveigh.. The Tsabaists were hyloists, who held that the celestial bodies moved through space, and preserved order and regularity in all their motions, by their own energies, and by powers, properties, and qualities, existing in themselves. To these material powers and properties they accordingly and consistently offered their homage; for if matter can govern itself by its own laws, there is no occasion for the interference of a spiritual director and preserver. If we say, that the material energy is a *vis insita*, it is a shift and a subterfuge, (if it be not, indeed, a contradiction,) to call that *vis insita* a *vis impressa*. It seems then, that the Tabernacles, or portative Temples, of the Tsabaists were types of the material

Universe, and that the *Elohim* there represented were mere emblems of material powers and properties; whereas in the Tabernacle or portative Temple, constructed by Moses, the Universe was indeed typified, but typified as governed and pervaded by the infinite immaterial Being, of whose agency there can be no cessation. The literal interpreters have mistaken the type for the thing; and have, in my humble opinion, most erroneously supposed, that the God of the Universe was carried about in a Tabernacle, or portative temple, fashioned by human hands. The tabernacle seems to me to have been nothing else, than a sensible and material symbol, which was intended to represent the universal system, of which the ideal and immaterial exemplar is in the eternal contemplation of the Deity, who, according to that exemplar, called the Universe into existence, and preserves and sustains that which he hath created.

13. The conversations which are stated to have taken place between the *Summum Numen*, and Moses and David, concerning the Tabernacle and the Temple, appear to me altogether astonishing, if the sacred writers were not speaking allegori-

cally. I have little doubt, that both the Tabernacle and the Temple were built in imitation of the temples already constructed by the Egyptians. It appears from Lysimachus (cited by Josephus against Apion) that the Egyptians had many temples, ere the Israelites crossed the Red Sea. There was a Priest of *On*, and probably that Priest worshipped his God in a temple. In fact, Diodorus Siculus says, that the temple at *Heliopolis* was of extreme antiquity. I observe besides, that the Egyptian temples were furnished nearly in the same manner as the temple of Jerusalem. Clemens Alexandrinus [1] mentions the splendor of the Egyptian Temples, the Porches, Vestibules, Courts surrounded with columns, the gold, silver, amber, the precious stones, &c; and what is yet more striking, the veils which concealed the *Oracles.* Now at no period do I believe that the Egyptians would have copied from the Hebrews any of their emblems, or ornaments, much less would they have followed, in the construction of their temples, the example of a people, with whom they held it to

---

[1] Pædag. L. 3. C. 2.

K

be an abomination to eat. Ages before Clemens, Herodotus had spoken of the *Oracles* in the Egyptian temples, and the *Oracle*, or call it an *adytum*, of a Pagan temple could not be very unlike to that part of the Temple of Solomon, which the Jews call the *Dabir*. Josephus [1] says, that there was no door in the Jewish temple to the West; and, I believe, it is said in the *Gemara*, that the gate of the Tabernacle was to the East. Now we learn from Porphyry, (*de antro nympharum*) that the Egyptians built their temples with the door towards the rising Sun, and this seems to have been peculiar to the Jews and Egyptians. But I have no doubt, that the Tsabaists always endeavoured to symbolise the material heavens in the construction of their temples; and this, I think, even appears from the observations of *Vitruvius*. [2] The emblems, contained in the Jewish temple, could not have been very unlike to those in the Egyptian temples. We have seen, that the Jewish *Ark* resembled sufficiently the Egyptian Ark, in

---

[1] De bel. Jud. L. 5. C. 5.   [2] L. 4. C. 5.

which the hierophant kept the emblems of the celestial spheres. With respect to the *Cherubim*, I have little doubt, that similar images existed in the Egyptian temples; and I think it may have been to such an image that Apuleius alludes, when, in describing the Egyptian Pomp, he says—*gerebat alius gremio suo summi sui Numinis venerandam effigiem, non pecoris, non avis, non feræ, ac ne hominis quidem ipsius consimilem, sed solerti repertu, ipsâ etiam novitate reverendam.* It is pretty plain, that Apuleius did not know what to make of this image; but it is equally plain, that he here indicates all the figures represented in the images of the *Cherubim.* We are told, that the quadrangular altar in the Temple of Jerusalem had its four corners projected in the shape of horns.[1] Now the fashion of such an altar was not uncommon among the Gentiles.

Nec Triviæ templo molles laudentur Iones,
Dissimuletque Deum cornibus ara frequens.

Mart.

---

[1] Jos. de bel. Jud. L. 6. C. 5.

Miror et innumeris structam de cornibus aram.

Ovid.

The worship of *Apis*, or *Mnevis*, among the Egyptians probably first suggested the notion of making altars with horns; and this seems to afford some proof, that the temple, or tabernacle of the Hebrews, was formed after an Egyptian model. From whom, indeed, but from the Chaldeans and Egyptians, could the Israelites have got those curious mechanical representations of the motions of the heavenly bodies, which, (as Mr. Hutchinson has proved,) were placed on the tops of the Pillars called *Jachin* and *Boaz?* If, indeed, the Tabernacle and the Temple had not been constructed after the models of Egyptian temples, it seems difficult to account for the numerous astronomical symbols, which were placed in them by Moses and Solomon.

14. I have omitted to mention the palm-trees, the Urim and Thummim, and some other astronomical emblems. I conceive, indeed, that I have said enough to show, that the Tabernacle and Temple were types of the universal system.

As I am not aware, however, that any other person has suggested this notion, I wish to argue the question no more at present. If I be wrong, let it be shown, how all the astronomical emblems, which I have already mentioned, were introduced into the Temple. Whether, or not, I be correct in my references to ancient writers, may be easily determined by turning to them; and I can only say, that if, in the various reading which I was obliged to go through, I have made any mistakes, I am certain that no mistakes have been made by me, with the intention of misleading my readers. I fairly confess, that I consider the style of the Old Testament to be altogether figurative; and it seems to me not a little strange, that Christians should think it necessary to insist upon literal interpretations with the same zeal as if they were Jews. It may satisfy the vanity of the Jews to make it be believed, that the Deity actually abode in the Tabernacle, or Temple, which their ancestors constructed for his residence; but I do not see why Christians should think themselves obliged to maintain so monstrous a proposition. When the Christian looks into the Hebrew Bible for the prophecies concerning Jesus Christ, he does not hesitate to throw aside the shackles which the Jews would impose on him ; and he finds abundance of types illustrative of the truths, for which he is seeking. But this is to admit, that the Hebrew Bible is a typical book ; and if it be so, why should we not reason freely concerning what may be true, and what may be typical? When we meet with passages, that either are, or seem to be, irreconcileable to reason, why should we not exercise reason, in examining whether the author be, speaking symbolically, or not? When Isaiah, for example, describes his vision of God in the temple, it seems, to me at least, that he spoke typically. Let us suppose the temple to be the type of the universe, and then surely the vision of Isaiah will appear in a very different light from what it must do, if the Jewish place of worship were literally meant. We know that wings were the hieroglyphic, by which the Egyptians expressed spirit and intellect; and that a serpent was the symbol by which they denoted the revolutions of the stars. Now *Seraphim* signifies *serpents*, or rather *fiery serpents*. Instead then of understanding the Prophet to say literally, that he had seen God in the Temple of Jerusalem, surrounded by strange winged creatures, I suppose him to mean typically that he contemplated the Deity presiding over the universe, and surrounded by those spiritual intelligences, which emanate from him, which guide the orbs of heaven in their paths, and which hail him the threefold holy one, Lord of the celestial hosts. In like manner, when Ezekiel describes the glory of Jehovah as filling the temple, and relates all the wonders of the *Cherubim* and their *wheels*, I cannot possibly conceive him to be speaking literally. We have, indeed, already seen, that the *Cherubim* were types of the spiritual influences, which conduct the revolutions of the stars from solstice to solstice, and from equinox to equinox; but the word גלגל *gilgal*, which we translate *a wheel*, also signifies *the revolving heavens*. Thus our translators properly have written in another place, *the voice of thy thunder was in the heaven;* and the word answering to heaven in the original is *gilgal*.

I shall now leave it to my readers to judge, whether they ought, or not, to believe, that the sacred writers literally meant to represent the Deity as residing in a temple, on a box of Shittim wood, between two monstrous images with the faces of a man, a lion, a bull, and an eagle, with six, or four wings, and with the feet of an ox. If there be those who can believe this, I must be permitted to address them in the words of a Greek philosopher—ὦ ἀμαθεῖς ἄνθρωποι, διδάξετε ἡμᾶς, τί ἐστιν ὁ Θεὸς ἐν τοῖς ναοῖς ἀποκεκλεισμένος;—*O uninstructed men! will you teach us, what is the God shut up in temples?*

IV.

Dissertation,

&c. &c.

Dissertation

ON THE

BOOK OF JOSHUA.

———

THE passage of the Israelites into the promised
land, the extirpation of the original inhabitants,
and the distribution of the country among its new
possessors, are the principal events recorded in the
Book of Joshua.   There are few persons, I believe,
who allow themselves to reflect, or to reason, who
have not been struck with the extraordinary examples of violence, injustice, and cruelty, which are
here represented, not only as permitted, but as
approved and sanctioned, by the will of the Deity.
It is not for mortals to scrutinise too exactly the
mysterious plans, which, according to the sacred

writers, have been adopted by Providence; but it is impossible, at the same time, to dissemble, that the violation of every principle of justice and humanity only appears more terrible, when it is said to be authorised by the Supreme Being. The inhabitants of Canaan had remained for ages in quiet possession of the country, when it was suddenly overwhelmed and laid waste by the robbers of Israel, who, not satisfied with taking possession of the property of others, burned the cities, and massacred the people. If there be law, or right, or justice in the world, it seems difficult to excuse, much more to justify, such atrocities; and when, for all answer, we are told, that these horrors were perpetrated by the express command of God himself, we must either believe and renounce the use of our reason, or disbelieve and abandon the professions of our faith.

I cannot help thinking, that we generally bring ourselves into this dilemma, by adhering too closely to the literal sense of the scriptures. The writings of the Orientalists, (and those of their historians are not to be excepted) frequently abound in allegory. The histories of the ancient Egyptian dynasties, of their Gods and their Kings, are chiefly allegorical; and the same thing may be said of the sacred books of the Chaldeans, the Persians, and the Indians. In the ancient legends of all nations, indeed, the judicious critic will expect to meet with a mixture of truth and fiction—of fact and fable; but among the Orientalists this does not result more from the uncertainty of tradition, than from the taste, which so generally prevails in the East, for figurative language, for symbolical expressions, and for allegorical descriptions. We see from their *cabbala*, that the Jews were no strangers to types and enigmas; nor does it seem unreasonable to suppose, that their historians followed the example of all the East, in blending in their narratives real with fictitious events, and in veiling important lessons to mankind, whether in morals, or in science, under the guise of recorded facts.

To those, who are strangers to the manners and customs of the East, and who are unacquainted with the notions of the Orientalists concerning the art of writing, the statement which I have made may appear singular and paradoxical. The mixture of allegory with history, above all, must appear an improbable and unnatural association to those, whose reading has been limited to the chaster productions of European authors, and who have formed their notions of the object, character, and utility of history, from the models in that kind of writing, which we are the most accustomed to admire. In turning, however, to the remnants of ancient Oriental history, we shall quickly perceive, that our own notions of style, and our own laws of composition, could never have served as rules to the authors of those interesting works. Most of what we know concerning the astronomy of the Egyptians has been gleaned from the histories of their fictitious Gods and Kings :—To believe, that these were real personages, can only be excused to infancy or to dotage. The Zendavesta instructs us in the science of the Persians; and the Vedam in the wisdom of the Brahmans; and he, who would look in either for a true and simple relation of facts, had better satiate his credulity, by believing in the voyages of Gulliver, or in the stories of the Arabian Nights. In the fragments of Sanchonia-tho, we find rude traces of the notions of the Phœnicians concerning cosmogony; unless, indeed, we believe, that the historian was in good earnest, when he related, as a fact, the marriage of *Ouranos* with *Ghe*,—of the Heavens with the Earth.

The attention of mankind in the East was early directed to the study of astronomy; and accordingly we find, that many of the pretended histories of the Orientalists are merely astronomical records. The knowledge of the stars was, indeed, of the utmost importance to a people approaching by gradual steps to civilization. Agriculture and navigation have never succeeded, where astronomical science has remained uncultivated; and the necessity of fixing the seasons according to true time must soon be felt by men, when they quit the savage for the social state, and depend for subsistence on the produce of the soil. Accordingly the observation of the heavens, and the regulation of the Calendar, appear to have engaged the attention of the earliest legislators; and the first agriculturists were probably the first practical astronomers. As the wants of men increased in proportion to their progress in civilization, and as commercial speculators began to navigate the seas, the necessity of being acquainted with astronomy must have become every day more evident; and under

all these circumstances we cannot wonder at the
sedulous attention, which was given to this science
in climates the best adapted to its study.

There seem, however, to have been other
causes, which contributed to render the knowledge
of the stars the most important of all acquirements
in the eyes of the Orientalists. The proposition
may seem too general, but I believe it to be true,
that man cannot exist in a social state without a
religion of some sort; and the human mind cannot
easily rest satisfied without assigning extraordinary
effects to supernatural causes. But where men
are to seek for God in the book of nature, we must
expect them to stumble on a thousand errors, and
to indulge in a thousand superstitions, before they
discover the truth. As the events, which excite
their surprise, are various, and as the effects which
they contemplate are different; they look for many
separate causes, fancy the influence of distinct
powers, and arrive late, indeed, at the conclusion
to which true philosophy must always come; and
which can be no other, than that a sole and immaterial principle is the source, to which all the phæno-
mena of nature and of the universe must be traced.

In those fine climates, where so much of existence is passed under the canopy of heaven, we can scarcely wonder that the first settlers in Egypt and Chaldea sought among the celestial bodies for supernatural agents, of whose being, and of whose power, the experience of the world seemed to afford continual examples. All the operations of agriculture, the seasons of sowing and of reaping, of planting the vine and of gathering its grapes, were in reality connected with the rising and setting of some constellations, while the state of the weather, and the temperature of the atmosphere, seemed to be equally combined with the appearance and disappearance of others. The influence of the Sun upon the whole system of nature, the splendor of his orb, and the ardor of his fires, pointed him out to the untaught idolator as the source of light and life, as the Lord of the universe, and as the parent of all things ; nor, when he withdrew his burning beams, can we be surprised, that the milder planet of the night was hailed as the associate of his empire, and as the Queen of Heaven. The march and order of the celestial bodies, which seemed independent of all power which human sagacity could yet divine, was believed to be the

result of their own spontaneous energies; and
their influence on the affairs of our lower world
soon came to be acknowledged by the superstitious
nations. Among men, by whom the heavens were
continually observed, as was the case on the fruitful banks of the Nile and the Euphrates, the revolutions of the stars were associated with the inci-
dents of life, the fortunes of individuals, and the
fate of kingdoms. A few coincidences will always
form a sufficient basis, whereon superstition may
erect a mighty fabric; and it is probable, that
judicial astrology, of which the origin is more
remote than men seem generally to suspect, was
first founded upon some vague associations, and
some accidental occurrences.

The utility of religion to those who govern, can
never fail to be observed by the politician; but
where a religion is created and formed by the rulers
of the state, its advantages to them, at least, must
be incalculable. *Tsabaism,* or " the worship of
the Hosts of Heaven," pervaded all the nations of
the East. This, indeed, was nothing else than a
more scientific and sublime astrology, of which
the innumerable mysteries were known only to the

Priests, and to those who were initiated in the secrets of their abstruse mythology. In the recesses of their colleges, the learned Egyptians undoubtedly taught a pure and beautiful system of theology; but the light, which illuminated the interior of the temple, shed from without only a doubtful ray of science and superstition on the prejudiced and semi-barbarous multitude. Science itself was scarcely so much an object with the Priests, as the art of concealing it from the people. Hence the numerous and complicated symbols of the Egyptians;—hence the use of hieroglyphics even after the invention of letters;—and hence that singular mixture of wisdom and folly, of philosophy and fanatacism, of profound research, and of childish prejudice, which manifests itself in the laws, doctrines, customs, and institutions of ancient Egypt.

When we reflect upon this system of Priestcraft, we may be tempted to condemn it as the base offspring of ambition and hypocrisy; but since it must be confessed, that science can never be the portion of the vulgar, and must always be confined to the few, it may be doubtful, whether any real

advantages flow from a too ardent desire to propa-
gate knowledge among the lower classes of mankind.
It requires so much time and study, to master the
great questions in politics, morals, and science,
that the mass of the people, occupied with the
common business of life, can never be competent to
judge of them ; and I am not convinced, that they
are the least prejudiced reasoners, who maintain,
that the truth most surely results from the chaotic
strife of incongruous principles, and from the
fortuitous collision of jarring opinions. Be this as
it may, however, there can be no question, that
where the government is intended to be sacerdotal,
it is the policy of the priests to instruct themselves
in that knowledge, which is to be kept from the
eye of vulgar curiosity. This, indeed, was the
policy which gave such credit and influence to the
Priests of Egypt and Chaldea, and which, considered as a human and secondary cause, protracted
for a long period of time the existence and authority of the Jewish Hierocracy.

At the period when Moses was called upon to
exercise the functions of his legation, the Hebrews
appear to have been imbued in all the supersti-

tious notions of the unlearned among the Egyptians. They seem to have had no distinct ideas concerning the divine nature;—to have considered their God as a local and partial Deity,—and to have worshipped in *Jehovah Tsabaoth* a material rather than a spiritual and intellectual being. After their flight across the desart, and their miraculous passage through the Red Sea;—after all the signs and wonders which they had witnessed, they were still attached to the loved idolatries of Egypt, and still doubtful believers, either in the power, or in the beneficence of Jehovah.

I cannot help thinking, that in the whole of this miraculous history, there is much that is typical and allegorical; and that in abiding too strictly by the letter, we lose the sense and the meaning. The history of the emigration of the Israelites could not have been written for the generation that departed out of Egypt with Moses, and it may be presumed that it was composed for the benefit of their posterity. Now there seem to be some lessons, which it is natural and probable that the great reformer and legislator should wish to leave behind him to those, who were to teach and establish his laws. The great object of Moses was clearly to introduce the true religion, and to destroy idolatry among his countrymen :—The second and subordinate point, which he had in view, was the establishment of a Hierocracy in Israel. In order to accomplish the first of these purposes, he obtained the immediate assistance of heaven itself. That Jehovah is God, and the sole God, was announced to the Israelites by various miracles, which, however, appeared not to have convinced that stubborn and stiff-necked people. The establishment of the Hierocracy was, indeed, ordained by the Deity; but the confirmation and duration of its authority seem to have depended more upon human means. To the mass of the multitude it was sufficient, or appears to have been deemed sufficient, that general laws should be promulgated, that God should proclaim his unity and supremacy, and that the worship of idols, with all the rites and ceremonies instituted in their honor, should be strictly forbidden. These ordinances, accompanied as they were with proofs of power which spoke to the senses, were best fitted for the understandings of a stupid, ignorant, and bigoted populace. But when Moses founded a college of Priests, whose influence he desired to render permanent, it might be necessary to enter into many explanations, and to expound many propositions, which were above the capacity and beyond the sphere of the illiterate vulgar.

There seem to be two things, concerning which Moses could in no way fail to impart his sentiments to the Priests. *First*, it is obvious, that the people could not accurately distinguish between their God, and the Gods of other countries, and that *Apis*, or the Golden Calf, was reckoned by them as a Deity as well as Jehovah. In fact there were many circumstances that might tend to lead so stupid a race into error. The Tabernacle, as I have proved elsewhere, was indubitably a type of the universe. The figures in the Cherubim answered to the four signs of *Taurus, Leo, Scorpius*, (or the Eagle) and *Aquarius;* and in those signs the Solstitial and Equinoctial points formerly had place. The Bull, the Lion, the Eagle, and the Man with the Urn, were accordingly the four emblems chosen by the four leaders, Ephraim, Judah, Dan, and Reuben, in the camp of the Hebrews. Every thing in that camp, as well as in the Tabernacle, recalled to the people the material system of the heavens, and with it the doctrines and worship of the Tsabaists. At the period of the flight from Egypt, the vernal equinox took place when the Sun was in *Aries;* but the worshippers of Apis, either through ignorance, or perverseness, seem to have been unwilling to transfer their reverence from the Bull to the Ram, or Lamb. The Bull had been for more than two thousand years the Prince and leader of the celestial armies, and an unlettered people still adored him as such. Misled by similitudes, they even seem to have confounded this leader of the celestial armies with *Jehovah Tsabaoth,* " Lord of the hosts of heaven."

To the Priests, it seems evident, that Moses was bound to explain the real difference between the theism which he taught, and the polytheism which he decried. By the confession of the two most learned Jews who have written in Greek, Josephus and Philo, and by the further testimony of the most profound antiquary among the Christian Fathers, it has been proved, that the Jews were surrounded, while they performed the duties of religion, with the emblems of Tsabaism, and with

innumerable memorials of that very idolatry,
against which their Priests and their Prophets
never ceased to fulminate their curses. There
could hardly, then, have failed to have been a
secret and esoteric doctrine, known to those Priests
and Prophets, by which, in the midst of so much
ambiguous imagery, the true system of theology
could be separated from the false.

Secondly, it may be observed, that Moses established many laws and institutions, which were
peculiar to the Jewish nation. Of these, in spite
of the labors of some of our theologians, who have
sought to account for them, it appears, at first sight,
at least, that many are capricious, and that some
are cruel. But this could not have been really the
case. They must in fact have been all just, and
all adapted to the state of the people for whom
they were framed. The reason, then, which, under
the divine authority, guided the judgment of the
legislator, must have been explained to those, who
were to be his successors in administering the law;
for without that reason had been known to some,
we should not have been told that there were
Levites, who caused the people to understand the

law, nor should we have heard of masters in
Israel.

It is well known, that the error of the Tsabaists
lay in their believing, that the material heavens,
the Sun, the Moon, and the Stars, were conscious
and intelligent beings, that governed the earth with
all its inhabitants. It is not to be supposed,
however, that the sages of Egypt and of Chaldea
were themselves the dupes of so monstrous a
system. They appear to have been divided, like
the philosophers of later times, into spiritualists
and hyloists; and it is undoubted, that the former,
as Cudworth has clearly proved, were pure theists,
from whom the Greeks copied some of their most
sublime notions concerning the eternal and infinite
mind. Now, if I mistake not the plan of the
Jewish legislator, his intention was to represent
the Deity as an immaterial essence, by whose
power the external world had been fashioned into
shape, and by whose agency the order of Nature
and of the universe had been preserved. With
Nature and the universe, therefore, the Deity
must ever be associated in a true system of theology; and the type of the spiritual God governing

the material world, was, if I err not, that, which it was the object of Moses to place before his countrymen. Instead of that celestial army of shining and unconscious globes, and that rolling multitude of Suns and planets, which were adored as Gods by the Tsabaists, he pointed to the supreme and spiritual principle, whence emanates existence, and whence proceeds the order of all things. It is, indeed, this principle which is truly *Jehovah Tsabaoth*, the Being by whom all the hosts of heaven are conducted amidst the immensity of space, and in ceaseless revolutions, while he sees that it is good.

From this statement, it must be evident, that Moses could not teach his theology, without explaining the true system of nature, and without developing the connexion between God as the cause, and the order of nature as the effect. In distinguishing between the religion of the Tsabaists and his own, it was necessary to show in what Tsabaism really consisted. It was incumbent on him, I say, to explain, what was the difference between his own theology and that of the worshippers of the celestial hosts;—not, indeed, to the people, who were too gross and material in their conceptions, to have understood him, but to the Levites and to the Elders of the congregation; for without such explanation, what could those, who had leisure to reflect and to reason, have thought of the innumerable symbols of Tsabaism, which appeared in the religious institutions of the Jews? The Sun, the Moon, the twelve signs of the Zodiac, the two hemispheres, the planets, the solar light, were all typified in the Tabernacle by types that could not be mistaken. It cannot be supposed, that the college of Priests was ignorant of the reasons why these symbols were introduced. But I have to observe, that the step from polytheism to theism is not so immediate as many may suppose. To obtain any distinct notion of a perfectly pure and spiritual existence, and to abstract the thoughts from all contemplation of matter, may not be quite so easy as it appears to superficial examiners. We may be certain, that men have arrived very gradually at those conceptions of an immaterial essence, which, perhaps, even now, are only entertained as they ought to be by the most enlightened minds. I believe, that the sages of Egypt did entertain such conceptions of the Deity; and that Moses held the spiritual existence of God to be distinct from matter, I cannot for a moment doubt; but this was by no means the case among the multitude, whether Jews, or Egyptians. It may be even questioned, whether the Priests themselves always comprehended the doctrines of Moses; and whether they did not occasionally confound the spiritual agency of God, with the powers and energies which they attributed to matter.

The attachment of the people to the idolatry of the Egyptians could not have been altered by explanations, which their ignorance would have prevented them from understanding, and to which they probably could have no leisure to attend. Positive laws and injunctions were, therefore, infinitely better adapted to their state; but to reclaim the infatuated minds of those men, who were to serve the altar, and who were to compose the Hierocracy, was an object of the most serious nature to a lawgiver, whose chief care was to establish the true religion. Now in order to destroy Tsabaism, it was necessary to show, that it was a system of astronomy imposed on the vulgar as a system of theology. Nor was this all. The system of astronomy was as false as the religion. But Moses was learned in all the wisdom of the Egyptians; and how could he prove better the ineptitude of the religion, than by proving that the system of astronomy on which it was founded, was absolutely false and erroneous?

The Priests of Egypt and of Chaldea had made a progress in the science of astronomy, which will be found more astonishing the more it is examined. Their cycles were calculated with extraordinary precision; and their knowledge of the most important parts of astronomy must appear evident to all, who candidly consider the question. But the people appear to have been purposely left in gross ignorance on this subject. Their vague, and their rural years, were neither of them correct. The festivals were fixed according to calendars made for the people, and the religious institutions were only calculated to confirm the errors of the ignorant. The truths of science were the *arcana* of the Priests. The whole system of Tsabaism was founded on the erroneous astronomy, if astronomy it could be called, which was contained in the public calendars. On certain days of the year, the people worshipped the Sun under various names and attributes,—rejoiced at one time for his imaginary birth, and mourned at another for his fictitious death. But the year, by which they established the return of these ceremonies, was their vague year, and consequently the Sun was always worshipped out of his place.

Now surely Moses could not employ better the wisdom in which he was learned, than in exposing this false astronomy, on which the vulgar idolatry was built. If he showed to the Priests of Israel, that all the festivals which the partisans of Tsabaism were desirous to observe, were fixed for wrong periods,—if he proved, that these worshippers of the stars were so ignorant as to mistake and miscalculate their returns,—if he made it evident, that these adorers of the material heavens were utterly ignorant of astronomy,—it can hardly be doubted, that he would shake that respect, which it may be suspected, even the Levites and Elders yet entertained for the superstitions of the unlearned among the Egyptians.

Those, who are acquainted with the astronomy

and mythology of the Egyptians, must know full well, how much their religious institutions were connected with the establishment of the civil year, and of the civil month. The Priests themselves, who in their colleges had reformed the Calendar, did not permit the people to become acquainted with the secret; and they obliged every monarch, at his accession to the throne, to swear upon the altar of Isis, that he would allow no alteration to be made upon the duration of the month, or of the year. But since the use of the civil year, and of the civil month, was intimately connected with the superstitions of the Tsabaists, it seems extremely natural, that Moses and Joshua should show to the Elders and Priests of Israel, that the public Calendars of the Egyptians were altogether erroneous. This, I pretend, was done in the allegorical history of the flight from Egypt, and of the passage of the Israelites into the promised land.

I am very sensible of the peril, which I must encounter, in advancing such an opinion. The Europeans, not being acquainted with that figurative and symbolical language in which the Orientalists have always delighted, are generally attached to literal interpretations. To *matter-of-fact people* nothing is so intolerable as being told, that what they call real truths, real events, and real histories, ought to be explained away into figures, symbols, metaphors, and allegories. It sometimes happens, indeed, that they are obliged to acknowledge, that the facts are rather extraordinary; but in speaking of the scriptures, this difficulty is easily removed, by observing, that our duty with respect to sacred things is to believe, and not to criticise, or to reason.

This last argument, however, may not have much weight with some antagonists, who may insist, that without belief be authorised by reason, it is nothing better than superstition; and that he, who gives credit to his Bible, without consulting his judgment, would in other circumstances have equally respected the authority of the Edda, of the Koran, or of the Zendavesta. But although this reasoning appear conclusive to many; I must yet confess, that I like better the humility of those, who bow with blind reverence to the sacred Oracles, in acknowledging the difficulty of comprehending them; than the arrogance of certain teachers, who,

M

adhering to the literal sense of the scriptures, boldly pronounce, that every event recorded in them is probable, and consistent with the plans of eternal wisdom. It is, indeed, from these persons, that I have to apprehend the severest strictures. I would take away from them the belief of many things, which they hold it as a duty to credit and defend. I would persuade them, that Joshua did not rob, plunder, burn, and destroy,—that he did not massacre the men and cut up the bellies of the women and children,—in the name and by the order of the God of justice and mercy,—and for such an undertaking, I must expect reprobation. But this is nothing in comparison, of asserting, that the Orientalists were not *matter-of-fact people*, that they delighted in allegories, and that this may have been the case with some of the writers of the Old Testament. There is yet, however, a direr charge of which I shall be found guilty. Instead of believing in the historical truth of all those exploits, by which it has been so often proved to the satisfaction of the faithful, that Joshua was a lawless freebooter, and a blood-thirsty robber, who dared to justify his atrocious crimes, by asserting, that he was authorised to commit them by the God of the universe ; I pretend, that this same Joshua was a wise magistrate, a scientific teacher, and a true theist, who taught the arts to the people, instructed them in agriculture, pointed out the proper seasons when they ought to sow and to reap, while in the sacred college he reformed the Calendar, and proved the erroneous astronomy of the Tsabaists, and thence the vanity of their superstitions, and the grossness of their idolatry.

I have now stated the nature and magnitude of my guilt ; and must expect to be condemned by the *matter-of-fact people*, who are persuaded, that the Eastern prophets, who wrote three or four thousand years ago, composed their works upon the same model, and with the same regard to facts, as may be seen always attended to in the praise-worthy pages of the Annual Register, and of the London Gazette. But I must leave the *matter-of-fact people* to mistake shadows for substances, to confound the symbol with the thing symbolised, to realise metaphors, to convert allegories into true histories, and to misunderstand and misconceive the character and genius of the ancient Oriental writings, which are so strangely judged of according to standards of other times and other countries. I proceed to answer some objections, which have been already made to my theory.

1. It has been observed, that my explanations of proper names, and that the consequences I thence deduce, cannot be admitted, unless those proper names can be so interpreted, and similar consequences drawn, whenever, and wherever, they occur in the Bible. I am inclined to think, that this argument can be of no avail to those who urge it. I pretend, that those parts of the Hebrew Scriptures, which are usually called historical, are in truth partly historical, and partly allegorical. Not to insist further on the example of all the ancient Orientalists, we may observe, that the traditions of the Greeks sufficiently prove, that this mixture of history with allegory formed the basis of their ingenious and elegant mythology. Thus Hercules, and many others, were partly historical and partly allegorical personages. Castor and Pollux, for example, evidently had an allegorical existence, but it does not follow, that their real existence could never have been. When we read the

accounts which are still preserved of the ancient heroes, who florished in the early ages of Greece, we do not contend, that all is allegory, or that all is true history; nor do we confound the mythological with the historical personages. I read, and I believe, that there was a King of Athens, called Theseus, who deserved much of his country; but I do not mistake this real personage for the allegorical one, who slew the Minotaur, and who conquered the Amazons. I think it by no means impossible, that there were men called Perseus and Orion; and yet I am aware, that the traditions concerning them are chiefly astronomical fables. I cannot be persuaded, then, that I may not apply the same principle, and exercise the same judgment, when I turn from the ancient Greek to the ancient Jewish traditions, the more especially, that the love of allegory was yet greater among the Orientalists than among the Greeks, and that the books of the former are so often found to be compounded of historical truths and allegorical fictions.

2. It has been stated to me, that the proper names of various regions and cities were such as really

existed. How, then, it is asked, could the sacred writers be speaking allegorically, when they mentioned those places?—How could they be making allusions to astronomy, or to agriculture, or to religion, when they spoke of towns and districts, of which the situation may be pointed out in the map? There is abundance of evidence, it is added, that such names as we find in Scripture, were really given to the places therein mentioned.

Let this last proposition be admitted. I have stated, that the great object of Moses and of Joshua was to reclaim the Israelites from the idolatry of the Egyptians, and I have shown how much an exposure of the false astronomy of the Tsabaists must have tended to weaken the respect of the Priests and Elders for those worshippers of the stars. Moses, therefore, employed various types, taken from the Tsabaists, in order to explain the true system of the universe to the persons who were to hold the sacerdotal office. The religion of the idolators, as we have already seen, was intimately connected with the preservation of the civil month, and the civil year. The establishment of the solar year would go far to confound that idolatry, which was so much dependent on the false calculations of the Tsabaists. That Moses was acquainted with the true length of the year I have proved elsewhere; and that he was obliged to continue the use of the year of 360 days, is at once a proof of the prevalence of Tsabaism among the Israelites, and of the necessity under which he was to instruct the College of Priests in a better system of astronomy. In fact, the false system of religion, and the false system of astronomy supported each other ; and, therefore, the destruction of the latter was a matter of no small importance to the lawgiver, since the reformer of religion was compelled to become the reformer of astronomy.

It will be remembered, that I have already proved, that the twelve tribes of Israel took for their emblems the twelve signs of the Zodiac, even before they left the land of Egypt. When they are said to have entered the promised land, it appears, that the places were named after various stars, constellations, &c. I think, I shall prove, that the whole partition was made in allusion to astronomy, by the proper understanding of which, the idolatry of the Tsabaists, as far as human prudence could effect it, was most likely to be rooted out among the Israelites.

Before I proceed further, however, I have to make a remark, to which I should wish to call the particular attention of my reader. He may, perhaps, have already exclaimed, that to suppose a country to be laid out, its districts divided, and its cities named, in allusion to astronomy, is a wild and untenable proposition. It is thus, that men often hastily make conclusions. The philosopher should know his duty, be patient, and persevere.

Upon this plan, the land of Egypt, the country where Moses was educated, was certainly distributed; but it was so distributed in order to favor the superstitions of the multitude, which the Priests never failed to encourage. The civil year of the Egyptians consisted, like that of the Hebrews, of 360 days; and was divided into twelve months, each consisting of 30 days. This was an approximation of the lunar to the solar year, which appears to have been adopted very early; but which, by rendering the errors of the Calendar a little less obvious than they had been before, perhaps only aided the astronomical and religious deceptions, by which the people were kept in ignorance. The civil month was divided into three *decans*, and each day was consecrated to the God, or the genius, that the astrologers appointed over it. The whole of this system was deeply involved with Tsabaism. Now if my reader will turn to Kircher's Œdipus, he will find it sufficiently proved, that the land of Egypt was partitioned into three provinces, answering to the three decans, and into thirty nomes, or præfectures, corresponding with the thirty Deities ruling over each day of the month. In Egypt, then, the country of Moses, we find the exemplar of a territory divided and named according to the Calendar.

In fact, we find the nomes of Egypt were called Busiris, Lato, Hermon, Buto, On, Canobus, Mendes, &c. &c. and as we know, that these were all Gods of the Tsabaists, or, in other words, were planets and constellations represented by different symbols, we can no longer doubt, that the land of Egypt was partitioned with a view to the astronomical system, which the Priests intended for the worshippers of the celestial host.

If the lawgiver of the Hebrews, who was learned in all the wisdom of the Egyptians, desired to overthrow the false religion of the Tsabaists, which was built on their false astronomy; and if he sought to abolish those rites, which were practised on certain days of the sacred year, and which, by reason of the false calculations, never returned exactly at the proper periods; he would naturally establish the duration of the year according to the passage of the Sun through the signs of the Zodiac. The Israelites adhered to the civil month of 30 days, and it may be supposed, that those among them, who were inclined to Tsabaism, did not forget the division of Egypt into 30 nomes, called after the leaders of the hosts of heaven. But the true solar year, which it was contrary to the religion of the Tsabaists to admit, can only be fixed by marking the progress of the Sun through the Zodiacal signs. The Israelites had come from a country which was divided, and of which the districts were named, with an evident allusion to that astronomy, on which the idolatry of the people was built. It was then very natural for Moses to divide the new territory upon a similar plan, if by doing so he could give a blow to that very system, which it was the great object of his legislation to destroy. Now, by making every thing refer to the true solar year, he must have completely confounded and confused the calculators, who, going by the vague year of the Egyptians, established their sacrifices and festivals to the Gods of their idolatry, at times directly contrary to those in which they should have been celebrated. Thus it would be evident to those, who adopted the solar year, that the idolators, who followed the vague year, would in a certain period come to worship the vernal for the Autumnal Sun, and would weep for his fictitious death, when they ought to have been rejoicing at his imaginary birth.

We find then, that to name and divide the promised land with a distinct allusion to astronomy, is not quite so extravagant a fancy, as may be at first imagined. It had been certainly already done by the Egyptians; and, perhaps, by other Oriental nations.

3. Some persons have fancied, that the allusions to the celestial bodies, and especially to the signs of the Zodiac, which I have pretended to discover, cannot exist in reality in the books of Moses and Joshua, because, say they, the partitions and collocations of the signs, the grouping of the Stars, and the names of the constellations, as well as the symbols by which they are denoted, are of much later date. This is a *petitio principii*, which I cannot admit. I readily allow, that the planets and constellations were called by different names in Egypt and in Greece, and that some of them, at least, were expressed by different symbols. But I maintain, that the division of the circle into 360 parts, and of the Zodiac into twelve houses, was established by the Egyptians before the dawn of science in Greece. Some of the emblems were certainly changed, but some of them were as certainly preserved. It is chiefly, where they were changed, that we shall find a difficulty in explaining the allusions made to the celestial bodies in the book under our consideration; but since the Greeks were instructed in astronomy by the Egyptians, we may infer, and indeed we shall see, that they did not

alter the emblems so much as has been generally supposed.

If the persons, to whom I allude, will examine the ancient Zodiacs of the Egyptians, as exhibited and explained by Kircher, La Pluche, Bailly, Dupuis, &c. they will find, not only that the Greeks generally copied their astronomical symbols from the Egyptians, but that those symbols were invented at a very remote period of time.

4. It has been observed, that of some, and indeed of many, proper names I have not been able to give any explanation. I fully acknowledge the truth of this remark ; but let my reader take the following circumstances into consideration. The Egyptians and Chaldeans must have been the masters of the Israelites in astronomy; and consequently, the names of the stars and of the constellations were probably borrowed either from the Egyptian or the Chaldaic. It is vain, then, to seek for some of these names in Hebrew; and when we do, we very rarely succeed. We must, however, be aware, that many of these names have been disfigured by the Scribes, who, when they came to

words originally foreign, may have confounded and confused the orthography. Thus they clearly mis-spelt the name of *Poti-pherah*, as has been proved by Jablonski. The name of *On* is written sometimes with, and sometimes without, the *vau*. The city, of which the name is written *Leshem* in Joshua, is called *Laish* in Judges. Many examples of similar inaccuracy might be given; and if in some instances we can yet certainly adjust these names, and discover their import, this is nevertheless to be done with extreme caution. Thus the explanations of Scriptural proper names, as given by the author of the Onomasticon, by Rumelin, by Stockius, and by Gussetius, are sometimes incomparably absurd, because, determined at all events to make these names Hebrew, when they were Chaldaic, Syriac, Egyptian, or Persian, they give us the most anomalous compounds, without regard to grammar, or to common sense.

But it is time, that I proceed to lay before my reader my proposed explanation of the book of Joshua. If he still find, that this book contains no astronomical allusions, he will do well to account for the introduction of so many names, which seem to bear direct reference to the state of the heavens, the revolutions of the planets, the divisions of the Zodiac, the positions of the constellations, and the reform of the Calendar.

───◆───

More than two thousand years have elapsed, since the sign of *Aries* (called امرا *Emro* by the Syrians, and برا *Bara* by the Persians, both of which words signify *agnus*,) has ceased to answer, owing to the precession of the Equinoxes, to the first of the signs. The place, which *Aries* then held, is now occupied by *Pisces*. We see, however, that before this change, the year opened, and the vernal equinox took place, when the Sun was in this sign. Then was fixed the commencement of the civil year among both the Jews and Egyptians. If, however, we proceed to more distant times, we shall find that the vernal Equinox took place, and that the year opened, when the Sun was in the sign of *Taurus*. To reform the Calendar, as these changes happened, must have engaged the attention not only of astronomers but of legislators.

Tsabaism, or " the worship of the hosts of heaven," must have been the general religion of the East at so early a period, as to bring its establishment within that era, when the opening of the year, (fixed by all the Oriental nations at the vernal equinox) answered to the sign of *Taurus*. From the Mithraic, Egyptian, and Indian monuments, we cannot question how much Eastern idolatry was connected with the symbol of the *Bull*, or with the passage of the Sun in the sign of *Taurus* from the lower to the upper hemisphere. Now after the period had arrived, when it was no longer in the sign of the *Bull*, but in that of the *Ram*, or of the *Lamb*, that the Sun rose from the lower hemisphere, it was evident, that the Tsabaists, even according to their own system of idolatry, ought to have transferred their reverence from the former symbol to the latter. But what could be more humiliating to those partisans of Tsabaism, who still sighed after the idol of the golden *Calf*, or golden *Bull*, the symbol of Apis, than to find, that their calculations were wrong, and that they had mistaken the symbol, by which, even in conformity with their own false theology, they ought to adore their Deity? Let us attend to this; and in order to obviate an objection, which is made to little purpose, I shall here observe, that as nothing is certainly known of the date, when the Book of Joshua was written, it may, perhaps, be best guessed at from its own internal evidence. It is clear, that the vernal equinox must have been already transferred from *Taurus* to *Aries*, when Moses ordained that the civil year should open with the month *Nisan*. Whether the institution of the feast of the transition, which we call the feast of the passover, had any reference to the passage of the equinoctial Sun into *Aries*, I leave others to determine. It is certain, that while the year commenced with the Sun in *Taurus*, the Persians represented Mithras as slaying a young Bull; and we are not to forget, that the sign of the *Ram*, was called the sign of the *Lamb* by Persians and Syrians. I cannot help suspect ing, that the *Paschal Lamb* was a type of the *Astronomical Lamb*.

I have already stated my reasons for thinking,

N

that Joshua could not more effectually, by human means at least, destroy the superstitious reverence of the Israelites for Apis, or *the golden Bull,* than by showing that the Tsabaists, according to their own system, ought to have transferred their reverence from the *Bull* to the *Ram,* or *Lamb;* and that as their whole astronomy was false, so also was the religion which was founded upon it. The equinoctial Sun being then really in *Aries,* the Calendar ought to have been adjusted according to the retrograde motion of the signs ; and thus the *Ram,* or *Lamb,* might be metaphorically called the Preserver, the Deliverer, the Rectifier, the Reformer. Perhaps Joshua, the son of Nun, was no other than this Preserver, and may have been as much a real personage as the Egyptian Hermes, or the Grecian Hercules.

That the Sun rising from the lower to the upper hemisphere, should be hailed the Preserver, or Saviour, appears extremely natural; and that by such titles he was known to idolators cannot be doubted. [1] *Joshua* (יושע) literally signifies *the*

---

[1] The Sun, according to Pausanias, was worshipped under the name of the Saviour, at Eleusis.

Preserver, or *Deliverer*; and that this Preserver, or Deliverer, was no other than the Sun in the sign of the *Ram*, or *Lamb*, may be inferred from many circumstances. It will be observed, that the LXX write Ἰησοῦς for *Joshua*, and the *Lamb* has always been the type of Ἰησοῦς. Joshua is called the *son of Nun*. I find that נון *Nun* in Chaldaic, and ܢܘܢܐ *Nuna* in Syriac, signified the *great fish*, or the constellation which we call the *Whale*. The head of *Cetus*, or *the Whale*, is placed immediately under the *Ram*, or *Lamb*, and always rises and sets with that sign, but the rest of the constellation rises before *Aries*. Thus the *Ram*, or *Lamb*, the Saviour, was metaphorically called the son of that constellation, which is next to it, and which rises immediately before it.

C. 1. V. 2.

Now therefore arise, go over this Jordan.

There was as certainly the river called Jordan in Judea, as there was the river called the Nile in

Egypt; but as the Nile was employed for an
astronomical symbol by the Egyptians, who thus
denoted the vast constellation of *Eridanus,* I am
apt to suspect, that the Jews also, in their sacred
language, employed the name of the Jordan in an
astronomical sense. The 12 tribes, on whose
banners, as I have elsewhere shown, were displayed
the 12 signs of the Zodiac, passed the Jordan,
and took out of its bed twelve stones, which Joshua
replaced. Now, when we consider that the precession of the equinoxes had really changed the
position of the signs, and that it was in consequence
of this, that the Calendar required reform, we
shall, perhaps, understand the allegory. The word
ירדן *Jordan* is explained variously by the Rabbins.
Some make it out to be יאר דן, *the river of Dan.*
Others bring it better from ירד, and understand it
to signify *the great declivity.* I observe, however,
that ירד, or ירוד, in Chaldaic signifies *a serpent ;*
and a serpent biting his tail was the hieroglyphic
for the year, or for the Sun's orbit, as may be
proved by reference to the third volume of
Kircher's Œdipus. ירודן, or ירדן *Jordan,* with the
intensive, would then signify *the great serpent,*
the hieroglyphic for the Sun's annual orbit, or in

other words, for the circle, which we call the Ecliptic. The meaning of the allegory seems pretty plain. The style being changed, the equinoctial Sun, hailed the Saviour, and identified with the *Ram*, or *Lamb*, opens the year; and is feigned as leading the twelve Zodiacal signs along the Ecliptic.

V. 4. *From the Wilderness and this Lebanon.*

The endeavours of the Rabbins to explain the meaning of מדבר, which we translate " the Wilderness," and to trace it to its root, have been far from successful. It is evidently compounded of two Oriental words, which are not Hebrew, of which a fuller account is given by Bochart. I mean מדי, and ברא. The true signification of מדבר then is *the boundary of the land.* The boundaries of Judea were chiefly desarts, and this accounts for the meaning usually given to the word. But if there be any astronomical allusion here, the term may have been applied to the horizon.

Lebanon. There was a mountain known by this name; but I suspect that *Lebanon* was as much an astronomical symbol as *Atlas,* which also served for the name of a mountain. לבנה *Lebana* signified *the Moon,* which the Rabbins say was thus denominated from its whiteness; but I imagine, that לבן, the root, answers rather to the Latin *Candidus,* and might even be translated *erubescens.* The word לבנה *Lebana,* " the Moon," occurs but rarely in the Bible; and I am inclined to think, that it was employed for the rising Moon. *Lebanon* I conceive to have been a name given to the Sun, and probably to the rising Sun.

Even unto the great river, the river Euphrates.

The Nile and the Jordan, as we have already seen, served for astronomical symbols. If I mistake not, we shall find the same thing to be true of the Euphrates. The original meaning of נהר is not *a river,* but *splendor,* or more exactly *the flux of light.* The *Pharet,* or Euphrates, I conceive to signify *fruit-bearing,* or, perhaps, *a fruit-tree.* The name may have been given to the river from the fertility of its banks; and this is the general opinion of the Rabbins. But a fruit-tree was certainly a symbol of the starry heavens; and the fruits typified the constellations. In the ancient astronomical monuments of the Persians, fruit-trees are generally represented. We see traces of this in the mythology of the Greeks, and especially in the astronomical allegory concerning the golden apples brought by Hercules from the gardens of the Hesperides. In the 36 decans taken from the Egyptian astrologers, frequent allusions are made to fruit-trees and fruits; and the astronomical Gods, for such they were in fact, of the Egyptians are generally represented with fruits. Thus Horus carries a *cornucopia* in his hand, and Harpocrates is represented with a *persea* on his head. On the ancient coins and other monuments of the Tsabaists, and even of the Israelites, we see fruit-trees represented. The *Sephiroth* of the *Cabbalists* were disposed in the form of a tree, as is stated by *R. Shabte ;* and of course under this form they intended to represent the universal system. The fruit-tree, mentioned in the Apocalypse, has been supposed by some to be a type of the Zodiac, as it bore twelve fruits, and one each month. In the apocryphal Gospel of Eve, spoken of by St. Epiphanius, it is said, that the tree of life bore one apple each month. The Arabians typify the Zodiac by a fruit-tree, and on the twelve branches of this tree the stars are depicted as clusters of fruit. The Cabbalists represent the tree of life as marked with the emblems of the Zodiac, and as bearing twelve fruits. When we consider these things together with the reverence of the Tsabaists for groves and trees, we shall hardly doubt, that trees, and especially fruit-trees, were symbols of the starry heavens. The splendor of *Pharet*, " the fruit-tree," might have been understood to mean the light of the Zodiacal constellations, by the initiated; while the people may have thought that the promise related to the river Euphrates. But if the Jews ever had any possessions on the banks of the Euphrates, which is a disputed point, it could have been only for a short period, and not before the reign of Solomon.

All the land of the Hittites.

The proper name חתים is confounded by Josephus with the proper name כתים, for which the Jewish historian is reproved by Bochart. I must confess I am equally puzzled by both names, if we follow the Rabbins. These good people seem to have no idea, that their progenitors could have employed words which they do not understand, and the absurd confidence with which they talk deserves pity. התים, *the Hittites*, if we believe Rumelinus, ought to signify *the terrors*, or *the consternations*. Surely no people in the world ever took such a name. All I can do for this word, at present, is to observe, that it is frequently connected with others, which bear a distinct reference to astronomy. This will appear presently.

C. 2. V. 1.

And Joshua sent two men out of Shittim.

This seems clearly enough an astronomical allusion. שטים comes from שטה, and שטה was one of the Deities of the Tsabaists. The house, or temple of *Shittah* שטה (Bith Shittah) is mentioned in the Book of Judges. But let my reader attend to the words of Parkhurst; " בית השטה, *the house of declination*, or *of the declinator*—not improbably so called from a temple dedicated to the heavens, considered as causing the declination of the earth."

He may also see more in Hutchinson, M. P. part 2, and in the 4th volume.

Go view the land, even Jericho.

This chapter seems to contain an account of the first attempt to reform the lunar month. יריחו is evidently from ירח, *the Moon.* But as it is written יריחו *Jericho,* with the *vau,* it becomes a collective noun; and must mean the Moon in her different quarters.

Rachab signifies *space,* or *latitude;* and was worshipped as a Deity by the Tsabaists, who built a temple to *Rachab,* called *Bith-Rachab.* [1]

It will be remembered, that when Jericho was taken, it was compassed round seven times, with more mysteries relating to the number seven.

Now let us consider in what way we may under

---

[1] Jud. 18. 28.

stand the capture and destruction of Jericho in an astronomical sense.

The lunar month consisted of 28 days, and consequently the lunar year consisted of only 336 days. The first reform in the Calendar was made by a more exact calculation of the Moon's motions, and her revolutions with regard to the Sun; and the year was thus found to contain 356 days. But still a very short period was sufficient to prove, that the use of the lunar year would go to reverse the order of the seasons. Another, though an imperfect, reform was made by adding two days to each lunar month of 28 days, and by fixing the number of days in the year at 360. This was the civil year of the Egyptians and of the Hebrews. Joshua sent two men out of *Shittim*, that is, out of those that decline; and by them, according to Parkhurst and Hutchinson, we must understand the heavens as causing the declination of the earth, and thereby, says Parkhurst, the succession of the seasons. In fact, the succession of the seasons is caused by the obliquity, or declination of the Ecliptic. But the Ecliptic is divided into twelve parts, each of which contains 30 degrees; and before the establishment of the civil year, each of these parts must have contained only 28 degrees, according to the calculation for the first and original lunar month. The two men seem to represent the two degrees added to each sign, or the two days added to each lunar month. The word *Jericho* either means the Moon in her several quarters, or the lunar month divided into weeks. The Hebrews compassed the city seven times. Does not this allude to the seven days of the week, or to one of the Moon's quarters? It seems to me that the abolition of the lunar month of 28 days, by the addition of two days, is typified by the destruction of Jericho.

C. 3. V. 10.

He will without fail drive out from before you the Canaanites, and the Hittites, and the Hivites, and the Perizites, and the Girgashites, and the Amorites, and the Jebusites.

The literal interpreters are pleased to believe, that these were so many distinct nations, against whom the God of the universe declared a *bellum internecinum.*

The first to be driven out were the Canaanites הכנעני, whom the Rabbins will have to be a nation of merchants. כנע signifies *to put down,* and when a merchant sells his goods, he puts them down before you. This nation of merchants was, therefore, called *Canaanites,* because they put down their goods. But in spite of this ingenious derivation, I am inclined to think that the origin of the word is totally different. The God of time was worshipped under the names of *Chon, Chiun,* and *Chaon,* by the Egyptians, the idolatrous Jews, and the Syrians. These names are clearly taken from כון *to establish,* or *constitute.* But כון עון, or without the *vau,* כן עו, *Canaan,* would signify, " he who established, or directed the time." The Canaanites are then those who fix the time, and probably no others than the astrologers, whose false Calendars misled the people.

I have already pointed out the absurd meaning affixed to החתים, the *Hittites,* by the Rabbins. I believe, the *Hittites* signified *the worshippers of the solar fire.* From חת I derive the radical *aith,* or *ait ;* because I think the harsh aspirate ה was generally softened by strangers. This may be proved from the names *Adad, Eve,* &c. Concerning *aith* my reader may consult Bryant; and for חת, Parkhurst *in voce* חתה.

The *Hivites* appear to be worshippers of the Serpent, more generally called Ophites. The idolatry of these Ophites was extremely ancient, and was evidently connected with Tsabaism. The great constellation, which we call *Hydra,* is named חויא, or חוה, by the Chaldeans. [1]

The *Perizites* פרזי are understood to signify *villagers.* But why should these harmless villagers be driven out by the power of Jehovah? I strongly suspect this proper name to be an Egyptian word, which the interpreters did not understand. רז, prefixed by the Egyptian article פ, would signify in Chaldaic, Ethiopian, and Egyptian, the *mystery,* or

---

[1] See Castelli, and Bryant.

cabbala. Perizites seems then to mean *the Cabba-lists,* whose mummery was all originally founded on the idolatry of the Tsabaists. *Razael,* or *Riza-el,* was apparently the God of these Cabbalists, who called him the angel of Adam.

Rumelin derives גרגשי *Girgashites,* from גרש, *expulit.* What then becomes of the second ג? Bochart brings the name from גרגש which he says signifies *clay.* This is not strictly accurate; but in all events I must doubt the existence of this argillaceous people. I know not the meaning.

האמרי, *The Amorites* must signify either *speak-ers,* (i. e. teachers, expounders,) or *branches,* or *lambs;* any one of which names appears very strange when applied to a people. But when we recollect, that the celestial hosts were typified by branches of trees, and that the Sun was worshipped under the form of a Ram, or Lamb, we may suspect that the Amorites were Tsabaists—worship-pers of the branches, or types of the celestial hosts— or possibly of the Lamb, אמר *Amor,* by which name the Chaldeans called the sign of *Aries.* [1]

---

[1] See Castelli.

The *Jebusites*, היבוסי. If we derive this name from יבש, or יבס, it would seem that we ought to translate *the driers up*. This would be a very singular name for a people. I rather think, that the Jebusites were a sect of the Tsabaists, who worshipped בשת, or בסת, who was no other than the Moon, and who was called *Busta*, or as the Greeks had it *Bubastis*. But see Jablonski; Castelli *in voce* יבס; and Castelli and Parkhurst, *in voce* בש.

C. 4. V. 19.

And the people came up out of Jordan on the tenth day of the first month, and encamped in Gilgal in the east border of Jericho.

We have seen that the people to be driven out were the Tsabaists ; or those, who under different emblems taught the worship of the celestial bodies; but I think it evident, that the extermination was asserted not of the people, but of their idolatrous systems. In fact, by a reference to the Scriptures we shall find, that the people were not driven out.

The *Girgashites,* for example, whom I suppose to have been Tsabaists, though I cannot trace the etymology of the name, possessed their country in the time of Christ.[1]

The allegory now conducts us to the siege of *Jericho,* that is, in fact, to the overthrow of the lunar month consisting of four times seven days. The people go up out of Jordan, where they have placed the twelve stones ; and this I have shown to be an allegorical description of the establishment of the solar year, according to the progress of the Sun through the signs of the Zodiac. But the people encamp in Gilgal ; and גלגל, *Gilgal,* means *the revolving sphere,* or *the heavens,* which seem to turn round the earth.   Thus קול רעמך בגלגל is properly rendered " the voice of thy thunder was in the heaven"—instead of " the voice of thy thunder was in Gilgal." But when the twelve tribes of Israel, who bore the twelve signs of the Zodiac on their standards, as I have proved in another place, are said to have

---

[1] Matth. 8. 28.

encamped in *Gilgal*, the revolving sphere of the heavens, and on the border of the Moon, it seems difficult to say that there is no astronomical allegory.

V. 23.

As the Lord your God did to the Red Sea.

In the original we find ים סוף which is generally understood to signify *the weedy sea;* but how can this weedy sea be the Red Sea, where I have been assured weeds are rarer than perhaps in any other sea? It has then been called the sea of weeds, because it has so few, or, if we believe Bruce, because it has none—*lucus à non lucendo.* We learn from Josephus, L. 8. that a sea, and particularly the molten sea in the Temple, was a type of the hemisphere. Now I suspect this ים סוף to be an astronomical type. The word סוף I conceive to be very like סף, which means any thing concave, and which, if I err not, signified symbolically *the concave vault of heaven.* I cannot help thinking, then, that ים סוף, which we make to be the Red

Sea, was really the concave hemisphere. I observe, that the universal system was represented by the Jews in what they call their *Sephiroth,* and at the top of these was the *in suph,* אין סוף, which may be a corruption for יַם סוף, *im suph.*

C. 5. V. 9.

This day I have rolled away the reproach of Egypt from off you, wherefore the name of the place is called Gilgal unto this day.

The word חרפה can only signify *reproach* in a metaphorical sense. I should rather translate it *the winter.* By the use of the vague year, and by their false calendars, the Egyptians had reversed the order of the seasons; and he, who reformed the year, might not improperly say, that he rolled away the winter of Egypt. But I question much if Egypt was always really literally meant by the word מצרים. I bring the name from צר; and I suspect, that, instead of *the reproach of Egypt,* we ought to translate the winter or season of condensing colds. (Consult Parkhurst and Hutchinson). But this change of the seasons could only be produced by the revolutions of the heavens, and, therefore, the place was called *Gilgal*, " the revolving heavens."

It will be observed, that this declaration follows the circumcision of the Israelites. Now there is some ambiguity in the words of the second verse of this chapter ;—

עשה לך חרבות צרים

which are rendered " make thee sharp knives," and which may be translated " constitute to thyself the desolations of the frosts."

It is evident, in the first place, that the rite of circumcision was common to the Egyptians and Jews, and it is difficult to understand how, by re-establishing it, Joshua rolled away the reproach of Egypt. In the second place, the rite was re-established at the time when the Sun entered the sign of the *Lamb*, when the frosts of winter cease ; and Moses ordained, that none should eat of the Paschal

Lamb, at the feast of the Transition, which was celebrated in the month of *Nisan*, when the Sun passed into the sign of the *Lamb*, except those who were circumcised. There seems then some reason to suppose, that the rite of circumcision was a ceremony practised, not for convenience or cleanliness only, but as a mark by which those might be known, who were to be admitted to eat of the *Lamb*, at the feast of the Transition, when the Sun quitted the lower hemisphere, and passed into the sign of the *Lamb*. [1]

C. 6.

I have already remarked the frequent repetition of the number seven, and which, when applied to the siege of Jericho (the lunar month consisting of four times seven days) presents a very obvious meaning. But after what I have stated, the blowing with the horns of a *Ram* must appear particularly striking. The *Ram*, or *Lamb*, was the solar

---

See Parkhurst, in voce צר.

symbol set up by the reformer of the Calendar in opposition to the sign of *Taurus*, because the transition of the vernal equinox from the *Bull* to the *Ram* had already taken place. This, however, is not all. The trumpets of rams' horns are called in the original שופרות היובלים, and the ram's horn is named קרן היובל. Thus we find, that the *Ram*, with which the year commenced according to the new style, is called יובל *jubel*, and from this Hebrew word comes *Jubilee*. If there were no allusion to the Calendar, or to the reform of the year;—in short, if this be not an astronomical allegory, it is very strange, that accident should have brought together all these names and all these symbols. In all events, I think it unnecessary to say any thing more concerning the siege and capture of Jericho, of which the walls fell down, when the trumpet was sounded—that is, when the *Jubilee* was proclaimed, and the new year adopted.

C. 7.

It appears, that after the fall of Jericho, or destruction of the lunar month, Joshua proposed to overthrow *Ai*. But the children of Israel committed a trespass in the cursed thing; for Achan, the son of Carmi, the son of Zebdi, the son of Zerah, of the tribe Judah, took of the cursed thing; and the anger of Jehovah was kindled against the children of Israel. Let us examine whether or not this language, like that of the preceding chapter, be allegorical.

One great object in fixing the true period of the year is to regulate the proper seasons of agricultural labor. No legislator can overlook this object; and I think we shall find the sin of the children of Israel, in the example before us, to have consisted in this, that they did not abide by the civil year, but seem, like the Egyptians, to have had a rural year of their own.

The cultivation of the vine has been always connected with the mythology of the ancient Orientalists. Witness the fables concerning Dionysus. If we can form a judgment from the scriptures, the time of gathering the grapes ought to have been, when the Sun was in the sign of *Leo*, and this, as we have seen, was the emblem of Judah. But if by a wrong computation the grapes were gathered too early, the vintage was necessarily spoiled; and in a country of vines this was an object of great importance to the people. Now I think, that the allegory before us represents the people as still continuing to follow the old style, and consequently making their wine at an improper season; for which they are figuratively said to have incurred the anger of the Deity, and by which is only meant, that they suffered what the laws of God and Nature necessarily inflicted on them. It is difficult for the philosopher to believe, that a theft committed by an individual, should have kindled the anger of Jehovah against a whole nation. To me all these histories appear as mere allegories. I cannot believe, that the Supreme, eternal, and infinite Mind, either goes into a passion at one time, or comes out of it at another.

It is clearly to be proved from the Septuagint, and from the reason of the thing, that עכן *Achan* should be written עכר *Achar*. Now let us follow the text.

עכר in a moral sense signifies *perturbation;*—

and in a physical one *fermentation*. This would be a strange name for a man.

כרמי, *Carmi*. This word is composed of כרם, *a vine*, and י for יה. *Carmi* is consequently the vine of *Jah*, the *Iao*, *Iacchus*, and *Bacchus*, of the Gentiles.

זבדי, *Zebdi*, is literally *the gift of Jah*.

זרח, *Zerah*, signifies *the Orient, the East*. This Zerah was of the tribe of Judah, and Judah commanded the Eastern division of the camp of the Hebrews, where were displayed the twelve signs of the Zodiac.

The words before us literally signify—*Fermentation, the son of the vine of Jah, the son of the gift of Jah, the son of the East, of the tribe of Judah, took of the accursed thing*. This really seems to me to be an allegory relating to the vintage, and to the season for making wine.

We are told at verse 21, that the accursed thing consisted of a goodly Babylonish garment, two hundred shekels of silver, and a wedge of gold of fifty shekels' weight. This has the air of being more historical, than the preceding passages. But let us inquire, before we decide.

The Jewish lawgivers were endeavouring, for many useful purposes, to introduce the knowledge of astronomy, and of the real duration of the year, among their countrymen. But they seem to have been opposed by the ancient usages and prejudices of the people.

Now I think the trespass of Israel was in not adhering to this year. The words אדרת שנער אחת טובה are rendered " a goodly Babylonish garment." But I find, that אדר, *splendid, glorious,* &c. was a title frequently addressed by the Tsabaists to the objects of their adoration. The Sun was worshipped under the name of אדר מלך *Adra-Melech.* The Moon was adored by the title of *Adra-Daga.* The month of February, when the Sun was in *Pisces,* was called *Adar;* and I conceive it was so named in honor of *Adra-Daga,* (literally *the glorious Fish*) otherwise called *Dagon.* The word שנער has been explained in a former Dissertation. I then suspect that *Adaroth Shan-aar* has totally a different meaning from that usually given to it. *Adaroth*, like *Ashtaroth*, was probably an idol of the Moon. The Arabian writers tell us, that ادريس *Adris* was the *idol of a star*, and I suspect, that this is a corruption of *Adaroth*. [1]

And two hundred shekels of silver.

The Jews represented different symbols on their shekels, such as the *gomer*, *Aaron's rod*, &c. and it may be supposed, that the Tsabaists had their money struck with symbols which were peculiar to themselves. The shekels, which are said to have been found at Jericho, probably were stamped with emblems in honor of the Moon; and I cannot help suspecting, that the emblem particularly alluded to was that of the Moon worshipped under the form of *Adra-Daga*, or *Dagon*, when the Sun was in the sign of *Pisces*, and when the month was called *Adar*. It appears, that the Persians have

---

[1] Isis, the symbol of the Moon, was represented by the Egyptians in the sign of *Virgo*, and *Virgo* is called *Adarah* by the Arabians.

named a certain fish from *keseph,* which they call *kesephti ;* and the two hundred shekels of *keseph,* which we translate *silver,* may have borne some relation to the idolatrous worship of the Moon. In Chaldaic *keseph* signifies any thing of which the color may be expressed by *candidus* in Latin ; and hence metaphorically signified blushing, shame, confusion, &c. as well as desire, which seems to be a very common meaning of the word in Hebrew.

And a wedge of gold of fifty shekels' weight.

לשון signifies a *tongue.* A golden tongue, weighing fifty shekels, seems a very odd exhibition of riches. But Stockius remarks, that a tongue was the type of flame; and gold, according to Clemens, was the symbol of light. This tongue of gold then was probably an object of the idolatrous reverence of the Tsabaists. But let us proceed.

Joshua had sent men to view *Ai.* Now this word signifies *a heap ;* and this heap probably was no other than the Calendar of the Tsabaists, for it is well known that their Calendars were piles of stone, on which their astronomical observations were engraved. But some of the Hebrews still retaining the *Adaroth Shan-aar*, and other symbols of the ancient worship, continued to calculate by the lunar month, as that ancient worship required. While the people persisted in this, the lawgiver could not succeed in his design of overthrowing *Ai*, the pile, or heap, or Calendar, which misled the populace.

Ai was situated between *Bith-Aven*, (read *Bith-On*) and *Bith-El;* and these were temples of the Sun, under his different titles of *On* and *El.*

It is evident, that the language which now follows can be understood to convey no very distinct meaning, if it be not allegorical.

And the men of Ai smote of them about thirty-six men.

The Hebrews having made false calculations themselves, and abiding by the lunar year, were incapable of reforming the Calendar. The men of Ai smote about 36 of them. This number 36 answers precisely to the number of the decans, into which the Orientalists divided the Zodiac.

For they chased them from before the gate, even unto Shebarim.

לפני השער. I doubt whether this be properly rendered *from before the gate;* but allowing that לפני may be translated *from before,* I wish to know, how שער comes so often to signify *a gate,* which meaning it certainly often bears in the scriptures. Doctor Parkhurst gives us a verb שער, *to stand erect,* and derives שער, *a gate,* from this verb; but I have never found any example of the existence of such a verb, nor do I think his quotation from the Targum proves it. The verb שער signifies *to estimate.* Not to detain my reader, I shall remark, that שעיר signifies *a goat;* and that, as Dupuis has observed before me, the sign of *the goat,* or *Capricorn,* was called *the gate of the Sun* by the ancient Orientalists.

Unto Shebarim—that is,—unto fractions.

Whether, or not, this denote the numerical calculations, may be best gathered from the context. "The men of the heap, of the Calendar, smote 36, amounting to the decans, the divisions of the Zodiac, and of the year, and chased them even to fractions; and the reason was, because the Israelites took of the accursed thing, the symbols of the lunar year."

C. 8.

In this chapter Joshua is said to have taken *Ai*, (העי) *the heap*, by stratagem; and it appears, that he commanded 30,000 men of valor, that he placed 5000 men in ambush, and that he slew 12,000 of the inhabitants of *Ai*. Now I find, that some ancient nations both of Asia and Europe, had an enigmatical manner of denoting any period of time by a year, and that cycles, and months, and days, were called years; and I likewise find it indubitably proved, that they employed the term a *thousand*, for one; and that where they count by thousands, we must, if we would understand them, count by units. Thus in the mysterious language of the ancient Persians, 1,000 years denoted one month. We are told in the Zendavesta, that the supreme God first created the Man and the Bull in a high place, where they remained during 3,000 years. These 3,000 years comprehended the *Lamb*, the *Bull*, and the *Twins*. In this manner the twelve signs of the Zodiac are comprehended in 12,000 years. Ormuzd reigns during the first 6,000 years, and Ahriman reigns during the 6,000 which follow. *Aries, Taurus, Gemini, Cancer, Leo, Virgo*, are allotted to the former; *Libra, Scorpius, Sagittarius, Capricorn, Aquarius, Pisces*, to the latter. It is clear, then, that by 1,000 years, the Persians understood one month, or the passage of the Sun through a sign of the Zodiac. According to Suidas, the ancient Tuscans taught, that God employed 12,000 years in creating and governing the world, and that he distributed the 12,000 years into twelve periods, answering to the twelve solar mansions, or to the twelve signs of the Zodiac.

The aggregate of four ages, (said Menu, in what are termed his oral instructions,) amounting to 12,000 divine years, is called an age of the Gods. When we recollect, how early was the partition of the year into four seasons all over the East, we shall, perhaps, be inclined to think, that the 12,000 divine years amounted in fact to only twelve months. Berosus fixed the period when the Babylonians commenced their observations at 490,000, and Epigenes at 720,000 years before the passage of Alexander into Asia. Bailly remarks on this, very shortly—Ces années ne sont que des jours. It is evident, then, that there were ancient nations, among whom the Priests, or learned men, in order to conceal their knowledge, employed this kind of mysterious calculation, and that, where they counted by thousands, we must count by units, if we wish to get at the truth. Let us apply this remark to the chapter before us.

It is evident that by adopting the rule which I propose, we shall bring out the numbers in the text thirty—and five—and twelve. Now if I have been right all along, in supposing that the history of the reform of the year, is related in this book, we shall find that these are precisely the numbers which we want. Thirty answers to the number of days contained in each month of the civil year:—five to the five intercalated days—and twelve to

the months of the year as established by the Calendars. But multiply thirty by twelve, and you get
360, the number of days of the civil year; to
which add *about* five, and you get the number of
days comprehended in the solar year.

V. 30.

Then Joshua built an altar to the Lord God of
Israel in Mount Ebal.

עיבל, *Ai-Bel* (which our interpreters write Ebal,
from following, as they generally do, the vicious
punctuation of the Masorites) signifies " the heap of
Bel." We must beware of confounding *Bel* with
Baal. The latter was a solar title; but the former
seems to have been the emblem of the great Serpent,
or Dragon, of astronomers. It is to be observed,
that this Dragon was the type of the Moon's
course,—the nodes were called the Dragon's head
and tail, and the greatest elongation of the Moon
from the ecliptic was named the Dragon's belly.

Joshua appears to have abolished the lunar year, as fixed by the common calendars, and with it, probably, many of the idolatrous rites practised by the Chaldean Tsabaists in honor of Ashtaroth, or the Moon; and in place of the heap, or Calendar, of *Bel*, which was made in conformity with the use of the lunar year, he built an altar, perhaps another pile, or Calendar, to Jehovah God of Israel. In fact, Joshua wrote upon the stones a *copy* of the law of Moses, or as I should translate, the second part of the law of Moses. But Moses changed the year, and was the first who instituted its commencement with the Month *Nizan*, and with the entrance of the Sun into the sign of the *Ram*, or the *Lamb*.

Six tribes were appointed to bless upon mount *Gerizim*, and six to curse on mount *Ai-Bel*. We have already remarked, that six signs of the Zodiac were allotted by the ancient Persians to *Ormuzd*, the principle of good, and six to *Ahriman*, the principle of evil.

C. 9.

The first proper name occurring in this chapter, which has not been already explained, is *Gibeon*. I know not why Dr. Parkhurst fancied, that גבע signifies any thing *conical*. It means any thing that is either *convex*, or *concave*, or, perhaps, better, any thing *gibbous*. I suspect that the Moon was sometimes indicated by *Gibeon*, though it might more commonly mean the great *concave*, the *cope* of heaven.

V. 10.

Sihon, King of Heshbon.

If we follow Rumelinus, we ought to render these words, *amotio rex supputationis*. It would appear, that allusion is made to the removal, or more properly the suppression, of the true calculation in the Calendars. But I am not quite satisfied about the signification of סיחון *Sihon*. In

Chaldaic חשבון *Heshbon* certainly signifies " supputation, calculation, or arithmetic."

Og, King of Bashan.

עוג, *Og*, signifies *he who hath drawn the circle.*[1] This word is Chaldaic. *Bashan,* בשן,[2] according to Buxtorf, is a contraction for בית שן *Bith Shan.* The sense of *Shan* has been already explained. He, who draws the circle, King of the temple of the personified year, or annual Sun, must, I should think, be himself an astronomical personification.

V. 17.

Chephirah, כפירה. This word is generally derived from כפר, *a village;* but it seems rather to belong to כפיר, *a young lion.* I know not whether any allusion were made to the sign of

---

[1] See Buxtorf's Chaldaic Lexicon, *in voce* עוג.

[2] See Hutch. Vol. 4. Parkhurst, *in voce* שן, and Buxtorf's Chaldaic Lexicon, *in voce* בשן.

Leo. באׄרות *Beeroth,* " *wells.*" I cannot help suspecting, that the orthography of this word is incorrect, and that we ought to read ברית. In all events I agree with Mr. Bryant in thinking, that *Berith* and *Beeroth* indicated the same place. Now *Berith* was named after a God of the Tsabaists called *Baal-Berith.* What was the distinctive attribute of this God among the hosts of heaven has been discussed by Hutchinson and Parkhurst. The symbols of the celestial bodies were often expressed by trees, as I have had frequent occasion to remark. The symbol of *Chephirah* may have been a pine;—that of *Beeroth,* or *Berith,* a cedar.

קרית יערים, *Kirjath jearim,* signifies *the cities of the woods.* On the representations of the starry hosts by woods, groves, trees, branches, &c. I have already spoken at considerable length ; but I ought before to have cited the following verses from Orpheus :

Θαλλῶν δ' ὅσσα βροτοῖσιν ἐπὶ χθονὸς ἔργα μέμηλεν.
Οὐδὲν ἔχει μίαν αἶσαν ἐπὶ Φρεσὶν, ἀλλὰ κυκλεῖται
Πάντα πέριξ· στῆναι δὲ καθ' ἓν μέρος οὐ θέμις ἐστίν.
Ἀλλ' ἔχει, ὡς ἤρξαντο, δρόμου μέρος ἴσον ἕκαστος.

Now I think, that by the operations of the branches, the mystic poet indicates the influences of the stars. In fact, when we consider how much trees vary with the seasons, we shall less wonder at their being employed as symbols by the Tsabaists. The representations of the palm-trees in the temple of Jerusalem might lead strangers to think, that the religion of the Israelites did not materially differ from that of those, who worshipped the hosts of heaven under the symbolical forms of groves, woods, and trees.

Interpres legum Solymarum, et magna sacerdos Arboris.

C. 10. V. 3.

Adoni Zedek. Every school-boy knows that the *Adoni* of the Phœnicians, whom the Greeks called *Adonis*, was no other than the Sun. The epithet of *Zedek*, " the just," was of course given to him by the idolaters.

ירושלם, *Jerusalem.* Some bring this name from ירש, *to inherit*, and שלם, *peace;* others compound it of ירא, *to fear*, and שלם. Josephus tells us that Jerusalem was anciently called *Solymah*, which must have been written שלומה, that is, *retribution.* The Sun, the just Lord, King of retribution (the seasons having been established in due order) became by the reform of the Calendar King of the inheritance of peace.

הוהם, *Hoham.* So we write the word, because the Masorites have misled us by their points. In the Samaritan character, which was employed by the Jews before the captivity, the orthography must have been, ᛉᛉᛉᛉ, and consequently in Roman letters EOEM. This is, perhaps, the same with the mystical word *Om*, which I imagine to have been a solar title among the Egyptians, and which is still held in the highest veneration by the Hindoos.

Hebron signifies *alliance, conjunction, union.* Its ancient name was *Kirjath Arba,* " the city of the four." The true return of the four seasons, being determined by the reform of the Calendar, the city of the four might not improperly be termed *Hebron.*

פראם, *Piram.* This word is not Hebrew, and I believe it to be Egyptian. If upon this point I follow Jablonski, I must translate *Piram* "the solar rays;" but perhaps I could express the thought better in French—*le Soleil rayonnant.*

ירמות, *Jarmuth.* This word, according to the *Onomasticon,* signifies *altitudines. Piram, King of Jarmuth* is the radiant Sun, King of altitudes.

יפיע, *Japhia,* is a corruption from יפעה, *splendor.*

לכיש, *Lachish,* is not to be found in Hebrew; but in Samaritan, ܨܓܓ signifies *inflammation, flame,* &c. I know not the meaning in the passage before us.

Debir, King of Eglon.

We have seen, that the temple was a type of the universe, and the *Debir,* דביר, was the oracle, or *adytum.* עגלון, *Eglon,* signifies *a circle.* Mr.

Harmer observes, that an Arab camp is still always round, when the disposition of the ground will admit of it, the Prince being in the middle, and the Arabs about him, but so as to leave a respectful distance between them. Now *Debar*, or *Debir*, as M. Court Gebelin remarks, was the ancient Arabic name for the planet *Mercury*, the orbit of which may be said to include the *adytum* of the solar system. *Eglon*, being written with an intensive, means the immediate circle; but *Debir*, or *Mercury*, is King of that circle, of which the Sun is of course the centre.

V. 5.

Five Kings of the *Amorites* are here described as making war against *Gibeon*, the great concave, or vault, of which Joshua, the saviour, or reformer, had obtained possession. The civil year contained only 360 days; and the five Kings in the text seem to represent the five intercalated days. I have said so much on this subject in another place, that I shall be excused from entering further upon it, and shall only observe that the story of the five Kings in the Book of Joshua appears to be nothing else than an astronomical allegory relating to the five intercalated days, sufficiently resembling the story of the five Kings in the fourteenth chapter of the Book of Genesis.

V. 10,

בית חורן, *Bith Horon,* " the house or mansion of great heat." But *Horon,* otherwise written חרון, appears to have been a solar title, as I think Mr. Hutchinson has observed. It is possible that Horon was no other than the Egyptian *Hor,* or *Horus.*

עזקה, *Azekah,* " the zone, the ring." This ring was probably an astronomical circle.

מקדה, *Makedah,* signifies *the division.*

V. 12.

Sun, stand thou still upon Gibeon, and thou, Moon in the valley of Ajalon.

Gibeon seems here to mean the cope, or vault of heaven. *Ajalon* signifies a *Ram*. The allusion to *Aries* in the Zodiac can hardly be mistaken. But wherefore did Joshua command the Sun to stand still in the vault of heaven, and the Moon in the sign of *Aries?* Ought he not to have commanded the earth to stand still rather than the Sun? This passage has always embarrassed *the matter-of-fact people*. When Joshua commanded the Sun and Moon to stand still, I understand an allegory. If my reader will consult Bailly, he will find that the Egyptians did not admit the five intercalated days as making part of the year. This will appear yet more evident from the statements made by Jablon-ski, Dupuis, &c. The course then of both the solar and lunar years was held to be suspended during the period of the intercalation; and the Sun and Moon were consequently, (though figura-tively) represented as arrested in their course. I pretend, that by the five Kings, the five interca-lated days were typified. The meaning of the allegory then comes out clearly enough.

So the Sun stood still in the midst of Heaven, and hasted not to go down about a whole day.

The mystical writers of the East did not always strictly understand 24 hours by a *day*. In fact, they often generally denoted by it a period of time. The period of time here implied was probably *about* 126 hours. If, however, the literal interpreters please, I will readily allow that about a whole day may *also* be taken in its usual acceptation. Though it be true, that the solar year consists of about 365 days, and about six hours, yet it must have been obvious to astronomers, that the sidereal year was about one day longer. That the Jews knew the length of the sidereal year is evident from a passage in Clemens Alexandrinus, which I have cited elsewhere.

V. 29.

לבנה, *Libnah*, "the Moon." What do our literal interpreters say to this? Did Joshua fight against the Moon? The sense is obvious enough, if we take the history as an allegory. *Jericho*, being the word ירח with a *vau* post-fixed, means the Moon considered collectively with respect to her several quarters. By the taking of *Jericho,* therefore, we were to understand the reform of the lunar month. *Libnah,* " the Moon," so called from its color, seems to denote the rising Moon. After the old Calendars were destroyed, in which the duration of the lunar month had been wrongly stated, it was still necessary to rectify the observations, and to fix the rising of the new Moon by surer calculations.

V. 33.

הרם, *Horam.* Mr. Hutchinson thinks that this was the real name whence the Greeks made *Hermes.* This *Horam* then was probably no other than an astronomer, who came to help *Lachish,* of the meaning of which I am ignorant, unless it signify *flame.* We cannot, however, doubt that an astronomical allusion was intended. *Horam* is called King of *Gezer.* Now *Gezer,* גזר, signifies *a segment;* and hence augurs and astrologers were called גזרין *Gezerin* by the Chaldeans, as observers of the segments of the sphere.

V. 41.

Kadesh Barnea. ברנע *Barnea,* is a word to which I can affix no sense.

עזה, *Gaza.* The real existence of *Gaza* as a city cannot be questioned. Rumelinus thinks that it signifies *a fortified place,* and עזה may certainly be so understood. But I have already remarked, that both Palestine and Egypt were divided, and their districts and cities were named, with a distinct reference to the astronomical divisions, and to the mythology of those, whose business it was to study science, and whose policy led them to involve that science in a system of mystery, which showed itself in every branch of their government, and in every part of their institutions. We find in Egypt, that *Mendes* was a district of country; but we also find that Mendes was a type of the Sun in the sign of Capricorn, and that Mendes signified *a goat.* I observe that עזה *Gaza* may signify *a goat,* and that اعز was *an Arabian idol;* and, in the midst of so many astronomical allusions, I suspect that *Gaza* may have been transplanted from heaven to earth.

גשן, *Goshan.* Mr. Bryant has proved that this signifies " the house or habitation of *Shan*—the annual Sun." *Goshan* was consequently the Zodiac.

C. 11. V. 1.

יבין, *Jabin.* According to Rumelinus, this word ought to signify *an intermediate space.*

חזור, *Hazor,* means *the hall,* or *interior.* Evident allusion is here made to the divisions of the temple, which was the type of the universe.

יובב, *Jobab.* This word clearly comes from יבב. In Hebrew it seems to bear no sense but *vociferation;* and this would be a very odd name for a King. But I must take refuge in allegory. In Syriac and in Geez, *Jobab* signifies *jubilee.* The name, therefore, suits the subject, if I be right in my interpretation of this book.

מדון, *Madon,* signifies *the great measure, extension,* also *mensuration.* The meaning seems to be, that the author of the *jubilee*, or new year, is called the King of the measure, or of mensuration. Can this be an historical personage? The Arabians worshipped an idol by this name المدان. But *Jobab* was probably erroneous in his mensuration, and was therefore leagued with the astrologers against Joshua.

שמרון, *Shimron*, "the great guard, the keeper of the watch"—*custos*.

אכשף, *Achshaph*—signifies "a necromancer, an astrologer, &c."

V. 2.

כנרות, *Chinneroth—the lyres*. I confess myself puzzled with this name. It probably denotes the stars in the *Lyre*.

דור, *Dor* originally signifies "any thing circular in its form."

V. 3.

חרמון, *Hermon.* This word comes from חרה, *arsit;* and seems to signify *great heat.* The Sun was called *Baal Hermon,* probably the same as *Hor.*

מצפה, *Mizpeh* is " a place of speculation, or observation"—probably *an observatory.*

V. 5.

מרום, *Merom.* Stockius thinks that this signifies *exaltation.* There are many of these names which it is difficult to explain; but we can understand enough to perceive, that perpetual references are made to astronomical symbols.

V. 8.

צידון, *Zidon*—"The hunter." Sagittarius, Bootes, and Orion, were denominated hunters among the constellations. The hunter *Adonis* was the God of the Zidonians, who seem to have called their city *Zidon,* " the hunter," after their God.

Misrephoth must come from שרף, a *fiery serpent,* and I have little doubt that the שרפים were types of the starry hosts. A serpent was the hieroglyphic, by which the course of the stars was expressed.

V. 17.

חלק, *Halek* signifies *an equal partition.*

שעיר, *Seir* signifies " a goat;" and might have denoted the sign of Capricorn.

בעל גד, *Baal Gad.* A cluster of stars in Capricorn was called *Gad.*

V. 21.

ענקים *Anakim*—" collars, zones, circles." These have been converted into giants by the commentators; but it is pretty clear, that they signify the circles employed by astrologers.

עֵנָב, *Anqb* signifies a *grape* in Hebrew, and why should not a mountain be called *a grape?* Let us observe, that the season for gathering grapes was when the Sun was in the sign of *Leo*, the emblem of Judah.

V. 22.

גַּת, *Gath*, according to Bochart, signifies *cattle;* according to the lexicographers, *a wine press.*

אַשְׁדּוּד, *Ashdod.* I cannot help thinking that an idol of the Tsabaists was thus called. My reader may, however, consult Parkhurst *in voce* שׁד. But I will fairly confess, that the latter part of this chapter appears by no means so distinct, or to bear allusions to astronomy in so clear a manner as the preceding parts of the book. This may be, because the mystic language of Oriental science can only be partially understood at the present day.

C. 12. V. 1.

אַרְנוֹן, *Arnon* signifies *an ark, a chest,* &c. also *an elm-tree.* There certainly was a river called

Arnon ; but so were there rivers called the Nile, the Gihon, the Niger, and the Eridanus, which yet served for astronomical symbols. I think, that נחל ארנון signifies *the valley of the river of Nun ;* and that ארנון is written for יאר נון; nor is this without authority. We find אר defective for יאר in Amos, c. 8. v. 8. But the Nile, by which name both the river of *Aquarius*, and the river of *Orion*, were known, was called יאר. Again, the Syrians and Chaldeans called both *Cetus* and *Pisces* by the name of *Nun*. The rivers of *Aquarius* and of *Orion* were joined in the Egyptian planispheres. The river of *Nun*, or of the *Fish*, consequently extended along the border of *Pisces* to *Piscis Australis,* and to *Cetus,* or the *Whale.*

V. 2.

ערער, *Aroer* in Hebrew signifies *naked ;* but in Chaldaic it signifies *a griffin, an eagle,* a kind of *hawk,* &c. Is this then the constellation which we call Phœnix? Perhaps *Aroer* is the same with the Egyptian *Arueris.*

The Phœnix is a name generally supposed to have been given by modern navigators to the Constellation so called on our globes. This, however, does not appear to me to have been the case : the Constellation must have been visible in Egypt, and the brilliant beside it could not have failed to attract the attention of the Arabians, who, I am led to believe from many circumstances, have known it under the name of the eagle, griffin, or Phœnix, from the most remote antiquity. Our astronomers probably called the Constellation Phœnix from the example of the Arabians.

The following observations are submitted to the reader :

1. It appears, that the ancient Arabians adored an idol under the form of an eagle, and this eagle was an image of one of the celestial signs. Consult Hyde Hist. Vet. Pers. and Golius, in voce نسر. Now I think this was neither the eagle, nor the vulture, but the Phœnix.

2.   We learn from Herodotus, l. ii. c. 73. and from Pliny, l. x. c. 2. that the Phœnix was fabled to have come from Arabia.   The Constellation so called by us, with the great star beside it, *Acharnar*, is distinctly visible during the summer months in Arabia.

3.   The Phœnix was the type of the Sothic year among the Egyptians.   See Tacit. Ann. l. 6. Be it observed, that when Sothis rises, the Constellation of Phœnix comes to the meridian.   It is then entirely visible in the Thebais.

4.   It seems probable, that the Phœnix was marked as a distinct Constellation by the Egyptians; for though it contains a small number of stars visible to the eye, yet if we reckon *Acharnar* among them, we shall find one star of the first, and three stars of the second, magnitude in this Constellation.

5. The Egyptians feigned the Phœnix to come from Arabia. In fact, the Constellation so called authorises this fable by its course through the Heavens.

6. Erasmus says, that the Phœnix was the symbol of the year, or of the annual revolution. This Constellation, in fact, rose to the Egyptians shortly before the commencement of their sacred year. Had they known no such Constellation, the observation of Erasmus must be unfounded; and Erasmus was not a person likely to speak lightly on such subjects.

7. The Phœnix is placed not far from the Altar, with respect to latitude. The relation between the Constellations of the Phœnix and the Altar seems to be pointed out by some of the Roman authors. Thus Tacitus, who probably did not consider the Phœnix as a Constellation,

expresses himself in words which are by no means distinct, if the Egyptians did not consider the Phœnix as a Constellation in the same region of the Heavens with the Altar; (inque Solis Aram perferre, &c.) Then Claudian in his Phœnix has the following words :

———————————— Jam destinat aris
Semina reliquiasque sui ; myrrhata relucent
Limina ; divino spirant altaria fumo.

8. But there is a passage in this same Claudian, which I cannot understand, if the Phœnix had not been reckoned a Constellation by the ancient Arabians and Egyptians.

——————— Rutilo cognatum vertice sidus
Attollit, crispatus apex, &c.

גלעד, *Gilead.* This word has been variously interpreted—*scaturigo perpetua,* and *acervus testimonii.* Now if my reader will turn to the Egyptian planispheres edited by Kircher, he will find that an altar, and a river, are designated as two iconisms belonging to the sign of *Aries,* or *Ammon.* I must remark again, that among the Egyptians, the river of *Orion* seems to have been represented as a continuation of the river of *Aquarius.*

יבק, *Jabbok.* I know not the meaning. This was, however, the border of *Ammon,* or of the Sun in *Aries.* This brook flowed by *Gilead,* and it would seem, (Cant 4.) that Solomon alludes to its bordering on *Ammon,* when he speaks of the flocks shorn and washed there.

V. 3.

בית ישמות, *Bith Jeshimoth.* Mr. Hutchinson has written at great length on these words. I cannot follow him in all his whimsical though ingenious notions. I understand, generally, that *Bith Jeshi-moth* signifies " the temple of the heavens."

אשדות הפסגה, *Ashdoth Pisgah.* I derive *Ashdoth* from שדי.[1] The שדי, or שדים, were certainly idols worshipped by the Tsabaists; and I suspect *Ashdoth* to have been of the number. *Pisgah* signifies a *hill* in Hebrew, but in Chaldaic it may be rendered *the segment of a circle.*

V. 4.

נבול עוג. Instead of *the coast of Og*, I under-stand *the boundary of a circle.* This boundary of the circle, or border of the Zodiac, is figuratively called King of Bashan, which is *Bith-Shan,* " the temple of the annual Sun." But we have seen that the Sun's annual course had been falsely calculated by the astrologers and Tsabaists. It is added, that *Bashan* was of the remnant of the Giants, that dwelt at *Ashteroth* and at *Edrei.* Now I am not

---

[1] See Hutchinson, Vol. 4.

convinced, that רפאים is properly translated *giants*. I rather think with Parkhurst, that the *Rephaim* were so called as restorers of the worship of the Moon. They dwelt at *Ashteroth* and at *Edrei*. *Ashteroth* was a name very generally given to the Moon by the Tsabaists. אדרעי, *Edrei*, is a word to which I can affix no meaning. It is probably a corrupt spelling for אדרי.

V. 5.

סלכה, *Salcah.* I have the authority of the Onomasticon for saying, that the letters in this name are transposed; and, indeed, *Salcah* is a word to which I can give no sense. The true reading then is כסלה, and this was probably of the כסילים, " constellations," which arose in the cold season in the month כסלו, and perhaps might have indicated כסיל, *Orion.* This constellation is a paranatellon of *Taurus.* If *Hermon* be the same as *Hor,* I ought to observe that the station of *Hor* was in *Taurus,* which rises in the month *Chisleu,* or November, about the beginning of the night.

נשורי, *Geshurites.* This word is apparently a compound. I have already had occasion to remark that the נ prefixed to another word, seems to indicate a mansion. It is possibly a contraction from the ancient Persian جـ. There is no such word as *geshur* in Hebrew, and I am, therefore, the more confident of the truth of the etymology, which I am about to propose. נשורי, *Geshurites* ought, according to my observation, to be composed of נ for נא, *a mansion,* and שורי *bulls,*—" the mansion of the *bulls,*" by which I understand the stars included in the sign of *Taurus.* I have something further to remark. We write *Geshurites,* but there is no proof, that the first syllable was not pronounced *ga,* or *go,* or *gu.* Now be it observed, that according to Anquetil, the sign of *Taurus* was called *Gao,* or *Go,* by the ancient Chaldeans and Persians. Be this as it may, however, I have no great doubts, that the sign of *Taurus* was indicated by the word before us.

מעכתי, *Maachathites.* These *Maachathites* probably appertained unto *Maachah,* " a Deity of the Tsabaists," whose temple is mentioned in the second Book of Samuel. What might have been the place of *Maachah* among the constellations, I cannot pretend to say.

V. 14.

ערד, *Arad* signifies *a snake, a serpent.* Probably the constellation *coluber.*

I have already given the explanations of many of the names contained in the remainder of this chapter; but some of them are to me, at least, incapable of affording any meaning. There seems, however, to be pretty clear proof, that the whole relates to astronomy. Out of 31 names we find the following.

Jericho, " the Moon's quarters."

Ai, " the pile, heap, or Calendar."

Eglon, " the circle, or sphere."

Arad, " the serpent, or adder."

Libnah, " the Moon."

Bith-El, " the house, or temple of the Sun."

Madon, " measure, measurement." [1]

Achshaph, " an astrologer, astrology."

Gilgal, " the revolving sphere, the celestial sphere."

Without entering further into the question, I may be permitted to observe, that these names seem to bear more reference to the heavens than to the earth. But I have remarked that Egypt was partitioned into 30 districts, answering to each day of the month in the civil year. Here we have 31 Provinces; and I shall leave it to my reader to find out the enigma, by the help of the five Kings of the Amorites.

C. 13. V. 2.

פלשתים, *Philistines,* the *revolvers,* or *wanderers.* These *revolvers* were probably belonging to the celestial hosts—possibly the planets.

---

[1] It would seem, that the Sun was adored under this name. The Arabians had an idol called *Madan.*

V 3.

שיחור, *Sihor* signifies *the dawn.*

אשקלנ, *Eskalonites,* the *Balancers.* I know not whether an allusion be here made to the sign of *Libra.*

עוי, *Avites,* the *oblique ones,* the *obliquities.* Does this refer to the obliquity of the Ecliptic?

V. 5.

גבלי, *Giblites,* " the borderers."

חמת, *Hamuth,* " the pitcher;"—possibly the urn of *Aquarius.*

V. 9.

מידבא, *Mideba,* 'the stream of water"—possibly the river of *Aquarius.* [1]

---

1 See Rumelin.

דיבון, *Dibon,* " the great bear"—*Ursa Major.*

V. 15.

We now come to the allotments made to the tribes of Reuben and Gad, and to half the tribe of Manasseh. It will be remembered that *Aquarius* was the emblem of Reuben.

I have already had occasion to remark, that in the Egyptian Zodiacs, the river of *Aquarius,* and the river of *Orion* seem to have been united. I have also observed, that *Nun,* or *Non,* was a name not only given to *Cetus* but to *Pisces.* The coast of Reuben, then, was from *Aroer* (Phœnix) in the Valley of the river of *Nun* (the *Fish* either *Cetus,* or *Pisces,*) and all the plain by *Medeba,* which signifies *a stream,* according to Rumelinus, and by which I understand the constellations combined of *Eridanus* and the river of *Aquarius,* generally called *the River.*

Among the cities allotted to Reuben, whose emblem was *Aquarius,* I find the following.

Dibon, " the great bear."

Bith Baal Meon. " The house of the Lord of Meon." I find that the Egyptians called the sign of *Aquarius Mon*,[1] with the Latin termination *Monius*.[2]

Bamoth Baal, " the high places, the altars, of the Lord, the Sun." Janus, or the Sun in *Aquarius*, was represented by the Etruscans, who derived their religion from the East, as seated on a throne composed of twelve altars.

Kedemoth signifies " the Eastern parts."

Zareth-Shahar, " the splendor of the dawn."

Bith-Peor. *Peor* was no other than *Hor*, or *Or*, with the Egyptian prefix.[3] Now the station

---

[1] See Dupuis, Vol. 5.

[2] *Maon, Meon, Mon*, were solar, and *Maonah, Menah, Monah*, lunar titles of the most remote antiquity. But see Court Gebelin. Vol. 4.

[3] See my Essay on a Punic Inscription.

of Hor was in *Taurus;* and when *Taurus* comes to the Meridian, *Aquarius* begins to rise.

Midian signifies *measure, mensuration.* [1]

Zur, " *splendor.*"

Hur, " *brilliancy.*"

Reba, " a fourth part." Reuben commanded a fourth part in the camp of the Hebrews.

Balaam. I derive this word from בלע, " to swallow up." *Balaam* was probably the astronomical dragon, of which I have already spoken.

The emblem of the tribe of Gad was *Aries.* Some of the names of the cities are not intelligible to me, though they are explained in the *Onomasticon.* The truth is, that any signification, however absurd, is adopted by the lexicographers, who

---

[1] Perhaps the same with *Madon.*

have been misled by the Masorites. Thus we find *Jazer* made to signify *auxiliabitur Deus*. But has this word no connexion with עזרה, which was a part of the temple,—the temple being a type of the universe? I only give this as an example, and much more striking ones might be adduced, of the absurd etymologies which have been given of names, many of which are not Hebrew.

Aroer—already explained. See the celestial globe for the relative positions of *Aries* and *Phœnix*. I pass over several names which have either been explained, or which are of easy solution.

Betonim, or *Botenim*—literally the *Bellies.* This is a strange name for a place; but observe, the stars forming the belly of *Aries*, are still called *Boten* by the Persians and Arabians. [1]

Nimrah, from *nemer* נמר, " a leopard." The constellation which we call the wolf is named

---

[1] Alfrag. c. 22. Ulug Beig. p. 58.

nemer by the Arabians. It is a paranatellon of *Aries.* We may, therefore, understand what is meant by Gad's having possessions in the valley of *Bith-Nimrah.*

In the valley of *Bith-Aram* (a most vicious orthography) Gad of course had possessions, at least, if I be right in thinking that חרם were those belonging to *Hor.* The station of *Hor* was in *Taurus,* and the tail of Aries occupies the interval between the signs, which figuratively may be called the valley.

Succoth (or Succoth Benoth).

This is the Syrian name of the *Pleiades,* which are on the back of *Taurus,* close to *Aries.* [1]

Zaphon signifies " the North."

---

[1] But perhaps *Succoth* here may be derived from the Chaldaic סכה, which signifies " to speculate, to observe, &c." In another place we shall find that the men of *Succoth* indicated the observers of the stars.

R

Mahanaim, " the encampments of the celestial hosts."

The half tribe of Manasseh seems to have inherited half the portion of Simeon and Levi, whose joint standard displayed the sign of *Pisces.* My reader will remember, that the *Ram* encroaches on *Pisces.*

Jair, יאיר, Rumelinus makes this signify *the Lord will illustrate.* But it seems a corruption for יאר already explained.

Machir, מכיר, this is not from מכר, *to sell,* but from כר, *agnus, Aries.*

Moab, I believe to have been a title of the Moon. The Sun was hailed *Ab, the Father. Mo-ab—like to the Father.*

C. 14.

This chapter contains an account of the petition of *Caleb,* who obtained *Hebron* for his inheritance.

But כלב, *Caleb* is the name by which the *Dog-star*, or *Sirius*, is known in Hebrew, Syriac, and Arabic. *Caleb* received *Hebron*, " union, conjunction," which had formerly been called *Kirjath-Arba*, " the city of the four," for his inheritance. Now a short extract from Bailly will, perhaps, explain this allegory. " Le changement du lever de cette étoile (Sirius) qui retardoit d'un jour tous les 4 ans, donna lieu aux Egyptiens de former une petite période de 4 années, qui étoit précisément celle de nos années bissextiles ; période qu'ils désignoient sous l'emblême d'un arpent de terre, marquant la première année par un quart d'arpent, la seconde par deux quarts, &c." *Caleb*, or *Sirius*, is figuratively represented in the text, as obtaining possession of *Hebron*, which had been called the city of the four, with an apparent, if not an evident, reference to this canicular period.

C. 15.

The sign of *Leo* was the emblem of Judah.

V. 1.

אדום, *Edom* signifies *redness.* The country of *Idumæa* was thence named. But it is to be observed, that allegory was seldom lost sight of in the names and divisions of districts. In the quadrilateral camp of the Hebrews, the *lion*, the standard of Judah, was displayed at the North-east corner; and the *man with the urn*, or *Aquarius*, the standard of Reuben, at the South-east corner. Now *Edom* may be either from אדם, *a man*, or אדם, *a ruby*, and a ruby was the stone consecrated to the tribe of Reuben; and *a man* was the emblem displayed on his standard. *Leo* and *Aquarius* are opposite signs.

The wilderness of Zin.

I have already explained the meaning of מדבר. *Zin* is not so easily interpreted. According to some it signifies *a thorn*, or *palm-tree.* But I observe, that צנה in Chaldaic signifies *cold*, and

צנצנת signifies *an urn*. Can it bear this meaning from the colds brought by the *urn of Aquarius?* [1]

V. 2.

ים מלח, *the salt sea.* Josephus clearly shows, that *the sea* was one of the enigmatical types, by which the hemisphere was expressed, and that the brazen sea in the temple was thus intended.

V. 3.

" And it went out to the south side to *Maaleh Acrabbim.*" This does not appear to be the meaning of the original. I translate, " and it went out opposite from the south side to *Maaleh Acrabbim.*" Now *Maaleh*

---

[1] *Zin* is also a solar title, the same with *Zoan, Zan,* &c. This name is Egyptian, for the Egyptians, as may be seen from the remarks of Bochart, frequently changed the *aleph* and *jod.*

Acrabbim signifies " the ascent, or height of the Scorpions." In fact the emblem of Dan, which was taken from the sign of *Scorpius* was placed to the north in the quadrilateral camp of the Hebrews.

Adar, read *Adarah*, already explained.

Karkaa, I know not the meaning; but the floor of the temple (which was a type of the universe) was called *Karkaa*.

V. 4.

" From thence it passed towards *Azmon*." Rumelinus makes Azmon signify *validus*. I know not the meaning.

V. 6.

Bith Hogla. There is no such word as חגלה, *Hogla*, in Hebrew. I derive it from the Syriac

‏ﻞﻐﺣ‎, and translate *Bith-Hogla* " the house of the circle, or the temple of the circle," which seems to have been personified and deified by the Tsabaists. [1]

Bith-Arabah. This *Arabah* appears to have been another Deity of the Tsabaists. [2]

Bohan, בהן. This word, according to the lexicographers, may signify either " a thumb, or a great toe." This is a very odd name for the son of Reuben to have taken. I know not the meaning.

אדמים, *Adumim.* " The red ones." Can these be the *Hyades.* Scaliger and Bayer say that *Aldebaran* was called אדם *Adum* by the Hebrews.

En-Shemesh, " the fountain of the Sun."

---

[1] But see also Hutchinson, vol. 4.

[2] If I recollect rightly, Court Gebelin says that *Arba,* or *Arabah,* or *Urbah,* was the ancient oriental name of the planet Venus; but as he does not give the original characters, I know not whether the word be the same.

Without entering into the *metaphysical* speculations of Mr. Hutchinson, I shall agree to his
physical explanation of the word *Shemesh*, or
Shemosh, which I understand to signify "the solar
light, receding from the fire at the orb of the Sun."
It would seem, however, that the Tsabaists personified and deified *Shemesh*, and that they principally
adored this irradiation, or solar effulgence, at the
rising of the Sun. The fountain of *Shemesh* may,
therefore, indicate the Orient; and I understand
this to be the meaning in the passage before us.
Towards the waters of En-Shemesh may be, therefore, taken either literally, or metaphorically; but
in the midst of so much allegory I am inclined to
adopt the figurative sense.

En-Rogel, "the fountain of the fuller," according
to the Rabbins. Their manner of obtaining this
sense is truly very ingenious. רגל *regel*, signifies
a foot. Now when a fuller washes clothes in a
fountain, he treads on them *with his feet*, in order
to clean them. What is so clear then, as that the
fountain of the *foot*, is the fountain of the *fuller?*
But further, the LXX and Jerome write Ρωγὲλ,
and *Rogel;* and the infallible Masorites authorise

this reading by their punctuation. But I find that רגל never signifies *a fuller*, except when question is made of this fountain; and in spite of the authority of R. Solomon, and R. Kimchi, I shall translate the word רגל, without the least regard to distinctions, which did not exist until near a thousand years after the Hebrew ceased to be spoken. In a word, I look upon the Masoretic punctuation to be the most impertinent imposition that ever was practised. For *En-Rogel,* I read *Ain-Regel ;* and I observe that *Regel* is the name still given to the brilliant star in the left foot of *Orion.* I must further observe, that the word *ain,* which we find so often improperly written *en* in the English Bible, signifies originally an *eye.* Now eyes were certainly symbols, by which the celestial orbs were frequently denoted. The story of Argus is a pretty clear illustration of this assertion. One of the symbols of Osiris, or the Sun, was an eye. Sallust, the philosopher, called the Sun the eye of heaven, and his mythological knowledge can hardly be disputed. —But I must return to my subject.

V. 8.

Hinnom, " the son of *Hinnom,*" (i. e. of lamenta-tations,) possibly indicated the Sun, when the Tsabaists mourned his fictitious death at the autum-nal equinox, and wept for him under the various names of Osiris, Adonis, Thammuz, Æsarah, &c.

V. 9.

נפתוח, *Nephtoah,* נ appellative, and פתוח. Now פתוח, or פתח, appears to me to have been precisely the same with the *Phtha* of the Egyptians; nor do I doubt that the Πάταιχοι, mentioned by Hero-dotus, were any thing else than images of this Deity. *Phtha* was the Vulcan of the Egyptians; and I have no hesitation in believing that the true name was written פתח *Phthah;* But we find the guttural was often either dismissed, or softened, or changed into an *aleph,* or into a *shin.* Thus Hero-dotus ought to have written Πάταιχοι, but he wrote with the single letter, and thus softened the sound. The Æolic Greeks and the Latins continually changed the aspirate into an *s*, as when they wrote *sex* for ἑξ, &c. The Copts seem to have done the same thing; and they appear to have written ΦΘⲀⳡ *Phthas* for *Phthah*, and I observe that the Greek sometimes write Φθὰ, and sometimes Φθάς. But I hasten to what it is most important for me to observe. The Phœnician פתח *Phthah*, and the Egyptian *Phtha*, *Phthah*, or *Phthas*, were the same Deity with the Ἥφαιστος of the Greeks, and with the Vulcan of the Latins. Now by this God the Stoics typified their primordial fire; and I am led to agree with La Croze in thinking, that the Egyptians also indicated by this *Pthah* the *Tsabaoth*, or " hosts of heaven." The name of *Pthah* seems clearly to be included in נפתוח; but I cannot trace the allusion further; nor point out more precisely what is meant.

עפרון, *Ephron.* Rumelin translates this name *oppidum pulverulentum.* I shall have occasion to speak again on this subject.

בעלה, *Baalah*. This was a title of the Moon, as *Baal* was of the Sun.

Seir, " a goat"—Probably *Capricorn*

Mount Jearim. The mountain of woods was probably a type of the starry heavens, worshipped by the idolators under the symbols of trees, groves, woods, &c.

V. 10.

Chesalon. In the Onomasticon this word is translated *spes, fiducia*, &c; and a very pretty name for a place it is, whether we make it *Hope*, or *Confidence*. But I cannot help observing, that כסלח, in spite of its intensitive, and in spite of the *masorah*, is not very unlike to כסל, whence is כסיל, " the constellation of *Orion*." We shall have more of this presently.

תמנה, *Timnah*. This word is Chaldaic. It signifies " an octant, or eighth part of the circle"—it may also mean a portion.

V. 11.

ש רון, *Shicron*, (written שכרונה in the original)
is clearly a derivative from שכר. I have already
shown that *Cancer* was the emblem of יששכר Issachar,
(שכר with the *jod* appellative.) I have now to
observe, that the Egyptians made *Cancer* the
station of *Hermanubis*,—or of *Hermes* with the
head of a *hawk*, or of an *ibis ;* and that the sign
was often designated by the head of a hawk, or
ibis, as may be seen in Kircher. But on turning
to Buxtorf's Chaldaic Lexicon, my reader will
find that שכר signifies *a hawk*. We may write
שכרון *Shicron*, or יששכר *Issachar*, and we may follow
the vicious punctuation of the Masorites, but to
the Hebraist, יששכר issachar (ishcar) is only distinguished from שכר by a jod appellative, as שכרון
Shicron is still the same word with an intensive ן.
By *Shicron*, then, I understand the *hawk*, or *ibis*,
by which the sign of *Cancer* was anciently denoted
by the Egyptians, who likewise were accustomed
to place there a *beetle*, which the Greeks seem to
have mistaken for a crab.

יבנאל, *Jabneel.* The lexicographers make this name to signify *ædificare faciet Deus.*

אל, *El* in the composition of these Canaanite names does not signify *Deus,* but *Sol.* I shall now leave the literal interpreter to make what he can of *Jabneel.*

V. 14.

ענק—*Anak*—" the collar, or necklace, &c." But the Rabbins tell us that *Anak* was a celebrated giant. What could induce this giant to call himself *anak, a necklace?* Perhaps the literal interpreters can inform us. In the text, however, we find הענק, *the necklace;* so he was *the necklace* κατ' ἐξοχήν.

I observe that *Caleb, Sirius,* takes possession of the country of *Anak.* I suspect then, that *Anak* has some reference to astronomy. The verb ענק signifies " to bind, or to girt round;" and the substantive, therefore, may be translated " a belt, a zone," with as much propriety as a necklace. What then if *Anak* be an astronomical zone?—the Ecliptic for example. Now we know, that the Sothic year, or cycle, was determined by the heliacal rising of Sirius; and by this canicular period as it was called, the true duration of the year was determined, and the conjunctions of the Sun and Moon were fixed in the same points of the heavens.

V. 14.

And Caleb drove thence the three sons of *Anak* (the circle or zone) *Sheshai*, and *Ahiman* and *Talmai*.

Rumelinus, and the lexicographers, make these names bear very singular significations. *Sheshai* means *the decrepit of God—Ahiman*, the *brother is like—*and *Talmai*, is a *furrow*. The explanations of Bochart are scarcely more to the purpose; and I must consign these names to the obscurity in which I found them, only observing that *Ahimon*, according to Munster, was an idol of the Tsabaists.

V. 15.

Kirjath-Sepher. "The city of the book, or record,"—by which was probably meant the false calendar.

I shall pass over the remaining names that occur in this episode concerning *Caleb,* to none of which I can give any meaning, for I cannot, in contradiction to common sense, and even to the true etymology, translate *Achsah,* " *the stocks,*" *Othniel,* " *the gentleness of God,*" and *Kenaz,* " *loss,*" as has been done by the lexicographers. It is evident that these, like the rest, were allegorical names, the meaning of which can no longer be traced. I return to the inheritance of Judah, whose emblem was *Leo.*

V. 21.

Kabzeel, קבצ־אל, literally *the congregation of the Sun.* *Leo* is the station of *Sol.*

עדר, *Eder*, means *a herd of any animals*. This would be a strange name to give to a place. The animals of the Zodiac were probably understood.

יגור, *Jagur*, is composed of י formative, and גור, *a lion's whelp*. The Sun in the first decan of *Leo* was possibly represented under this form; and this may have been named גור בעל *Gur Baal*.[1] We also hear of *Maalah-Gur*, " the ascent of the lion's whelp."

V. 22.

Kinah. The lexicographers bring this word from קין, and they render it *lamentatio*. I cannot consider the *jod* as a radical; I read קינה, for קנה, *a measuring rod*, or, according to Rumelin, *scapus in staterâ, unde bilances dependent*. The allusion may then be to *Libra*.

Dimonah. *Terra à fluxu excrementorum dicta*. *Rumel*. I cannot believe it. The tribe of Judah

---

[1] 2nd Chron.

S

would have refused a possession so offensive to their olfactory nerves. It appears to me, that *Dimonah* was a title given to the Moon. *Di* is a radical of remote antiquity, to be found in many languages, signifying, *day, light,* &c. which was thence given to their Deities by the *Tsabaists.* *Monah,* or *Manah,* or *Menah,* is a name not less common to the Moon. Concerning both words my reader may consult M. Court Gebelin, vol. 4. *Dimonah* then is *Dea Luna,* or perhaps, *lux Lunæ.*

Adadah. As this word is written עדעדה, it is difficult to determine the meaning. We know, however, that *Adad* was a solar title, and though the orthography does not authorise the inference, the sound may lead us to conclude, that *Adadah* was a title of the Moon. The word *Adad,* the solar title mentioned by Macrobius, must have come from אחד.

V. 23.

יתנן, *Ithnan,* is compounded of י formative, and תנן, *a serpent,* or *dragon.* The allusion seems to be to the great constellation *Hydra*, under the feet of *Leo*.

V. 24.

זיף, *Ziph*. This word is not Hebrew. Rume-linus makes it signify *a pledge ;* but this is a forced meaning, if it can be obtained at all from the Chaldaic.

טלם, *Telem*. There is no such word in Hebrew. In Chaldaic it signifies *oppression ;* but this would be a strange proper name.

Bealoth—Ladies—but as these ladies were idols of the Moon, or lunar emblems, I must consider them as such.

V. 25.

חדתה, *Hadattah ;* this word is Chaldaic, and signifies *the new moon*.

V. 26.

אמם, *Amam*, " mother." Possibly the Moon, under her character of the *magna mater*, may be meant : But of this we shall speak presently.

שמע, *Shema*, " *auditus*." *Onom*. This would be a singular proper name. I suspect the word to be wrongly written.

I observe that the Arabians name the two brilliant stars in *Virgo*, which we call *Spica* and *Protygeter* (not *Arcturus*, as Golius has it) السماك الأعزل and السماك الرامح. Now whether the Arabians have changed the radical *ain* for the radical *kef*, I cannot venture to decide, but it is possible that the ancient name of *Spica* was שמע, and that the Arabians have altered the sound to سماك. Kircher says that the station of the Moon in this part of the sign is called *Zamach*.

מולדה, *Moladah*, " the offspring," from ילד. We

have seen that *Amam* signifies *a mother*. I have said that allusion might be made to the *Magna Mater*. But the *Magna Mater* was no other than the *Dea Multimammia*, the Phrygian Cybele, the Ephesian Diana, and the Egyptian Isis. Again, in the apparently whimsical spirit of mythology, these were all feigned to be virgins. Isis had the same place in the Egyptian Zodiac as *Virgo* in our's. But in the ancient Oriental Zodiacs the *Virgin* was represented as a *Mother*. The two following passages will not fail to strike the reader. *In primâ facie Virginis* (translated from the Jewish astrologer Avenar) *ascendit Virgo pulchra, longis capillis, et duas in manu spicas continet, sedetque supra sedem, et nutrit puerum adhuc parvulum, et lactat et cibat eum.* The next passage is from Albumazar, an Arabian astrologer. *Oritur in primo Virginis decano puella, Ambice dicta, Aderenosa, id est, virgo munda, virgo immaculata, corpore decora, vultu venusta, habitu modesta, crine prolixo, manu duas aristas tenens, supra solium aulæatum residens, puerum nutriens ac jure pascens, in loco, cui nomen Hebræa, puerum dico à quibusdam nationibus nominatum* IESVM, *signi-*

ficantibus Issa (nempe יישע vel ישע, "salvatorem")
quem et Græcè CHRISTVM dicunt. [1]

If then any allusion were intended to be made
to the sign of *Virgo,* it could hardly be done in a
clearer manner than by mentioning *Amam,* " the
mother," and *Moladah,* " the progeny."

V. 27.

Hazar Gaddah—Both words have been already
explained.

חשמות, *Heshmon.* It is clear, that the letters in
this name have been transposed, and probably for
a mysterious purpose. In the *Onomasticon,* the
word *Heshmon* is brought from משח, *unxit,* and
even the English reader will easily see that this is

---

only a transposition of the radicals in חשמ-ון. The
Jews in fact pretend, that one *Messiah*, (משיח,)
was to be born of the tribe of Judah, and another
of the tribe of Ephraim. This *Heshmon* seems
to indicate him, who was *the anointed* of Judah,
and who, indeed, is called *ben-Jehudah*, "Judah's
son." Let us inquire if there be any astronomical
allusion here. Immediately on leaving the sign of
Leo, the emblem of Judah, the Sun passes into the
sign, where, as we have already seen, the ancient
Persians, Arabians, and Syrians, depicted *Virgo*,
with a male infant in her arms. Now I observe
that the Arabians make مسابيل *Mesaiel*, the protect-
ing *Genius* in the sign of *Virgo*. [1] This *Mesaiel*
seems a manifest corruption from משיח-אל *Mesiah-
El*. It is vain to talk of the *shin* being *dageshed*
by the Masorites, of its being written with a س
instead of ش in the Arabic, or of the aspirate
being suppressed. We ourselves suppress the
sound of the aspirate in *Eve, Messiah,* and many
other words. Besides, the Syrians certainly often

---

[1] See Kircher's Œdipus, Vol. 3. p. 245.

softened the harsh aspirate; and the Arabians may have caught the sound from them. *Mesai-El,* (مسابيل) then appears to be a corruption for مسيح-ال, משיח-אל *Messiah-El*—" *the anointed of El,*" the male infant, who rises in the arms of *Virgo,* who was called *Jesus* by the Hebrews, that is ישע, " the Saviour," and was hailed the anointed King, or the Messiah.

V. 27.

בית פלט, *Bith-Palet.* Mr. Hutchinson properly refers the word *Palet* to ילד, and we are not to forget, that we have just had the derivative מולדה *Molidah.* The mansion, or temple of *Palet,* clearly relates to a station of the Moon, but of the Moon worshipped as the Goddess of Parturition, and known by various names, *Ilythia, Juno Lucina,* &c. [1] I am inclined to think, that the Moon was particularly adored under the title of

---

[1] See Selden de Dis Syris, and Bochart, Vol. 2. c. 291.

Palet, " the deliverer," on the last night of the month. I remark, at least, that the Arabians call the last night of the month غلَتَ. [1]

V. 28.

חצר שועל, *Hazar-Shual.* Literally, *the hall of the fox.* I can only offer conjectures on this singular name. I observe that the constellation of *Bootes,* in which is the remarkable star *Arcturus,* so nearly placed to *Virgo,* is sometimes called *Lycaon* by the Greeks, and *Lycaon* is evidently derived from λύκος, *a wolf,* and as the translators differ whether *shual* be a *fox,* or a *jackal,* the Greeks may have made it a *wolf.* The Hebrews called this constellation כלב אנובח *Caleb Anubach,* " the barking dog," in evident allusion to *latrator Anubis;* and the Egyptians (as appears from Kircher's planisphere) made Anubis the slayer of the wolf, which constellation we now combine with

---

[1] See Golius, *in voce;* and consult Parkhurst, *in voce* פלט.

that of *Centaurus.* The Latins, [1] among other names, called Bootes *Canis.* Perhaps, then, the *Fox* in the text was no other than *Bootes,* or the most luminous star in this constellation, commonly called *Arcturus.* This star is remarkable for its red and fiery appearance. Now I find that in Arabic شعل *shal,* signifies *to inflame, to set on fire.* The radicals here are the same as in שועל. Then I suspect, that *Arcturus* may have been so denoted. This is not all. *Arcturus* rises with *Virgo,* and with her ears of corn. The heat of the season is excessive, and the lightnings frequently burn and scorch the corn and the vines, while the Sun continues in the sign of *Virgo.* It would seem that there may be something in the story of Samson and his foxes connected with the observations, which I have been making. Samson, שמשון, literally signifies *the Sun.* But I shall say more on this subject in another place.

באר שבע, *Beer-Sheba.* This is translated *the well of the oath. Onom.* That the words may

---

[1] See the tables of Dupuis.

bear this meaning is true; but I ask the literal translator, whether it may not signify *the well of seven?* What if באר *beer*, be a metaphorical word? In its primitive sense [1] it signifies, when used as a verb, *to elucidate, to give light, to render clear.* שבע *sheba*, certainly may signify *an oath*, and as certainly it signifies *seven*. *Beer-sheba* may then either be rendered *the well of the oath*, or *the lustre of seven*. The seven may be the planets, or they may be the *Pleiades*, or they may be the seven stars of the Wain, which the Orientalists, according to Hyde, still call the *seven* without any other distinctive appellation.

בזיותיה, *Bizjothjah*. The lexicographers make this word to signify *contemtus Domini*. This is surely a strange name for a city. I find, that the Arabians call the constellation of *Centaurus*, the proximity of which to *Virgo* my reader must already be aware of, by a name, which, I think, will bring us to the one in the text. They call *Centaurus* بَنِز, in Chaldaic characters בזה. [2] Now

---

[1] See Stockius, *in voce*.　　[2] See Castelli.

בזיותיה *Bizjothjah*, is clearly a compound word, of which the first part must be traced to בזה, the ancient Arabic name of the constellation which we call *Centaurus*. We find the additional name of יה *Jah*, whence the *Iacchus* and *Bacchus* of the Gentiles. This may, perhaps, explain, why *Centaurus* (as in Bayer's forty-first table) is represented with a *thyrsus*, and a flagon of wine. I rather think, that this name comes out pretty clearly, as that of the constellation indicated. I request of my readers to remember, that I am the *first*, who has attempted to give these elucidations to the proper names contained in the ancient, and very mystical, book before us. Where they think I have failed, let them examine the subject with care, and new lights will appear, which can only help to guide them in the course which I have pointed out. If I meet with an opponent, who really understands the question, I think he will be puzzled with the mass of collective evidence, which I have brought together. No Orientalist will pretend to deny, that בזה, the ancient Arabic name for *Centaurus*, forms the primary part of the word before us; and that the name of the God *Iao*,

Iacchus, &c. came from *Iah*, I believe, will be at least generally admitted. [1]

V. 29.

Baalah, " the Moon."

עיים, *Jim*. This word may bear several meanings, *piles, heaps, strong ones*, &c. I suspect a false orthography.

עצם, *Azem*. See what I have said, *in voce Gaza*. I understand *Mendes*.

V. 30.

אלתול, *Eltolad*. By עצם *Azem*, I have understood *Mendes*, or the Sun in the sign of *Capricorn*,

---

[1] See Plutarch. Sympos. L. 5. prob. 5. and Tacitus, L. 5.

for the final *mem* is servile and intensitive, and the root is עז *Az*, " a goat." Now the goat was adored by the Tsabaists as the symbol of *Sol Generator.* It would be idle to waste time in proving this. I shall, therefore, only add, that *El-tolad* signifies *the Sun,* or *the God of generation.*

כסיל, *Chesil,* is the Hebrew name for the constellation of *Orion.* Will it still be said, that there are no astronomical allusions in the text?

V. 31.

צקלג, *Ziklag.* "*The effusion of the fountain, or stream.*" *Onom.* Does this mean the river of *Aquarius?* In fact, Aratus calls this river *effusio aquæ.*

מדמנה, *Madmanah.* In the *Onomasticon* this word is made to signify *dung.* But why not render it " a dimension of the portion, a measure of the allotment?" *Mad-manah,* " a measure of the share given to the tribe of Judah," does not sound so strangely to the ear, as a place called *Dung*, in which the inhabitants were yet content to live. But I suspect, that מנה *manah*, is that same ancient word for the Moon, of which I have already spoken ; and that the word expresses *a proportion or dimension of the Moon,* or perhaps, *of the month.* [1]

סנסנה, *Sansanah.* " The branch of a palm-tree." Trees, in the most ancient dialects, appear to have received their names in allusion to the God, to whom they were sacred. Thus an oak seems to have been called אלה in honor of אלה, or אל, under which names the Tsabaists worshipped the Sun as their principal God. The palm-tree was a well-known solar symbol, and might have been named after that Deity so anciently, and in so many tongues, called Son, San, Sonne, Sun, Zan, Zen, Zoan, &c. [2]

V. 32.

לבאות, *Lebaoth.* " The lions". In the Egyptian

---

[1] See M. Court Gebelin, vol. 4.   [2] Consult Bryant, vol. 1.

Calendar, which I believe is chiefly taken from Avenar, I observe that there are three different lions introduced into the symbols of the sign of *Leo.*

שלחים, *Shilhim,* may mean " messengers, swords, and branches, or shoots of trees." I suspect the orthography.

עין, *Ain,* has been already explained.

רמין, *Rimmon.* " The exalted one." This was a Syrian Deity, and probably indicated the Sun in his highest exaltation, in the sign of *Leo,* in which the Summer solstice must have had place when this book was written.

V. 33.

The allusions seem now to be directed to the constellations at the Autumnal Equinox, when the Sun descends to the lower hemisphere. The first place in the valley is named אשתאול *Eshtaol.* In the *Onomasticon*, and Rumelin's Lexicon, this word is said to be compounded of אשתה שואל, and to signify *dispono me in sepulcrum*. The first word may be a noun with א formative prefixed. שואל answers in signification to *Hades*. The mythologist has no need to be reminded of more. The descent of the Sun to the lower hemisphere is clearly typified. For the meaning of שאול consult Parkhurst.

צרעה, *Zoreah*, " the leprosy." This *Zoreah* was part of the portion of Dan, whose emblem was *Scorpius*, the accursed sign. Herodotus [1] remarks, " that he who has the leprosy, or white scab, among the citizens, neither enters the city, nor mingles with the other Persians; for they say, he has it, for having committed an offence against the Sun." *Zoreah* may also signify *a wasp*, or *a hornet;* and perhaps it may have also denoted *a scorpion.*

אשנה, *Ashnah*, signifies *darkness.* [2]

---

[1] L. 1.   [2] See Castelli.

זנוח, *Zanoah*, seems to signify, " something that repels," or perhaps it is *Zan-och*—the name of the Sun combined with the title *och*, for which see Bryant. [1]

תפוח, *Tapuah*—in the *Onomasticon* is properly rendered *an apple*. This, however, would be a strange name for a place, if there were no mystery. But *Tapuah*, or " the apple," was a symbol of one of the Deities of the Tsabaists, who had a temple erected to Tapuah, called *Bith Tapuah*. This Tapuah then was an astronomical symbol; for the Tsabaists had no other Gods than the Hosts of Heaven. Now observe, that *Coluber*, the adder, placed on the back of *Scorpius*, and the emblem of Dan, was called *Eve* by the ancient Persians, as Chardin attests; and let it be remembered, that a dragon guarded the apples in the gardens of the Hesperides, in the astronomical fable of Hercules. Tapuah was then probably the symbol of Eve's apple; and when it is considered that this fruit ripens about the time, when the Sun

---

[1] Vol. 1.

enters *Scorpius*, and verges on the serpent, as he descends to the lower hemisphere, the region of Typhon, or of Ahriman, the principle of evil, we may, perhaps, combine enough of circumstances to understand, why Tapuah has been connected with the religion of the Tsabaists.

I passed over the preceding word, *En-gannim*, because I thought this would be a more proper place for its explanation. The 12th labor of Hercules, or the fiction concerning the gardens of the Hesperides, relates to the passage of the Sun into the sign of *Cancer*. But this same story is not unconnected with that of *Hercules ingeniculus*, or *Serpentarius*, which constellation, according to Theon, sets as *Cancer* rises. Now in the same position, where we find *Tapuah*, the *Apple*, we also meet with *En-gannim*, " the fountain of the gardens." It will be remembered that Hercules passed the river *Evenus*, or *Even*, after he had obtained the golden apples, and it was there that he slew the Centaur Nessus. This *Even*, as Court Gebelin observes, is literally " the water of the Sun." Now it appears, that *Hercules ingeniculus* and *Centaurus* set about the time, when the river, or fountain, of *Aquarius* rises. The next word *Enam* means likewise " a fountain."

V. 35.

ירמות, *Jarmuth*, " altitude." *Onom.*

עדלם, *Adullam*. Even Rumelinus authorises me to find the sense of this word in the Arabic اعتدل, which signifies the *Equinox*.

שוכה, *Socoh*. In its general sense this word seems to signify *a thorn*, or *pointed branch*. It occurs under this form but twice in Hebrew, as far as I know ; and consequently I think it may have occasionally been used in senses, which are now lost. We must remember, that genuine Hebrew has never been spoken since the captivity, and that all our knowledge of the language is derived from a single volume. Many senses of words have consequently been lost; and it is only occasionally, that they can be recovered by a reference to the cognate dialects. A thorn would be a strange name of a place. But if I have succeeded in showing, that the names from verse 33. relate to the constellations connected with the descent of the Sun to the lower hemisphere, at the Autumnal Equinox, we shall easily find a solution of the word before us. شوكة in Arabic signifies *a scorpion's sting*. The star in *Scorpius* so called is of about the fourth magnitude. By consulting Castelli and Golius, the reader will find that, in spite of the diacritical points, which are placed over the ة, and which give it the sound of a *tau*, the Hebrew and Arabic words are the same.

עזקה, *Azekah*. This word seems to mean " any thing that *surrounds*, *fences*, or *hedges in*." Could this name have been given to the circle of stars, which we call *Corona Australis?*

V. 36.

שערים, *Sharaim*. These were idols in the form of satyrs worshipped by the Tsabaists.[1] Bochart[2]

---

[1] See Parkhurst, *in voce*. [2] Hieroz. p. 641.

has brought together much curious learning on the subject. It would appear, that these *Sharaim* were considered as Demons, and since they were made objects of worship at all, it is not surprising, that honors should be rendered to them when the Sun descended to the lower hemisphere. שערים may also signify *gates*, but I scarcely think that this is the meaning here.

עדיתים, *Adithaim*, literally signifies *ornaments*. [1] But there probably is some latent meaning, which is now lost to us; and from the Arabic عدى I am led to think, that *Adithaim* may have meant sepulcral stones, nor would this be incongruous, if we were to drop the *jod*, and read עדתים, *the testimonies*, or *monuments*.

נדרה, *Gederah*, and נדרתים, *Gederothaim*. These words are expressive of inclosed places. Can

---

[1] See Rumelinus.

there be any allusion here to the place of inter-
ment of Apis, which took place always at the season
of the year, when the Sun descended to the lower
hemisphere? This sepulcral spot was in a temple
near to Memphis, and none might pass the sacred
precincts, but at the time when the symbol of the
departed Sun was there interred. Were there not
so many astronomical and mythological allusions
already so clearly made out, I should not have
offered these merely conjectural suggestions on the
words before us. Perhaps, the constellation which
we call the *Altar*, and which is close to *Scorpius*,
may have been indicated.

V. 37.

צָנָן, Zenan, may signify either *a shield*, or *a
sting.* [1] Is the allusion here to the sting of *Scorpius?*

---

[1] See Buxtorf, *in voce.*

It is possible, that Zenan may be no other than Zan, or Zoan, with an intensitive.

חדשה, *Hadasha.* This word signifies *the new Moon.*

מנדל גד, *Migdal-Gad*, " the tower of Gad." The asterism of Gad has been already mentioned. Ten stars in the sign of *Capricorn* are known by this name to the Orientalists.

V. 38.

דלען, *Dilean.* I find that this word signifies *a gourd*, or *a cucumber*, in Chaldaic. It would be an odd name to give to a city; but I observe, that the urn of *Aquarius* is variously called *Deli, Dalu, Delo, Delu*, in Hebrew, Syriac, and Arabic; and I suspect, that the word was originally written *Delu*, which with the intensitive would be *Delun.* It is to be observed that the Syriac *waw* and the Phœnician *oin* had nearly the same open sound.

A stranger, therefore, who wrote from his ear, might easily convert דלח into דלע. This might the more readily happen, that the great urn, which in the other dialects would have been called *delun*, would have been דלין *delin* in Hebrew.

Mizpeh. " The place of observation." I rather think, that allusion is made to the time of a solstice, when this word is introduced. The place of observation, or observatory, is placed by *Joktheel*, the aggregate of *El*, or of the Sun. By this, I suppose, was meant the aggregate time of his passing from one solstice to another.

V. 39.

Lachish. I have already observed that this word is not to be easily explained. Rumelinus makes it signify *musk;* but I must still render it *flame*, though this may not be the sense.

בצקת, *Bozkath.* This word seems to signify *fermentation.* But I believe it chiefly refers to farinaceous fermentation. The produce of the harvests seems to be indicated, and consequently the season of the year : for after the mention of this word, we find several relating to agriculture and its effects.

Eglon may mean *a circle,* as we have already seen ; but it also signifies *a waggon,* and *an ox.*

Kabbon and *Kitlish* are two words to which I will not venture to affix a sense; because the first seems capable of bearing various meanings; and because I am unable to trace the second to its root. *Lahmam* signifies *bread.* But *Lahmam,* or *Lehem,* was a Deity of the Tsabaists, whose temple is mentioned several times in scripture. *Lehem* was probably the same with Ceres. I know not why *Gederoth* is introduced, unless it indicates sheep-folds, a sense which, I believe, it will bear. *Bith-Dagon,* in this place, deserves particular notice. A Deity of the name of *Dagon* was worshipped under the form of a monster, which had the head and arms of a man, and the tail of a fish. This appears to have been the symbol of the Sun in *Pisces ;* and was considered as the principle of fecundity. Hence *dagon* seems to have been employed to signify " the corn and fruits of the earth." It is perhaps in this sense that we ought to understand the word here. *Naamah* means " the amenity of the country." But this was also a Deity of the Tsabaists. Buxtorf, in his Chaldaic lexicon, states her to have been the same with Cybele, or Rhea, the *Mater Deorum*. *Makkedah* has been already explained. *Libnah* is the *rising Moon*. *Ether* means *abundance, fertility*, &c. *Ashan* is a Chaldaic word signifying *fruit*. *Jiphtah ;* this is the word פתח, which we have had before with a *jod* appellative, and it apparently signifies " the universal principle of fire, or heat," of which *Phtha* was the symbol. *Ashnah* signifies *mutation ;* and *Nezib*, on the contrary, " what is stationary."

Of the remaining words in this chapter, which serve as proper names, I have already explained all to which I can affix any meaning.

My reader ought not to forget, that Judah, or the Sun in *Leo*, was the leader in the camp. This was according to the Egyptian Calendar. In the above account we are to consider, not only the decans in the sign of *Leo*, but its paranatellons, and likewise the course of the Sun through the Zodiac, as commencing at the Summer solstice. With very little trouble, the reader will find, by the help of the celestial globe, how well, as far as we can trace them, the symbols here given answer to the movements of the celestial bodies, to the revolutions of the seasons, and to the agricultural pursuits connected with them.

We are now to look at the allotments of Ephraim, whose emblem was the Bull, and of the half tribe of Manasseh that took the share of Levi, partly appertaining to *Pisces*, and partly to *Aries*.

C. 16.

The first name, which has not been already explained, is לוזה *Luz*. This means *obliquity ;* and the equinoctial point being then in *Aries*, the obliquity of the ecliptic is the first thing which is properly noticed.

אָרְכִּי, *Archi*, " the longitudes"—the degrees of longitude. The lot passeth along unto the boundaries of the degrees of longitude unto *Ataroth*. Now *Ataroth*, the *Crowns*, I conceive to be the stars of *Atarah*, the *Crown*, by which name *Corona Borealis* is still known to the Hebrews. When *Taurus* rises, the *Crown* sets. It is, therefore, true, that the degrees of longitude render it necessary, that the *Crown* and *Taurus* are always opposite, and that when the one rises in the east, the other sets in the west. Can any thing be clearer, than that this is an astronomical allotment? Let not my reader, then, be occasionally discouraged, because I cannot always so clearly explain the meaning of symbols, in use three or four thousand years ago, in a language, which has ceased to be a living one for more than half of that period, and in which only one book has been written.

יַפְלֵטִי, *Japhleti*. Strike off the two servile *jods*, and you will get *Palet*, a title of the Moon of which I have already spoken.

V. 3.

Bith-Horon, " the nether, the lower station of *Hor*, or of the Sun in *Taurus.*"

גזר, *Gezer.* " The segment of the circle."

V. 5.

Ataroth Adar. This seems to signify " the crowns of splendor." But I take *Adar* to have been a Deity of the Tsabaists. *Ataroth* can be nothing else than the constellation *Corona Borealis;* and if my reader will turn to Dupuis, [1] he will scarcely fail to see the propriety of the name here given. In fact, the Arabians still call *Virgo* by the name of *Adra*, or *Adara*, as Hyde attests. The *crown* is the crown of the *Virgin;* and seems to have obtained this appellation from its rising immediately after *Virgo*.

---

[1] Vol. 5.

V. 6.

המכמתת. Our translators make this word sound *Michmethah.* This is of little consequence; but when the lexicographers translate *desiderium,* I find myself obliged to seek for the root in כמה. Now I find this to be the same word with כימה *chimah,* for the *jod* is surely no radical; and *first,* instead of *desiderium,* I would translate " genial heat;" and secondly, I would observe, that כימה *Chima* is the name given to the *Pleiades* in the Book of Job. I suspect then, that our word must bear some relation to those stars; but let my reader judge for himself

תאנתשלה, *Taanath-Shiloh.* The lexicographers seem puzzled with the word תאנת. It is clearly derived from אנה. *Shiloh* I must still consider as the star in *Scorpius* so often mentioned. I translate *near to Shiloh,* and as *Taanath* is translated *prope* in the Onomasticon, I am not quite without authority. Now it is true that *Scorpius* and *Taurus* are so placed, that when the latter descends to the Western horizon, the former rises in the East. Thus the boundary of Ephraim, whose emblem was *Taurus*, went Eastward to the neighbourhood of *Shiloh*.

" And passed by it on the east to *Janohah*."

יגוחה, *Janohah*. The serviles being thrown away, this word resolves itself into נוח *noch*, *quies*. This was the name of the Patriarch, whom we improperly call *Noah*, instead of *Noch*, or *Nuch*. I agree with Court Gebelin, in thinking, that the words νὺξ, *nox*, *nuit*, *night*, &c. came originally from this Hebrew word. In fact, it will be found, that the Gentiles confounded *Noah* with *Dionysus*, *Saturn*, *Janus*, and other types of the Sun in the lower hemisphere. *Noch* indicates repose, connected with night and darkness; and the lower hemisphere is feigned by the mythologists to be the region of silence and night,—of darkness and rest. By the word *Janohah* then, I understand the symbol of the lower hemisphere.

V. 7.

Ataroth, " Corona Borealis."

נערתה, *Naarath.* " *Puella.*" I conclude that *Virgo* is here indicated.

The remaining names have been already explained.

C. 17.

The first proper name, which has not been explained, is *Abiezer ;* but as it is compounded of *Abi,* " a father," a common title of the Sun, and עזר *ezer,* already explained, it can occasion no difficulty.

V. 2.

חלק, *Helek,* may be translated " an astronomical portion." This seems, at least, to be a common sense in which the word is understood in Chaldaic.

U

אשריאל, *Asriel.* This word seems capable of admitting several meanings—" the blessings of *El* (the Sun);—the steps, or progress, of *El;*—the groves of *El.*" But consult Buxtorf. [1]

שכם, *Shechem* signifies *the dawn.*

חפר, *Hepher.* Rumelinus makes this name signify *opprobrium ;* but who would take such a name, or what parent would give it to his child? חפר in Chaldaic signifies *to redden,* and metaphorically *to blush ;* hence, it would seem, the word came to import *shame,* &c. I understand the word before us to allude to the redness of the evening sky, opposed to *shechem,* " the dawn."

שמידע, *Shemida.* I cannot conceive on what principle this name is translated *agnovit Deus* in the Onomasticon. It means literally *the name of Science.* I admit, that this seems a very strange name; but it had a Cabbalistical meaning, which

---

[1] *In voce,* אשר.

I am unable to explain.[1] Manasseh had allotted to half his tribe a portion of the *Amorite*, that is, of *Aries;* and as the astronomers by their science had been enabled to reform the year, and to fix its opening at the true time of the vernal equinox, which had passed from *Taurus* to *Aries*, there may be some allusion to this in the name before us.

V. 3.

צלפחד, *Zelophehad*—literally *the shadow of fear.* I imagine some allusion is made to the night. This *Zelophehad* has several daughters, all of whom we shall find to have been symbols of the Moon, or of her wanderings.

מחלה, *Mahlah.* This was one of the four names, given to the four mothers of the devils by the

---

[1] See Buxtorf's Chaldaic Lexicon, p. 937.

Jews. [1] It comes from חלה, and signifies *disease*. This name is associated with that of *Lilith, Ilythia*, the same with the *Juno Lucina* of the Latins. [2] There can be no doubt, therefore, that *Mahlah*, or *Malhat*, as the Rabbins write it, was a lunar symbol, but of bad omen.

נעה, *Noah*. I translate this word *motus* with Rumelinus. But there were אלהי הנע, " Gods of the motion." [3] In fact, the *sistrum* in the rites of Cybele and Isis was called *Menana* מנענע, evidently from this word *Nah*, or *Noah*. But I observe that the three words *Nah, Hoglah, Milchah*, which are divided as three proper names in the translations, seem connected with each other in the original, the particle *vau* not being employed to separate them. It would appear, however, that the first word *nah* means the motion of the *sistrum*, which we know was a symbol of the Goddess of the Night. My reader cannot have

---

[1] See Elias Levita.

[2] See Kircher's Œdipus, vol. 1. p. 321.   [3] 2nd Kings, 18. 34.

any need of explaining to him the form of the *sistrum*, or the nature of the rites practised in honor of the Moon by the Priests of Isis, *sistrataque turba.*

The next word חגלה *Hoglah*, has direct allusion to those rites. חגלה is composed, as Mr. Hutchinson observes, of חנה–גלה. Now this is literally a description of the circular dance of the worshippers of the Moon when they celebrated her orgies with *sistrums*, drums, cymbals, &c. It signifies " tripping the circle, or the circular dance."

מלכה, *the Queen.* That *Milcah,* " the Queen," was a title of the Moon, must be known to every one who has read the Bible. It is evident, then, that the three words before us signify " the motion of the circular dance of *Milcah,*" under which name the Moon was adored by the Tsabaists. The allusion in the text, to her erratic course, is as clear as it was in the practice of the mysteries, which were celebrated in her honor.

תרצה, *Tirzah.* After the mention of *Malhah* and *Milcah,* two lunar titles, or symbols, we can

scarcely suppose that *Tirzah* was a real personage.
This name indicates desire, or concupiscence; and
was probably a name given to the idol of the Moon.
Solomon says to his beloved, [1] " thou art beautiful
as *Tirzah ;*" and shortly after he adds, " thou art
fair as the Moon." We have seen, that the name of
Jerusalem served for a solar type, and *Tirzah*, I
believe to have been a lunar symbol. For a list
of names given to the Moon, as Venus, Juno, &c.
consult Apuleius. [2]

V. 4.

Eleazer. This word is compounded of *El,*
" the Sun," and עזר, which last word seems to signify
the same thing with עזרה, " the court of the temple."
Now the temple (I must still repeat it) was a type
of the universe.

V. 8.

Tappuah—already explained.

---

[1] Cant. 6. 4.   [2] *Metamorph.* L. 2.

V. 9.

קנה, *Kanah.* I believe I have neglected to explain this word, where it occurs before. It means *a reed, a cane, a measuring rod.* In the ancient Zodiacs, the sign of *Libra* was repre-sented by a man holding a measuring rod.[1] *Libra,* the emblem of *Asher,* is the opposite sign to *Aries,* a part of which was portioned unto the half tribe of Manasseh. But mention is here made of the river *Kanah.* The *nahal,* translated sometimes " a river," sometimes " a valley," as caprice directs, is the ancient name of the Nile; and the celestial river, or constellation, which we call *Eridanus,* is termed *nahal* in the astronomical tables of the Egyptians who, lest there should be a mistake, term it *Nahal Mizraim.* Now *Nahal,* the *Eridanus,* is suffi-ciently near to *Taurus* and *Aries ;* and it is called

---

[1] See Kircher's planisphere; Rumelinus *in voce,* קנה; and Castelli *in voce,* כנו.

the river of the measuring rod, for a reason which appears obvious. The measuring rod was placed in the hand of *Serapis Niloticus,* [1] and this symbol was properly referred to the *balance,* because it was when the Sun was in this sign, that the river began to decrease. Consequently, it was when the *balance* came to the Meridian at midnight in the Spring, that the river commenced its annual augmentation. This seems to be the reason, why it is called *nahal kanah,* "the river of the measuring rod."

V. 10.

Issachar and *Asher.* Their emblems were *Cancer* and *Libra.*

V. 11.

Bith-shean and her towns. Shean is the same with *Shan,* already explained. The lexicographers,

---

[1] See Kircher and Jablonski,

however, will have it to be different, and translate, " the house of tranquillity."

Ibleam is derived from בלע, already explained.

Dor, already explained.

Taanach, already explained.

Megiddo, already explained. The remaining proper names in this chapter have been likewise explained.

C. 18.

Shiloh—a star in *Scorpius*.

V. 11.

Benjamin. His emblem was the *Twins*.

The proper names have all been explained down to verse 21.

קציץ, *Keziz.* This is the same in signification with קצה, by which the Chaldeans understood either tropic. I rather suppose, that of *Cancer* is here meant.

V. 22.

Bith-Arabah—already explained.

צמרים, *Zemaraim.* " The highest branches of a tree."

V. 23.

עיים, *Avim.* This word seems to signify *curves, obliquities,* &c. I observe that in Arabic عوا is the name of a station of the Moon in *Virgo.* [1]

---

[1] See Golius, *in voce.*

פרה, *Parah*, " a heifer." This was possibly an emblem of Isis, or the Moon.

עפרה, *Ophrah*. Rumelin pretends that this signifies *dust*. This would be a strange name to give to a city. In *Micah*[1] we find the following words—" in the house of Aphrah (or Ophrah) roll thyself in the dust." It is clear then, that there was an idol named *Ophrah ;* but who was this dusty Divinity? I confess myself unable to solve the question; but I am inclined to think that the worship of this Deity was connected with that of *Thammuz.*

V. 24.

כפר העמוני, *Chephar-haamonai.* " The village of the Ammonites." The Egyptians worshipped the Sun in *Aries* under the name of *Ammon.* Is כפר " Capar" (for so it may be expressed in Roman

---

[1] C. 1. V. 10.

letters,) connected with the Arabic *Cabar*, a title given to Venus or the Moon?

Ophni. I cannot trace this word to the Hebrew, unless, by a transposition of the letters, we bring it from ענף, *a branch.* Is any allusion made to the branch of the palm-tree in the sign of Virgo?[1]

גבע. *Gaba*, the *concave*—already explained.

V. 25.

Gibeon is the same word with an intensive.

Ramah, הרמה. *The high place—the sky.*

Beeroth, literally the *Wells.* This word has occurred several times; but I had not remarked before, that the Arabians call certain stars in Eridanus, the *Wells.*[2]

---

[1] See the Zodiacs of Dendera.

[2] See Hyde's Commentaries on Ulug Beig. p. 48 and 49.

V. 26.

Mizpeh, already explained.

כפירה, *Chephirah*—" a lion."

מצה, *Mozah.* I know not the meaning.

V. 27.

רקם, *Rekem*—signifies *embroidery* in Hebrew. This could hardly have been the name of a place. I cannot explain it.

ירפאל, *Irpeel.* Rumelin translates this name *remittat Deus.* This is an odd name for a place. I would rather translate *remittat Sol,* not only because *El,* when found in heathen names, generally signifies the Sun, but because I think an astronomical allusion suits with the rest.

תראלה, *Taralah.* Rumelin makes this word signify *maledictio dirissima.* But who would call a city by such a name? I imagine, that this is a corruption from the Chaldaic תור־אלה—*Taurus Dei,* or *Taurus Solis.*

V. 28.

צלע, *Zelah.* This word signifies *a rib,* or it signifies *limping.* Either of these would be a singular appellation of a city. But the Sun was represented under the form of a limping boy by the Egyptians. This singular symbol was named by them ϬΡ—ΨШҍ—ΡⱭΤ. [1]

אלף, *Eleph* signifies *dux,* also *bos,* [2] also *dux armenti.* The Bull in ancient times had been the leader of the zodiacal animals. His place was afterwards occupied by *Aries,* called by the Latins *dux gregis.*

---

[1] See Jablonski, *in Harpocrate.*   [2] See Buxtorf, *in voce.*

C. 19.

The lot of Simeon was part of *Pisces*. We must always recollect the constellations, which rise or set while the Sun is in any of the signs, in order to follow the author. In describing the lot of Judah, the annual circuit of the Sun seemed to be pointed out. In the other lots, the description is chiefly confined to the paranatellons of the sign, which is the emblem of the tribe. I shall pass over the names already explained.

V. 4.

בתול, *Bethul,* for בתולה, *Bethulah,* the name which the Hebrews gave to the sign of *Virgo.* When the Sun is in *Pisces,* the sign *Bethulah* comes to the meridian at midnight.

V. 5.

Bith-Marcaboth—" the house or temple of the Chariots, or Charioteers." It seems that the constellation *Auriga* is still called *Marcab*, " the Charioteer," by the Arabians. [1]

הצר סוסה, *Hazar Susah,* " the hall of the cavalry:" apparently the constellations *Pegasus* and *Equiculus* are indicated.

בית לבאות, *Bith-Lebaoth.* " The house of the Lions." Simeon had a share of the portion of Judah. In fact, *Leo* passes the meridian about twelve at night, when the Sun enters *Pisces*.

V. 10.

We are now to consider the lot of Zebulon, whose emblem was the ship *Argo,* and whose sign was *Capricorn*.

---

[1] See Castelli.

שריד, *Sarid.* In Hebrew signifies *superstes.* But I am inclined to think, that it may have meant a *sardonyx* here.[1] The *Sardonyx* was one of the twelve stones in the breastplate of the priests; and these twelve stones represented, according to Clemens Alexandrinus, the twelve signs of the Zodiac.[2] Kircher has shown that the Sardonyx was the precious stone on which was engraved the name of Reuben, whose emblem was *Aquarius.*[3] The possession of Zebulon, *(Capricorn)* was therefore contiguous to that of Reuben, *(Aquarius)* denoted by *Sarid,* a *sardonyx.*

V. 11.

The sea; employed as a symbol; this word has been already explained.

מרעלה, *Maralah.* Rumelin translates this name *quæ tremere facit.* This seems to be a strange name to give a place.

---

[1] Consult Castelli.   [2] Strom. L. 5.   [3] Œdip. vol.2.

x

דבשת, *Dabasheth*, " the lump on a camel's back."
Onom.

יקנעם, *Jokneam.* Rumelin translates, *compara-
bitur populus, vel nidulans factus est populus.* I
think it better to avow, that I am ignorant of the
meaning.

V. 12.

Some of the preceding words I have been unable
to explain, and have, therefore, resigned them to
the lexicographers, who have been pleased to think,
that there were really cities called—*She who makes
tremble,—The lump on a camel's back,—Nidulans
factus est populus,* &c. The name of *Chisloth-
tabor* recals us so clearly to astronomy, that I have
no doubt, that the former names related to it,
though we are now ignorant of their signification.
Chisloth-Tabor is clearly an exotic name; and I
cannot question, that כסלות תבר has the same sense
with כסילי תבר. The allusion must then be to
the month *Cisleu,* and to the stars of *Orion.* But

תבר *Tabor* is a proper name, to which I can affix no sense. Could it have been originally written הגבר? Certainly כסיל הגבר is a name by which we should immediately recognise the constellation of Orion. I observe that the LXX omit *Tabor*.

דברת, *Daberath*. *Dabar*, or *Dobar*, was an ancient oriental name for the Planet Mercury. [1] In fact دبار *Debar* is the Arabic for " Wednesday," *dies Mercurii*. But I rather imagine that *Daberath*, or *Debarath*, must have been an ancient name for the *Hyades*, of which the brilliant is called *Al-Debaran*.

Japhia, " splendor"—already explained.

V. 13.

Gittah, or *Gath-hepher* has been explained.

---

[1] See Pococke on Abulfeda, and Golius on Alfragan.

עתה קצין, *Ittah-Kazin* in Chaldaic signifies " *the curve of the tropics.*" [1]

רמון המתאר, *Remmon-methoar*. *Remmon* signifies *the high place*, or, as I understand it, *the starry heavens*. *Remmon-methoar* is translated by Rumelin *civitas circulo definita*. I, therefore, translate " the high place, or the heavens, encompassed by a circle." The Zodiac was probably meant.

To Neah. I rather think it should be *of Neah.* This word implies " motion." *Remmon-methoar-neah*, seems to mean " the moving sphere of the heavens."

V. 14.

חנתן, *Hanathon*, " the camp"—probably the camp of the celestial army, or hosts of heaven.

---

[1] See Castelli.

Jiphtah-El—already explained, " the fire of the Sun."

V. 15.

קטת, *Katath.* Rumelin makes this word signify *parva, humilis*, &c. but he is certainly mistaken, since קטת cannot come from קטן. I imagine this word has a similar signification with קיט in Chaldaic, and with قيظ in Arabic; and by which word the season of the year, from the rising of the *Pleiades* to the rising of *Canopus*, was denoted. [1]

נהלל, *Nahallal.* Rumelinus translates *ductus*, and brings the name from נהל. I pretend, that the second ל is radical, and that the נ is servile and appellative. Now I observe that the Arabians call the Moon هلال, and the ancient Hebrews denominated the Morning star הילל *Hilel.* The root then being הלל, I am led to think, that נהלל

---

[1] See Castelli and Golius.

has the same meaning with הילל. In the first, the prefixed נ is appellative, and in the second the inserted י is merely formative. I translate *nahalal,* " Lucifer, the morning star."

Shimron has been already explained.

ידבלה, *Idalah.* Rumelin makes this word signify *a place of execration.* But why should men be supposed to give such names to their places of abode; and surely the name does not authorise this translation. As the word is written I can give no meaning to it; but the readers of Bochart will allow me to say, that in the cognate dialects the *jod* and *aleph* often changed places. Indeed this happens very frequently in the Hebrew itself. Now I find that אדאלה comes very near to the Syrian עדל *Adal,* or עדלא *Adala,* which is the name of the *Wain,* or *Great Bear.*[1]

Bith-lehem, already explained.

----

[1] See Castelli.

We now come to the lot of Issachar, whose emblem was *Cancer,* or *Hermanubis.*

V. 18.

שונם, *Shunem,* or *Sunem.* This seems to have been a solar title. [1] It is strange to find the lexicographers perverting the meaning of words, which either are not Hebrew, or can only now be found among the proper names. *Sunem* is probably the same in sense with *San, Son, Sun, Zan, Zoan,* &c. and then comes a lexicographer, who tells us, that *Sunem* was the name of a city, signifying *pinguedo.*

Chesulloth — " Constellation of Orion," already explained.

V. 19.

Haphraim—from חפר, already explained.

---

[1] See Bryant, vol. 1.

שיאון, *Shihon.* Why is the *aleph* aspirated?
This word is composed of שי, *a gift*, and און, *a
solar title*, of which I have frequently spoken. It
would then signify *Munus Solis;* but it is very
probable, that the word was originally of the same
class with *San, Son,* &c. mentioned above.
Rumelin makes *Shihon* signify *vastatio.* This
would be a strange name to give to a city.

אנחרת, *Anaharath.* The lexicographers make
this word signify *groaning*, or *snoring.* The latter
is in fact the sense, if the word come from נחר,
according to their derivation. But who ever heard
of a city named *snoring?* The meaning of *Anaharath* seems to me extremely obvious. It is
composed of אן, *the solar title*, and חרת, from חרה,
arsit.

V. 20.

רבית, *Rabbith.* " *Magna, multa.*" Onom. But
I rather imagine, that the word implies augmentation here. I translate *increment ;* and I believe

the name was formed in allusion to the season of
the year, when the Nile augments. This takes
place when the Sun is in *Cancer*, the emblem of
Issachar.

קשיון, *Kishion.* Rumelin translates *durities.* Of
course he derives the word from קשה. I cannot
help suspecting, that there is some error of orthography here. In all events I would rather refer
the word to קשה, a kind of vessel in the form of
a *patera*, which seems to have been employed as
a measure for liquids. Whether, or not, the word
before us, which I understand to signify *a great
measuring vessel*, could indicate the Nilometer, I
must leave others to determine. I find the following passage in Suidas at the word *Sarapis.* Τοῦτον δὲ
οἱ μὲν Δία ἔφασαν εἶναι, οἱ δὲ τὸν Νεῖλον, διὰ τὸ
μόδιον ἔχειν ἐν τῇ κεφαλῇ, καὶ τὸν πῆχυν, ἤγουν τὸ
τοῦ ὕδατος μέτρον. " Some say that he (Sarapis)
is Jupiter, others the Nile, on account of the
modius on his head, and the cubit, or measure of
the water." But I am apt to suspect, that Serapis
was also represented with a measuring vessel, or
patera, similar to that which I take to be meant by
Kishion. Certainly in the procession of Egyptian

priests, one is thus described by Clemens—*Ἔπειτα ὁ στολιστὴς τοῖς προειρημένοις ἕπεται, ἔχων τόν τε τῆς δικαιοσύνης πῆχυν, καὶ τὸ σπονδεῖον.* " Then the στολιστὴς follows the above-mentioned, holding the cubit of justice, and the cup of libation." [1] Apuleius describes a priest in the pomp, who carried *indicium æquitatis* in one hand, and a golden vase in the other, whence he poured forth libations. Abenephius, quoted by Kircher, says that the Egyptians adored the idol of Canobus under the form of a vase; and Canobus was a type of the Nile.

It seems extremely probable, that קשיון is here written for קישון. This was actually the name of a river, and may have been also one of the many appellations given to the Nile.

אבץ, *Abez* may signify either *increment*, or the reverse. [2] I cannot help thinking, that all these names allude to the state of the Nile, when the Sun was in *Cancer* the emblem of Issachar.

---

[1] Strom. L. vi. p. 456. in my edition. [2] See Rumelin, *in voce.*

V. 21.

רמת, *Remeth*, " altitude." *Onom.* Does this allude to the Nile's coming to its height?

En-gannim. " The fountain of Gardens."

En-haddah. " The fountain of joy." *Onom.*

בית פצץ, *Bith-Pazzez.* I know not the meaning. Rumelin translates *domus dispergentis;* but this does not appear authorised.

V. 22.

Tabor, already explained.

שחצומה, *Shahazimah. Leontopolis. Onom.* This was the boundary of Issachar, and in fact *Leo* is contiguous with *Cancer.*

Bith-Shemesh. " The house of the Sun." *Leo* is the domicile of *Sol.*

V. 24.

The next lot is that of *Asher*, whose emblem was *Libra.*

V. 25.

חלקת, *Halkath.* See *Helek*, already explained.

חלי, *Hali.* Rumelin translates *decus.* But this ornament was a necklace. [1] Now it seems strange to call a town, a necklace. There must be a meaning which is now lost. R. S. Iarchi says that חלי *hali* is originally an Arabic word. This of course is حلي, and I think it may have anciently signified *some kind of fruit*—perhaps *dates.* [2] The season

---

[1] See Buxtorf.   [2] See Castelli, p. 1249.

of the year, and the labors incident to it, namely the gathering of fruits, may be indicated by the names before us.

בטן, *Beten*, has two significations—*a belly*, and *a nut*. We have seen that the belly of *Aries* received this name; but I rather think here, that the nut is indicated. In fact nuts are generally gathered, when the Sun is in *Libra*, as well as other fruits.

אכשף, *Achshaph*. In Hebrew this word signifies *a necromancer*, or *an astrologer*; but in Chaldaic it also signifies *a prune*.[1]

V. 25.

אלמלך, *Alamelech*. This is so evidently a solar title, that it is not requisite to say more of it.

Amad and *Misheal* are two names about which I might say much; but as their meaning is not

---

[1] See Buxtorf's Chaldaic Lexicon, *in voce* בשף.

obvious, I pass them over, only observing, that Rumelin does not, as far as I can find, explain the first, and that his etymology of the latter is to me unintelligible. He explains *Carmel* as a country fit for sowing and planting; but כרמל is plainly a contraction for כרם—אל, " the vine of El, or of the Sun." שיחור ליבנת *Shihor-Libnath—Libnath* is only another feminine form of *Libnah*. The name must, therefore, mean the dark part of the Moon, or perhaps the *crepusculum*, which precedes her rising.

V. 27.

בית העמק, *Bith-Emek* is the first proper name in this verse, which has not been explained. It is evident that the constellations seen, while the Sun is in *Libra*, are now pointed out. *Emek* is generally rendered *a valley;* but the house of *the valley* seems to indicate the lower hemisphere.

נעיאל, *Neiel.* Rumelin translates *germinare faciet Deus.* I must always repeat, that *El* in heathen names signifies *the Sun.* I understand *Neiel* to signify *the germinating Sun.*

כבול, *Cabul.* Buxtorf translates this *compes;* and R. Solomon says that the country was so called because the soil was argillaceous, and people's feet are apt to stick in clay. This is absolute trifling. Rumelin makes *Cabul* signify *sicut id quod evanuit tanquam nihil.* A most singular name is this; but the explanation is not authorised by the word. *Cabul* must mean " a shackle, or ligament of some sort." Michaelis says the region was so called, because it was to have been ceded to Hiram in order to discharge the debt due to him by Solomon. But it was not ceded to him. Michaelis gets rid of this difficulty by saying, that it was named *Cabul* sarcastically by Hiram. I cannot believe, that the Jews would consent to call a district of their country by a nickname given to it by a stranger. I think we must find a better reason for the name than has yet been assigned. I have shown that the Provinces and Cities of Egypt were divided and named with reference to astronomy, and I have been endeavouring to prove that the same thing happened with respect to Judea. Now it has been remarked a little above, that the constellations, (seen while the Sun is in *Libra* the emblem of Asher, whose lot we are now considering,) appear to be indicated. When the Sun enters *Libra*, *Pisces* declines from the Meridian at midnight. In *Pisces* is the link, or ligament, called σύνδεσμος, by the Greeks, and still represented in our celestial globes. I think, that *Cabul* expresses this part of the constellation, after which the country was named.

The remaining names have been explained already down to V. 32. Among them we find, *Hebron*, " conjunction ;"—*Rehob*, "space, or latitude ;"—*Hammon*, the sign of *Aries ;*—*Zidon*, the great hunter, and possibly the hunter *Orion;* —*Achzib*, the name of a star, for which consult Castelli in כזב.

The next lot was that of ˉ*Naphthali*, whose emblem was *Virgo*.

V. 33.

Heleph has been already noticed, but I ought to have remarked, that it seems to have been an astronomical term among the Chaldeans. They had a kind of clock, which was called חלף סדרא, " the mutation, or transition of the series, or order"—I suppose, the order of time.

אלון, *Allon*—" a tree, an oak tree." It will be remembered, that Avenar placed a tree among the emblems of the sign of *Virgo*.

צעננים, *Zaanannim*. The word צען *Zan* is originally Egyptian, and the same with *Soan*, or *Zoan*, a solar title. [1]

Adami, already explained. But *Adami Nekeb* seem to signify " the red ones of the hollow or

---

[1] See Castelli; Kircher, vol. 1. p. 21. and Bryant vol. 1. p. 42.

concave place." I must leave my reader to find out the sense, as it does not appear quite obvious to me.

Jabneel—already explained.

Lakum—This word, brought by Rumelin from מקל, seems to express *exsiccation*.

Hukkok. See what I have said concerning *Cepheus* in another dissertation.

יראון, *Iron* is the next name which occurs, and which has not been explained. This name is probably another form for יראה, " an idol of the Tsabaists." [1]

Migdal-El-Horem. I understand this to signify " the tower, or station of the Sun of great heat —or the station of the burning Sun." Perhaps the station of *Hor* in *Taurus* was meant.

---

[1] See Buxtorf's Chaldaic Lexicon.

Bith-aneth. The lexicographers translate *the house of affliction.* But *Aneth* appears to have been a Deity of the Tsabaists. I suspect it to have been a lunar title.

Bith-Shemesh—" the house of the Sun."

The names in the lot of Dan have been for the most part already explained.

Ir-Shemesh. " The city of the Sun."

שעלבין, *Shaalbin*—" the dwelling of the foxes." This may easily be a false orthography, and the *ain* may have been written for an *aleph.* The word would then signify *the lower dwelling, the inferior abode*—in short, it would answer to *Hades,* which in the astronomical fables denoted the lower hemisphere. Perhaps allusion may be made to the stars in *Scorpius,* called شوله by the Arabians. The open sound of the *ain* may have often misled the ear, in writing proper names, and it may have been here inserted for a *vau,* or for a *jod.* But I think the first explanation the more probable of the two.

יתלה, *Jethlah.* Rumelin translates this name—
he shall suspend. A strange sense for a proper
name. I observe that תלי is the Chaldaic name
for *Serpens Ophiuchi,* the constellation which is
contiguous with *Scorpius.*

לשם, *Leshem.* The name of certain stars in
Scorpius. [1]

I shall now close my commentary on the Book
of Joshua. I have said enough either to prove
or to disprove my theory concerning it; and I
must leave the decision to the judgment of my
reader.

---

[1] See my former Dissertations.

V.

Dissertation,

&c. &c.

SKETCH OF A COMMENTARY,

OR

Dissertation,

ON THE

BOOK OF JUDGES.

———◆———

C. 1.

HAVING extended the last Dissertation to so great a length, I shall endeavour to be very concise in this; and shall only notice some parts of the Book of Judges, which seem to me to bear an immediate and distinct reference to astronomy. For the proper names explained in the preceding Dissertation, my reader will of course consult it.

V. 5.

אדני בזק, *Adoni-Bezek.* The solar title *Adoni*, or *Adonis,* is known as such to every schoolboy.

Bezek may signify either *lightning*, or *a lamb*. The Lord of lightning, or the Lord of the *Lamb*, or *Ram*, (by both of which names the sign of *Aries* was known,) evidently indicates the Sun, the principal Deity of the Tsabaists.

V. 7.

Threescore and ten Kings. The numbers 70 and 72 recur very frequently in the sacred text. It is to be observed, that the Orientalists divided each Zodiacal sign into three parts. The twelve signs of the zodiac were then divided in thirty-six parts. These parts were again variously subdivided. Considered with respect to the circle, they were divided by 10, and being multiplied by 12, amounted to 360, the number of days contained in the civil year. Considered with respect to the twelve signs of the Zodiac, they were divided and multiplied by 12. For want of better words, I shall call these 36 divisions of the Zodiac either *Decans*, or *Dodecans*. The three decans of each sign contained 10 degrees each, amounting to 30 for

each sign, and 30 × 12 = 360. The three dodecans contained 12 degrees each, amounting to 36
for each sign, and 36 × 12 = 432. The excess
of 432 above 360 is 72. But the 36 decans and
dodecans into which the whole Zodiac was divided,
being multiplied by 2, amount to 72; and this
number seems consequently to have become a
favorite one among the Cabalists. Now I
observe, that the Cabalists and calculators reckoned all periods as circles. They, therefore,
considered the first and last terms of a period as
unit. Thus they reckoned the first dodecan or
decan of *Aries*, as the same with the last dodecan,
or decan of *Pisces*; and consequently instead of
counting 36 decans and dodecans in the Zodiacal
circle, they reduced them to 35. Again, they
counted the first term, or degree, of the first dodecan in the sign, as one and the same with the last
term, or degree, of the last dodecan. Thus the
number of degrees in the three dodecans, amounted,
according to this mode of calculation, to 35, instead
of 36. Hence it happens, that when the degrees
of the three dodecans are multiplied by 2, we find
sometimes, 35 × 2 = 70, and sometimes

$36 \times 2 = 72$. Perhaps the hieroglyphic, by which the revolutions of time were denoted, will help to explain, how the first term and the last were considered as unit.

Here we see the tail of the serpent in his mouth; and the first and last terms of the circle united.

I have little doubt, that this explanation of the numbers 70, and 72, so often recurring, will elucidate many passages in the sacred text.

V. 34. 35. 36.

The Amorites. The word אמר, *amor, agnus,* was the Chaldaic appellation of the sign of *Aries.* But *Scorpius,* the opposite sign to *Taurus,* is preceded in its descent by the rising of *Aries* on the opposite side of the hemisphere. *Scorpius* was the emblem of Dan.

The *Amorites* would dwell in Mount *Heres* in *Aijalon.* *Heres* signifies " the Sun." *Aijalon* " the great *Ram.*" The allusion to the sign of *Aries* can hardly be questioned. *Akrabbim,* " the *Scorpions,* the stars of *Scorpius.*"

C. 4.

Sisera. Hiller translates this name " the exaltation of the Moon."

Harosheth of the Gentiles. But in the original the words are חרשת הגוים, *Harosheth of the Goim.* The ancient Persian and Chaldaic word for *a bull,* was *Go,* or *Gao,* and by this name they indicated the sign of *Taurus.* *Harosheth* will bear many meanings, but I find, that the lexicographers translate the words before us, "the woods of the Gentiles." The dwelling of *Sisera* was then a pretty spacious one. But the stars of heaven were continually indicated by trees, groves, woods, &c. I understand, therefore, by these woods of the Goim, the stars of *Taurus,* where was the dwelling of *Sisera,* the exaltation of the Moon. The 20 years may be reckoned 20 days.

Deborah. I take this prophetess to have belonged to those stars in *Taurus,* which we call the *Hyades.* See what I have already said concerning *Al-debaran.* But Rumelin makes *Deborah* signify a *bee,* and the meaning is really so uncertain, that I shall not pretend to fix it. If, however, we abide by the lexicographers, I would rather translate, *order, march, series ;* the march of the celestial hosts being typified.

לפידות, *Lapidoth*, " lights, torches, &c."
Whether the stars were indicated by this word, I
know not.

Barak, " the lightning."

Abinoam, " the father of amenity." Perhaps it
is meant that the father of the pleasant season is
the father of the lightning, as *Abinoam* was the
father of *Barak*.

The signs of *Virgo*, *Capricorn*, and *Taurus*, are
indicated by Naphthali, Zebulon, and Ephraim. I
have already confessed my embarrassment with
respect to the word *Tabor*. I think the *teth* and
the *tau* may have been exchanged. *Tabor* may
then signify " the middle or central part."

The river Kishon Sisera. My reader will
observe what I have before said of *Kishon ;* and
the word here translated *a river* is נחל—Certainly
the original name of the Nile, which answered in
astronomy to the river called by us the *Eridanus*,
and which in the Egyptian planispheres reached

from *En-Regel,* the fountain of the foot of *Orion,* to the urn of *Aquarius,* which was its source.

Jabin and *Hazor* are two words that relate to parts of the temple, the type of the Universe.

" *Heber* the *Kenite,* the child of *Hobab,*" signifies *conjunction,* the *balancer,* the son of the *beloved.*

Jael signifies *a kind of goat.* I know not whether the allusion be to *Capricorn.* It seems to me that the whole of this story relates to a reform in the Calendar, concerning the Moon's revolutions. In fact, the words of Deborah confirm this conjecture. The 20th verse of C. 5th, should be translated, " the stars fought from heaven, from their own exaltations they fought against Sisera—*i. e.*—the exaltation of the Moon."

C. 6.

The next allegory relates to the defeat of the Midianites by Gideon. I am of opinion, that this story refers to the harvest season, which by the use of the rural year had been miscalculated.

Midian, " the measure," seems to imply the measurement of the heavens, and consequently of time. The Midianites were probably those, who having made false measurements, or false calculations, concerning the rising of those constellations when the people were to sow and to reap, had occasioned a dearth in the country.

Amalekites. I have explained this word in a former Dissertation. It signifies " the people of the beetles, or locusts, or caterpillars." These animals so destructive of the harvests are brought in innumerable quantities by the South-East winds, which blow so frequently in Syria during the Summer and Autumn.

Ophrah signifies *dust.* It has been already mentioned; but it seems here to imply the clouds of dust brought by the same winds.

Joash signifies *Despair.*

Abi-Ezer seems here to signify *the father of help*—Despair begot the remedy.

Gideon signifies *cutting down*. The cutting down of the corn seems to be implied. But he who did this was compelled to go to war with the Measurers, or false calculators, and to destroy Baal, and the Grove, the emblems which these idolatrous and ignorant astrologers had set up as types of the Sun and the hosts of heaven.

פרה, *Phurah* may signify either *a fruitful branch*, or *a heifer*.

Bith-Shittah. " The house, or mansion of declination" — an astronomical term already explained.

Zererath. " The narrow place, or angle;" probably that formed by the ecliptic and equator at the autumnal equinox.

Abel-Meholah. The lamentation of *Meholah*, otherwise called *Mahlah*, " an idol of the Moon."

This *Mahlah* was feigned to have been one of the four mothers that brought forth evil spirits.

טבת, *Tabbath.* " The month of December, or the tenth Moon."

ערב, *Oreb.* " The evening."

זאב, *Zeeb.* This word signifies *a wolf*—but I have shown that it was a symbol of Mercury, or Anubis, and that it particularly indicated the crepuscular light. '

C. 8.

There seemed to be two objects yet to remain for Gideon, or the reformer who introduced the reaping of the harvests at the proper season. The first was to fix the sacrifices at the proper periods

---

Diss. on the 49th chap. of Genesis.

of the year; and the second might have been to determine the true time by the help of the gnomon, or dial. It would appear that the Midianites, or Measurers, had miscalculated the times for offering up sacrifices, and had also failed to place the dials in their just positions with respect to the Cardinal points.

V. 5.

סכות, *Succoth*. This name appears to come in this place from the Chaldaic word סכה, *to speculate, to observe*. The reformer applied for assistance to the men of speculations, or in other words to those employed in the observatories; but his request was refused by them.

זבח, *Zebah*. This word signifies *a sacrifice*. The reformer probably meant, either to regulate the seasons when sacrifices should be offered; or, perhaps, to abolish the celebration of sacrifices offered to idols.

צלמנע, *Zalmunah.* I find in the Onomasticon that this word signifies *the disturbed shadow.* I conclude, then, that allusion is made to the gnomons not being properly placed. It was of course necessary for the reformer of the Calendar to destroy this disturbed shadow.

Penuel. This word seems to me to signify *the aspects of El,* or *of the Sun.* The two roots are clearly פנה and אל.

Karkor, is translated *destructissimus,* by Rumelin &c. I rather imagine that it means the cold, or Winter season,—from קר, *frigus.*

נבח, *Nobach.* "*Latrator.*"[1] The *latrator Anubis* was the Egyptian symbol for the planet Mercury.

Jogbehah, is translated *exultabitur* in the Onomasticon. It is certainly from נבה; but as a proper name it probably implied some of the celestial host.

---

[1] See Bochart's derivation of *Anubis* from this root.

Ephod. This made part of the dress of the Priests. [1] Gideon had 70 legitimate sons. This type has been already explained. The first and last terms in the three dodecans, taken as unit, amount to 35; and $35 \times 2 = 70$. But the first and last terms are taken as unit to express the continuity of the circular rotation; and the tail of the serpent is placed in his mouth to show, that time is still resolved into time. When, therefore, the revolution of time divided by 36 is represented, the first and last terms are united, and the cycle, or circle is reckoned *quasi* 35. But upon the same principle, if the cycle or circle be 72 and the first and last terms be united, in order to express the circular continuity, the number will be 71. We find that Gideon had 70 legitimate sons, and one bastard.

Abi-Melech—This is a solar title composed, of *Abi*, " a father," and *Melech*, " a king."

---

[1] Consult the extracts which I have made from Clemens.

C. 9. 10. 11. 12.

My reader will easily follow the allegories contained in these chapters, even by the help of a common lexicon. I proceed to consider the history of *Samson*.

C. 13.

Zorah—This word, denoting the sign of *Scorpius*, the emblem of Dan, has been already explained.

Manoah, is derived from נוח, which I have already shown to be the ancient word for *night*.

נזיר, *a Nazarite*. Some of the lexicographers translate *separated*, but I understand the *Nazarite* to be *one who is crowned*.

שמשון, *Samson.* " The Sun."—Now if my readers be not aware that Hercules was a type of the Sun, they may turn to the works of Gebelin and Dupuis; and in those of the former they will find a curious parallel drawn between Samson and Hercules. Some things, however, have escaped the notice of Gebelin, which I shall briefly mention.

Eshtaol, " *Hades,* or *the lower hemisphere*"— already explained.

C. 14.

Timnath. I have already observed that this is an astronomical term in Chaldaic—it seems to signify *an octant;* but in its original sense it was probably used to denote a portion or segment of the circle. That the term was employed astronomically, even in Hebrew, appears from the words תמנת חרס, which signify *the Segment,* or *portion of the Sun.*

The Philistines,—" the revolvers, the wanderers, &c." Were these the planets?

Behold a young lion roared against him. The defeat of this lion by *Samson* reminds us of the combat of *Hercules* with the Nemean lion. In both examples it is the first of the labors. The Summer solstice being in *Leo* will account for this similarity.

Thirty companions were given to *Samson,* or the Sun. These were clearly the days of the civil month.

Ashkelon. " Ignis torrefaciens." *Onom.*

C. 15.

The story of Samson and the foxes is curiously illustrated by Gebelin. I shall, therefore, refer my reader to him. But though a similar fable may have been told of Hercules, I am inclined to think, that the whole has originated in a mistake occasioned by the resemblance in sound of two words, one of which signifies *a fox,* and the other *flame.* See what I have already said on the subject.

עטים, *Etam,* " an eagle." Rumelin. Every schoolboy knows the eagle to be a solar symbol.

לחי, *Lehi,* " a jaw-bone." It will be remembered, that in the first decan of *Leo,* an ass's head was represented by the Orientalists. [1]

רמת לחי, *Ramath Lehi.* " The high place of the jaw-bone."

En-hakkore. " The fountain of the palm-tree-pulp." קורא signifies that *pulpy substance of the palm-tree,* which the Orientalists consider as a delicious nutriment. But how came *Samson* to give the name of *En-hakkore* to the place? I know not, unless it were, that the palm-tree is sacred to the Sun; and particularly in the sign of *Leo.*

---

[1] See my Dissertation on the 49th chapter of Genesis.

C. 16.

Gaza. I have already observed, that *Gaza* signifies *a Goat*, and was the type of the Sun in Capricorn. It will be remembered, that the *Gates* of the Sun were feigned by the ancient astronomers to be in *Capricorn* and in *Cancer*, from which signs the tropics are named. *Samson* carried away the gates from *Gaza* to *Hebron*, the city of conjunction. Now Court Gebelin tells us, that at Cadiz, where Hercules was anciently worshipped, there was a representation of him, with a gate on his shoulders. This fact helps not a little to identify Hercules with Samson.

Sorec, signifies *a vine.*

Delilah. I derive this name from דלל, *to exhaust, attenuate,* &c. The story of Samson and Delilah may remind us of Hercules and Omphale.

As I write for scholars, hints are sufficient; and, therefore, I leave them to fill up the canvas, where my sketches are unfinished.

Thus it will be remembered, that the yellow hair of Apollo was the symbol of the solar rays; and Samson with his shaven head may typify the Sun when " shorn of his beams."

Samson had seven locks, and these answer, in number at least, to the seven planets.

But it is time to recollect, that my business is rather to encourage others to examine and explain these allegories, than to attempt to elucidate the whole myself.

VI.

𝔇𝔦𝔰𝔰𝔢𝔯𝔱𝔞𝔱𝔦𝔬𝔫,

&c. &c.

A

𝕾𝔥𝔬𝔯𝔱 𝔇𝔦𝔰𝔰𝔢𝔯𝔱𝔞𝔱𝔦𝔬𝔫

CONCERNING THE PASCHAL LAMB.

W E have already seen, that about 4,300 years ago, the Sun, at the vernal equinox, passed from the sign of *Taurus* into that of *Aries*. It was apparently while the equinoctial Sun continued in *Taurus,* a period of above 2,000 years, that astronomy was first cultivated in the East, and that the Tsabaists established their idolatrous worship of the Sun, the Moon, and the Hosts of Heaven. But the Orientalists, in general, seem to have dated the commencement of the astronomical year, if I be allowed the expression, from the vernal equinox ; and while the Bull was the symbol of the Sun in the first of the signs, it was considered as an object of the highest veneration. The monuments of all the ancient Oriental nations bear testimony to the respect, which was entertained for this symbol of the great God of the Tsabaists. Apis, Mnevis, the bull of Mithras, &c. were only so many types of the celestial Bull, or rather of the Sun in that sign. It was consequently supposed, that bulls, calves, and oxen, were most acceptable victims, when sacrificed at the shrines of the Sun, known in different regions by the various names of Osiris, Mithras, Moloch, Adonis, and Iao.

At the remote period of which I am speaking, the solstices had place, when the Sun was in *Leo* and *Aquarius*, and the equinoxes, when the same luminary was in *Taurus* and *Scorpius*. As the year then commenced at the vernal equinox, and as *Taurus* was the first of the signs, the Tsabaists founded their idolatrous worship on this order of things. In progress of time, however, the retrograde motion of the fixed stars must have made it evident to astronomers, that the solstices and equinoxes had passed into other signs, and that, consequently, the veneration of the vulgar for certain symbols became misplaced. Thus the Sun at the vernal equinox passed from the sign of *Taurus* to that of *Aries*, which became in its turn the first of the zodiacal constellations. But though astronomers might perceive this, it was probably not quite so easy to make the ignorant and superstitious people comprehend, why the principal symbol of their principal God should be changed from a bull, or calf, to a ram, or lamb.

It is to this source, that I am inclined to attribute the adoration, which was peculiarly offered up to bulls and calves, as principal symbols of the Sun, long after *Taurus* had ceased to be the first of the signs. The astronomers of Thebes in Egypt seem to have been the first, who obtained from the multitude that veneration for sheep, which is so remarkably noticed by Herodotus. In other regions, the Bull continued, through the lapse of ages, to maintain an unjust pre-eminence over the Ram, or Lamb, which had become the first of the signs. It is curious, indeed, to observe, that the Bull is still so much venerated in India, 4,300 years after the celestial bull ceded his place in the heavens to the Ram, or Lamb; nor is it less extraordinary, that there have been, perhaps, more adorers of the Sun in *Aries*, since that constellation ceased to be the first of the signs, than there were before.

It is evident from the idolatrous worship offered by the Israelites to the golden calf, that they were not so well instructed in astronomy as the Thebans. Moses, who was learned in all the wisdom of the Egyptians, must have known, that *Taurus* was no longer the leader of the celestial hosts; and in appointing the feast of the passover, he seems to have desired to amend both the religion and the astronomy of the Hebrews.

The word which we translate passover (Heb. פסח) properly signifies *transit*, and is sometimes taken for that which makes a *transit*. Hence the Paschal lamb was frequently called פסח *pesach*, as making the *transit*. I pretend that the feast of the *transit* was instituted as a memorial of the transit of the equinoctial Sun from the sign of the *Bull* to that of the *Ram*, or *Lamb*.

Before I proceed further, however, it will be

necessary to say something of the annual periods of the Egyptians.

It appears, that the Egyptians, besides their lunar year, of which I do not intend to take notice at present, had four different years. These I shall term the astronomical, the canicular, the civil, and the sacred.

The astronomical year of the Egyptians commenced with the vernal equinox. Aratus, having confounded it with the canicular year, has made *Cancer* the first of the signs, for which he has been reproved by Theon.

Wherefore, (says the latter)[1] *has he taken the commencement from Cancer, when the Egyptians date the beginning from Aries?*

The Rabbins acknowledge, that the Egyptians preceded the Hebrews in fixing the commencement of the year at the vernal equinox, when the Sun

---

[1] p. 69.

A a

was in *Aries. Incipiebant autem Ægyptii,* says R. A. Seba, *numerare menses ab eo tempore, quo Sol ingressus est in initium sideris Arietis,* &c. [1]

The Egyptians dated the canicular year from the rising of *Sirius. The commencement of the year,* says Porphyry, *is not dated from Aquarius by the Egyptians, as it is by the Romans, but from Cancer; for Sothis, which the Greeks call the dog-star, is near to Cancer, and the first day of the month, according to them, is fixed by the rising of Sothis,* &c. [2] Censorinus, speaking of this canicular year, says, *Græci* κύνικον, *Latini " canicularem" vocamus, proptereà quod initium illius sumitur, cùm primo die ejus mensis, quem vocant Ægyptii Thoth, caniculæ sidus oritur.* [3] This last expression of Censorinus does not appear quite clear to me. The month *Thoth,* as we shall presently see, answered nearly to our month of September.

---

[1] I am led to think that this astronomical year was that consisting of 360 days, to which the Priests annually added five days and a quarter. But see Diodorus Siculus, L. 1.

[2] *De antro nympharum.*   [3] *De die nat. C.* 18.

The civil year of the Egyptians commenced with the month *Thoth*. Alpherganius, in speaking of the Persian and Egyptian months, thus expresses himself. *At menses Ægyptii hodie aliter procedunt intercalando quarto anno: quare eorum menses jam Persicis dissimiles, at cum Græcis atque Syriis congruunt. Primus apud eos dies est 29us Augusti.* The 29th of August was, indeed, the day when the month *Thoth* commenced; but this establishment of the civil year, commencing with the month *Thoth*, is generally supposed not to have taken place until the time of Augustus Cæsar. I am, however, inclined to think, that the Egyptians had from the most remote antiquity a fixed year commencing with this month. The calendar of the Egyptians appears to have been reformed in the time of Augustus; but it seems strange to affirm that the Egyptians had no fixed year before that period. Joseph Scaliger severely reprehends Plutarch, for speaking of certain months as fixed in the ancient times of the Egyptians. It is true, that the sacred year was a vague year, as we shall presently see; but it does not therefore follow, that the Egyptians had no year that was fixed. The puzzle seems to arise from this: The word *Thoth*,

according to Jablonski, signifies *the beginning*.
Hence it was applied to the beginning of the year,
whether vague, or fixed; and thus the *thoth* might
be any month of the solar year, as denoting the first
month of the vague year; or it might be the first
month of an established year.

The sacred year of the Egyptians was vague.
Its *thoth*, or commencement, must have been
originally at the rising of *Sirius*. It was composed
of 365 days; and consequently a day was lost at
the end of every fourth year. This day the Priests
did not intercalate for the sacred year, which thus
became vague; and hence they obtained one of
their cycles. One thousand four hundred and sixty
one years, consisting of 365 days each, are equal
to 1460 solar years. This was called the Sothic
period, which shows, that the sacred year originally
commenced with the canicular.

Having thus briefly spoken of the Egyptian
annual periods, I shall only add, that if I have
named them wrongly, I trust it is of the less consequence, as I have pointed out their commencement. But I cannot agree with those authors,

who make the canicular year a vague year. The sacred year, which originally commenced with the rising of *Sirius*, was certainly vague; but it seems impossible to suppose, that the year, to which Porphyry alludes, was likewise vague. In fact, if this year had contained only 365 days, without intercalation, the rising of *Sirius* would, in the lapse of a few centuries, have been fixed nearer to the winter than to the summer solstice. Now when we consider how much importance was attached to the rising of *Sirius* by the Egyptians, we can hardly imagine, that they looked for it at any other time, than what their annual experience proved to them to be the true time. I have no objection, however, to state the matter thus. Let us call the canicular rural year fixed, and the canicular sacred year vague; for I admit, that the vague year originally commenced with the rising of *Sirius*. But the Priests appear to have intercalated a day every fourth year for the former, and to have omitted it for the latter. That the canicular rural year could not be vague is evident, I think, from the statement of Hor-Apollo. From the retrograde motion of the fixed stars, the Egyptians were obliged to add a day every fourth year, upon the same plan as we do in our bissextile years. It would be soon obvious, that the rising of *Sirius*, without having recourse to this expedient, would be retarded a day every fourth year. At the beginning of the fifth canicular rural year, this day was accordingly introduced. The emblem of this astronomical process was represented by an acre divided into four parts :—but see Hor-Apollo. [1] Now for the vague year, this quarter of a day was omitted ; and, therefore, after the expiration of the fourth canicular sacred year, it would require 1460 years to make the canicular sacred and vague year commence again precisely with the canicular rural and fixed year. The Egyptian Kings, according to an ancient writer cited by Jablonski, were obliged to swear, that they would not allow any intercalation in the year of 365 days, by which a day fixed for a festival should be changed ; and it is chiefly upon this authority, that I have marked the vague and sacred year of the Egyptians to have been the same. But it is time that I return to the Hebrews.

---

[1] L. 1. C. 5.

Before the departure of the Hebrews from Egypt, their civil year commenced with the month *Tisri*. The month *Tisri* is called ראש השנה, " the beginning of the year in the Talmud ;" but the author of the Chaldaic Paraphrase [1] observes of *Tisri*, also called *Ethanim*, that *it was the month which the ancients called the first, but which is now the seventh.* It follows, then, that *Tisri* answered to the Egyptian month *Thoth*, which was the first month of the civil year of the Egyptians, and which nearly answered to September. I cannot help thinking, that the Israelites took the use of this year from the example of the Egyptians.

When the Hebrews left Egypt, their legislator gave them another year. It commenced with the month *Nisan*, also called *Abib*. On the tenth day of this month the Paschal Lamb was separated ; and on the fourteenth the feast of the transit was held.

Now if this ceremony had nothing to do with the astronomical ram, or lamb, we shall find some

---

[1] 1. Kings, viii. 2.

curious circumstances, for which I shall leave others to account.

We learn from the author of the Oriental Chronicle, that the day, when the Paschal festival commenced, was that in which the Sun entered into the sign of the ram, or the sign of the lamb, as it was called by the Persians and Syrians. *Erat dies iste quo Sol ingressus est primum signum Arietis,* &c. R. Bechai, in commenting on the 12th chapter of Exodus, speaks to the following purpose. *Scripsit Maimonides, in ratione hujus præcepti, quod proptereà quòd sidus Aries in mense Nisan maximè valeret, et hoc sidus fructus germinare faceret, ideò jussit Deus mactare arietem,* &c. Here is a pretty clear avowal on the part of Maimonides, the most learned of the Rabbins, that the Paschal lamb was a type of the astronomical lamb.

But the Rabbins tell us, that the lamb was slain, in order to wean the Israelites from the idolatrous worship which the Egyptians offered to the Sun under the form of a ram. There can be no question, that Ammon, the type of the Sun in *Aries,* was worshipped by the Egyptians. Herodotus says,[1] that the statues of Jupiter Ammon had the head of a ram. We are told by Eusebius[2] that the idol of Ammon had a ram's head with the horns of a goat. Proclus (on the Timæus of Plato[3]) observes, that the Egyptians venerated the ram in an extraordinary manner, inasmuch as they affixed a ram's head to Ammon. Now, say the Rabbins, our forefathers were ordered to slay a lamb, in order to mark their abomination of Ammon; because the lamb was held sacred by the Egyptians, who never killed a sheep, it being the type of their God.

There is an objection to be made to this statement. It is not exactly founded upon fact. Herodotus[4] tells us, that in the temple of Mendes, and in the Mendesian nome, they preserved goats, and sacrificed sheep. Strabo[5] says, that in his time the Egyptians nowhere sacrificed sheep but in the Nitriotic nome. It is not quite accurate, then, to

---

[1] L. 1. [2] Preparat. Evang. L. 3, C. 12. [3] L. 2, C. 42. [4] L. 2, C. 42. [5] L. 17.

say that the Egyptians never killed sheep, and that for that reason the Israelites were commanded to slay the Paschal lamb.

We have seen by the avowal of the Rabbins themselves, that the Paschal lamb was a type of the astronomical lamb. What, if we were to find, that the feast of the transit was copied from a festival instituted by the Egyptians?

R. A. Seba, whom I have already quoted, admits, that at the time when the feast of the transit was first established among the Israelites, the Egyptians had already begun to count their months from the entrance of the Sun into *Aries;* and then he adds, *atque is mensis (Phamenoth) totus festâ solemnitate celebrabatur,* &c. In the Oriental Chronicle it is said, that the day, when the Sun entered into *Aries* was *solemnis ac celeberrimus apud Ægyptios.* But this Ægyptian festival commenced on the very day, when the Paschal lamb was separated. *Insuper die mensis decimo,* says R. A. Seba, *ipso illo die quo Ægyptii incipiebant celebrare cultum arietis, &c. placuit Deo ut sumerent agnum, &c.*

But, continue the Rabbins, the Egyptians adored the ram, or lamb, at this festival, whereas the Hebrews slew the lamb. This, therefore, only proves the more, that the Paschal lamb was slain in order to wean the Israelites from the idolatry of the Egyptians. I must observe, that this reasoning does not seem to be founded upon fact. Herodotus tells us, that once a year, on a certain day, at the festival of Jupiter Ammon, the people of Thebes in Egypt slew a ram. But Jupiter Ammon was no other than the Sun in *Aries*. This annual festival then must have been that, which the Rabbins acknowledge to have been celebrated at the same time with the feast of the transit. The Sun came into *Aries* on the tenth of *Nisan*, which month answers to the Egyptian *Phamenoth*. At the annual festival of Ammon, or of the Sun in *Aries*, a ram was slain by the Thebans. At the annual feast of the Jews, when the Sun was in *Aries*, a male lamb was slain. How will the Rabbins prove, that their ancestors did not copy this custom from the Egyptians, whose festival on this occasion they admit to have been instituted before their own?

But, say the Rabbins, there was nothing in the Egyptian festival, similar to the custom of the Israelites, in marking the doors, &c. with blood. My opinion is that there was something very like it. St. Epiphanius says, that about the vernal equinox, the Egyptians had been accustomed, from the most remote antiquity, to celebrate the festival of the ram, or lamb. At this festival, he adds, they used to mark every thing about them with red. I have not a copy of Epiphanius before me; but I am pretty certain that I have read a passage in him to this purpose.

It may be remarked, that פסח *pesach*, the *transit*, is sometimes employed to signify *the lamb.* It consequently follows, that the lamb was understood as at least the type of that which made the transit. But this becomes very intelligible, if the lamb were the type of the Sun making his transit into the sign of Aries at the vernal equinox.

When, indeed, we find that this feast of the passover, or transit, was instituted at the time when the Jewish lawgiver altered the Calendar, and when he made the first month of the year that very month, in which the equinoctial Sun passed into *Aries*, it seems difficult to imagine that the Paschal lamb had nothing to do with the astronomical ram. But this opinion, which I submit to the judgment of my readers, becomes strongly confirmed by the customs and practices of the Egyptians, from whom the Jews copied many of their ceremonies, and obtained the greater part of their knowledge.

The End.